Models for
Social Networks
With Statistical Applications

Advanced Quantitative Techniques
in the Social Sciences

VOLUMES IN THE SERIES

1. **HIERARCHICAL LINEAR MODELS: Applications and Data Analysis Methods, 2nd Edition**
   Antony S. Bryk and Stephen W. Raudenbush

2. **MULTIVARIATE ANALYSIS OF CATEGORICAL DATA: Theory**
   John P. Van de Geer

3. **MULTIVARIATE ANALYSIS OF CATEGORICAL DATA: Applications**
   John P. Van de Geer

4. **STATISTICAL MODELS FOR ORDINAL VARIABLES**
   Clifford C. Clogg and Edward S. Shihadeh

5. **FACET THEORY: Form and Content**
   Ingwer Borg and Samuel Shye

6. **LATENT CLASS AND DISCRETE LATENT TRAIT MODELS: Similarities and Differences**
   Ton Heinen

7. **REGRESSION MODELS FOR CATEGORICAL AND LIMITED DEPENDENT VARIABLES**
   J. Scott Long

8. **LOG-LINEAR MODELS FOR EVENT HISTORIES**
   Jeroen K. Vermunt

9. **MULTIVARIATE TAXOMETRIC PROCEDURES: Distinguishing Types From Continua**
   Niels G. Waller and Paul E. Meehl

10. **STRUCTURAL EQUATION MODELING: Foundations and Extensions**
    David Kaplan

11. **REGRESSION ANALYSIS: A Constructive Critique**
    Richard A. Berk

12. **PROPENSITY SCORE ANALYSIS: Statistical Methods and Applications**
    Shenyang Guo
    Mark W. Fraser

13. **MODELS FOR SOCIAL NETWORKS WITH STATISTICAL APPLICATIONS**
    Suraj Bandyopadhyay
    A R. Rao
    Bikas K. Sinha

Models for
Social Networks
With Statistical Applications

Suraj Bandyopadhyay

A R. Rao

Bikas K. Sinha

Indian Statistical institute

Advanced Quantitative Techniques
in the Social Sciences Series **13**

Los Angeles | London | New Delhi
Singapore | Washington DC

For information:

SAGE Publications, Inc.
2455 Teller Road
Thousand Oaks,
    California 91320
E-mail: order@sagepub.com

SAGE Publications India Pvt. Ltd.
B 1/I 1 Mohan Cooperative
    Industrial Area
Mathura Road, New Delhi 110 044
India

SAGE Publications Ltd.
1 Oliver's Yard
55 City Road,
London EC1Y 1SP
United Kingdom

SAGE Publications Asia-Pacific
    Pte. Ltd.
33 Pekin Street #02-01
Far East Square
Singapore 048763

Printed in the United States of America

Library of Congress Cataloging-in-Publication Data

Bandyopadhyay, Suraj.
Models for social networks with statistical applications /
Bandyopadhyay, Suraj, Rao, A R., Sinha, Bikas K.
     p. cm.—(Advanced quantitative techniques in the social sciences ; 13)
Includes bibliographical references and index.
ISBN 978-1-4129-4168-6 (cloth)
   1. Social sciences—Statistical methods. 2. Social networks. I. Rao, A. R
II. Sinha, Bikas Kumar. III. Title.

HA29.B36 2011
302.401′5195—dc22

This book is printed on acid-free paper.

10   11   12   13   14   10   9   8   7   6   5   4   3   2   1

Acquisitions Editor:	Vicki Knight
Associate Editor:	Lauren Habib
Editorial Assistant:	Ashley Dodd
Production Editor:	Brittany Bauhaus
Copy Editor:	Gillian Dickens
Typesetter:	C&M Digitals (P) Ltd.
Proofreader:	Christina West
Indexer:	Diggs Publication Services, Inc.
Cover Designer:	Candice Harman
Marketing Manager:	Stephanie Adams

TABLE OF CONTENTS

ABOUT THE AUTHORS

Suraj Bandyopadhyay (PhD, Sociology, McGill University, Montreal, Canada) was, before his retirement, professor of sociology and head of the Sociological Research Unit, Indian Statistical Institute, Kolkata. After retirement, for sometime, he was also affiliated with the Sociological Research Unit and Statistics-Mathematics Unit, Indian Statistical Institute, Kolkata, as an honorary visiting scientist. For his academic performance at McGill University he was awarded Bobbs-Merrill Award in Sociology in 1968. He has received a number of academic invitations and Fellowships from different international institutions such as the Canadian International Development Agency (CIDA, Ottawa), Centre for Developing-Area Studies (McGill University), International Data Library and Reference Service of the Survey Research Centre at the University of California (Berkeley, USA), and Overseas Development Group at the University of East Anglia (Norwich, UK). He has served as expert member in academic committees of different institutions and published more than thirty research papers.

A R. Rao (PhD, Indian Statistical Institute) was a professor in the Division of Theoretical Statistics and Mathematics of the Indian Statistical Institute at Kolkata. He was a visiting assistant professor at the University of Minnesota for one year. He published more than 25 research papers in graph theory, is a joint author of a book on linear algebra at the honors level, and edited the proceedings of three conferences on graph theory. His major interests were graph theory and its applications to social sciences and linear algebra.

Bikas K. Sinha (PhD, Statistics, Calcutta University) is currently a professor of statistics in the Applied Statistics Division of the Indian Statistical Institute, Kolkata. He was a recipient of PCMahalanobis Medal in 1980. He has served as an expert on mission in survey methodology for the United Nations and has also served as a consultant for the U.S. Environmental Protection Agency (EPA).

He has traveled extensively and visited a host of universities in the United States, Canada, Germany, Finland, Poland and other countries as a visiting faculty/research collaborator. He has authored more than 110 research articles in refereed journals, one graduate-level textbook (Wiley) and two research monographs (Springer-Verlag Lecture Notes Series in Statistics Publications). He is an elected member of the International Statistical Institute. His range of expertise includes survey theory and methods, design of experiments, statistical modeling, and statistical inference.

PREFACE

———•◦•———

This book is dedicated to the hallowed memory of our very dear colleague, the late Professor A R. Rao, who suddenly left for his heavenly abode while we were in the middle of this project. His thorough and disciplined specialized training in graph theory and his intrinsic interest in graph-theoretic and statistical aspects of social networks brought him close to one of us (SB) almost 30 years ago. His insightful critical comments have been instrumental in shaping the course of our thoughts in writing this book. He had very enthusiastically prepared the draft of the first few chapters, and we have tried to keep them almost intact. We have endeavored to complete the book in our own way—without having the tension to receive his critical comments. We fondly hope this has met his expectations.

The study leading to this book is rooted in experiences of a real-life situation of villagers in a typical rice-producing zone in Md. Bazar Community Development Block of Birbhum District in West Bengal. This was accrued in course of the project. "The Conditions of Rural Progress in India," undertaken by Suraj Bandyopadhyay (Indian Statistical Institute [ISI], Kolkata) and Donald Von Eschen (McGill University, Montreal, Canada). The project was funded by the Canadian International Development Agency (CIDA, Ottawa, Canada).

The study initially covered, during the years 1971 to 1974, 2,697 households in 21 villages. The final report of the study was submitted to CIDA in 1981, and an extended summary of its findings was published later (Bandyopadhyay & von Eschen, 1991 [see Chapter 1 for detailed reference]). The study report is available from the CIDA (see Chapter 1 for exact reference). Subsequently, some of the 21 villages were resurveyed after 25 to 30 years during 1998–2004 (under a project sponsored by the Indian Statistical Institute, Kolkata), and the data were analyzed by a team, including the present three authors.

The villages were marked by steep stratification by caste, class, and power. Again, the three systems of stratification were confounded with one another. This made the villagers, and the lower rung in particular, highly vulnerable to various crises and urgencies of life and living. The situation was further aggravated by the fact that a major source of livelihood of the village elite was appropriation, not production. Distrust of others and hopelessness about the conditions changing for the better in the near future characterized the worldview prevalent in the villages at that time.

Under such circumstances, it was sought to examine the commonly held view that the ethos of rural society, unlike that of urban society, is most likely to be conducive to promote mutual help and cooperation, which would enable the villagers, particularly the lower rung, to withstand at least partially the negative effects of steep stratification. Data on requests for help and cooperation provided from one household to another at the time of an emergency or crisis were collected in detail in each of the above 21 villages within a specified reference period. Articulation of the social relation of "help and cooperation" brought out "social networks" of help and cooperation among the households in each of these villages. Briefly speaking, the findings of social network analysis (SNA) belied expectations about rural society. The incidence of ties of help, especially the ties of mutual help, varied widely from village to village. In the lower rung of the society, the level of mutual help was found to be quite low. Even in the case of matters such as an emergency in daily family life, most of the households were dependent on the local elite. Asymmetrical relations dominated the social networks on the whole. The rural elite enjoyed not only high social position and economic strength, besides being bestowed with positions of power, but also were found to be more integrated among themselves by ties of mutual help and cooperation (Bandyopadhyay & von Eschen, 1988, 1995 [see Chapter 1 for detailed references]).

Recent official records claim that during the past few decades, a number of socioeconomic and administrative measures have been implemented in rural areas of West Bengal. Some examples include: land reforms, registration of rights of share croppers and distribution of surplus land among the landless, a three-tier system of Panchayats, an extension of minor irrigation and road transport facilities, a total literacy campaign, and others. Whereas the impact of implementing such measures for changes in socioeconomic conditions of the villagers may be explicitly manifested, there are hardly any studies of the impact, if any, on social relations among the villagers! One of the objectives of the resurvey was to ascertain whether the implementation of these measures in rural areas has made any perceptible impact on the pattern of social relations among the villagers. We intended to study this facet of societal change by an analysis of social networks of help and cooperation in the course of daily life.

The focus of the earlier study was to explore the methodology of the quantification of data relating to the flow of help and cooperation among the villagers and to measure the extent of reciprocity within the village community. Subsequently, it was expanded to include changing patterns of some important structural parameters of a group or community—namely, fragmentation, hierarchy, reachability (how far who can reach whom), power, potential sphere of influence, and so on. For our purposes, appropriate measures had to be derived since these were not readily available in the literature and, even if available in a few cases, suffered from limitations. Thus, we stepped into the study of characteristics of global (whole) social network. In this context, we gratefully acknowledge the interest shown by Professor Barry Wellman when he visited ISI, Kolkata, almost two decades ago. At that time, he discussed with us about the potentialities and constraints of whole social network analysis. He welcomed our endeavor to analyze a whole social network as a unit and to subsequently share our experiences with the community of social network researchers. We particularly mention that whole social network analysis, whether of a village or of an ethnic community, immensely contributes to deeper comprehension of various nuances of social reality. As for the present study, supplemented by ground data, it has revealed alterations in the distribution of social power. This has also indicated shifts in power centers, traditionally rooted in socioeconomically dominant strata in the community to its lower rungs (Chapter 1). We have shown how qualitative concepts of social characteristics can be measured by whole social network analysis and made amenable to quantitative analysis (Chapter 5) and how they may be applied to examine structural patterns of social networks (Chapter 6). Optimist social scientists have surmised that "community" has not been lost but transformed into social networks (Introduction to Part II on community in Wellman & Berkowitz, 1988, p. 125; see Wellman, 1988, at the end of Chapter 1 for detailed reference). We, however, find that a community remains a community while the distribution of ties in a network changes whether longitudinally over a period of time or horizontally across space. Ties of direct reciprocity that closely bind dyads or moderately sized groups of actors are transformed to indirectly bind together quite a large segment of the network (Chapter 6). In this context, the possibility of applying multivariate statistical methods to measure the structural similarity of social networks has also been demonstrated. Concern for methodology of whole network analysis has also prompted us to discuss elementary global social network models, problems of sampling and inference in the case of whole social network analysis, and model validation as well as application of methodology of computer simulation to estimate complex measures of whole social networks (Chapters 4, 6, and 7).

Evidently, such a venture could not be successful without interdisciplinary collective teamwork. It started with a sociologist's (SB's) query, which was taken up by a graph theorist (ARR) once a social network was recognized as a kind of digraph (courtesy of the late Professor B. P. Adhikary, then director of ISI, who had introduced SB to ARR), and later, a statistician (BKS) joined the endeavor. So far, we have a number of publications to our credit, covering some graph-theoretical and statistical aspects of the social networks. The references are cited in different chapters of this book. We express our grateful thanks to Professor J. K. Ghosh, the world-famous statistician, currently professor emeritus at the Indian Statistical Institute and professor at Purdue University, who has been kind enough to encourage us in our venture over all these years.

We must also acknowledge the encouragement and support we have received from Professor Donald Von Eschen of McGill University, Canada, for this study.

SNA deals with the pattern of flow/articulation of a relationship such as friendship or help/cooperation among individuals or households (HHs)—that is, societal units whatsoever, in a reference population. Although SNA deals with individual units (such as HHs), unlike socioeconomic surveys on individual HHs, SNA dwells on a study of dyads formed by pairs of HHs from a population. SNA is concerned with a dyadic relationship, marked by the "direction of flow" (involving various features of the community such as help and cooperation). Hence, the proper setting for studying social networks is what is called a directed graph, abbreviated as *digraph*.

Chapters in the book are arranged as follows.

In Chapter 1, the concepts and a few basic parameters related to SNA are discussed at length, along with the highlights of their interpretations. A comparative study of the social networks of a village at two time periods is also presented.

Chapter 2 is devoted exclusively to an introduction to graphs. In this chapter, we present in a systematic manner all relevant basic concepts involving both directed and undirected graphs and their extensions and generalizations. Also, various parameters of graphs are introduced, and their properties are discussed. This chapter forms a basis for exploring many workable graph-theoretic features of SNA. We have been able to concentrate only on a few of them in terms of proper exploration of their graphical and statistical aspects in this book. In Chapter 3, graph-theoretic (deterministic) and statistical (stochastic) models are introduced and discussed at length. This chapter constitutes the backbone of the book. The difficulty level in examining theoretical properties of many of the parameters related to the models is highlighted, and their extraction via simulation is indicated. The simulated distributions of various statistics under some of the probabilistic models are included to give the reader a good idea of what to expect from the models. Stochastic models for dyadic interactions are also discussed at the end of the chapter.

The validity of the statistical models introduced in Chapter 3 needs to be examined with reference to observed networks in terms of tests of goodness of fit and other valid statistical tests based on relevant data arising out of the networks.

Chapter 4 is devoted to an extensive discussion of model fitting and model validation. In Chapter 5, we discuss graph-theoretic and statistical measures at length. We broadly divide the measures in terms of (a) local measures of egocentric (i.e., related to an individual actor as the unit) characteristics, (b) local-cum-global measures of egocentric and global characteristics, and (c) global characteristics. Collectively, reciprocity, cohesion (density), expansiveness (out-degrees), popularity and power (in-degrees), connectedness and fragmentation (strong and weak components), reachability, cliques, centrality and hierarchy, and other such measures are discussed at length. Several of these measures have been derived by the authors and are appearing for the first time in a book. Although detailed theoretical derivations/proofs are omitted, the measures are presented along with the underlying assumptions and can be used without any advanced knowledge of either graph theory or statistics.

Chapter 6 contains two case studies based on actual field investigation and extraction of real-life network data. In the first case study, we have compared longitudinal changes in social structure with reference to the networks of the same village (Kabilpur) as observed during 1971–1972 and also during 1997–1998. We do this by SNA, obtaining the values of graph-theoretic measures of some global characteristics of social networks at two time periods. The second case study examines cross-sectional variation in the pattern of circulation of social ties of a community across villages. We have chosen the case of a minority religious group for this purpose in a few villages situated in the same region.

In addition, in Chapter 6, a section on the computation of a reciprocity measure based on a "weighted" digraph (i.e., weighted network) and its interpretation is also added. Last, fitting of some dyadic choice models to actual but small networks is also illustrated, and necessary interpretations are provided.

Finite population sampling and related inference is yet another very important topic. It has to be understood that for large populations, it is not at all an easy task to enumerate all the HHs and compile data on networks (with due attention to any nonresponse or any reporting errors whatsoever!).

Sampling of some of the HHs for collecting necessary data seems to be a viable alternative as it can be conducted competently and more cautiously to avoid any misreporting or nonresponse. By doing so, we do not make any attempt to create a prototype of a population network.

Creating a prototype is simply not possible. However, for some of the population parameters, we may attempt to provide "reasonably accurate" estimates based on a sample network, which is precisely the goal of a sampling expert. We present a reasonably complete account of this exercise in Chapter 7.

It is worthwhile to mention that Professor Vladimir Batagelj of the Department of Mathematics and Physics, University of Ljubljana, Slovenia, was amazed to know that the social network diagram of Kabilpur of 1970 was drawn by hand in 1972 by one of the authors (SB). He wondered how it was planned to handle that "enormous volume of ties." He commented highly about the diagram and said that Pajek came out much later.

The social network data of Kabilpur with brief notes of 1971–1972 and 1997–1998 are available on the following Web site: http://pajek.imfm.si/doku .php?id=topics:kabilpur.

This book is not a textbook or a handbook on SNA; rather, is expected to serve as a reference and text for demonstration of applying global SNA. A great deal of emphasis has been given to generate interest in this direction among students, teachers, and researchers in social sciences as well as for others who are interested in studying social networks. We believe this book has new material of interest to offer new ideas to graph theorists and statisticians equally, besides social science researchers. Last but not least, we derive much pleasure in thanking (1) an anonymous referee of the first draft of the manuscript for critically going through it and offering numerous constructive suggestions to bring our thoughts in proper perspectives; (2) the director of the

ISI for providing excellent research atmosphere throughout the tenure of this project; (3) the head of the Sociological Research Unit and head of the Stat-Math Unit, ISI, Kolkata, for providing adequate administrative support; (4) Dr. Prabir Ghosh Dastidar (a scientist in the Ministry of Earth Sciences, Government of India) for complying with our numerous requests for drawing the networks and the cover page of the book with extreme competence and courtesy; (5) Dr. Rabindranath Jana of ISI for complying with our requests, without losing patience, regarding technical assistance of various types as well as in keeping track of the manuscript pages while we were running back and forth among the many versions of the chapters; (6) Dr. Anil K. Choudhuri of the ISI, who provided us rich observations from the field on various angularities of articulating ties of help and cooperation among the villagers; (7) Mrs. Bandyopadhyay for hoping against hope that someday the project would eventually be over; (8) Professor S. B. Rao, our former colleague at ISI, Kolkata, and currently director of C R Rao Advanced Institute of Mathematics, Statistics and Computer Science (AIMSCS), Hyderabad, for giving us constant encouragement at very critical times, following the passing away of A. R. Rao; (9) Ms. Suchismita Roy for her assistance with our literature search; and (10) Ms. Lisa Cuevas and Ms. Vicki Night for reading our series of e-mails and responding to each one with extreme patience and encouragement. On behalf of Sage Publications, initially Ms. Cuevas and later Ms. Night did *not* lose hope on the book project, and here we deliver the manuscript, believing that we have accomplished the task to the satisfaction of all concerned.

—Suraj Bandyopadhyay
—Bikas K. Sinha
Indian Statistical Institute, Kolkata
August 28, 2009

ONE

INTRODUCTION TO SOCIAL NETWORK ANALYSIS

———◆◆◆———

1.1 INTRODUCTION

The study of social networks is a new but quickly widening multidisciplinary area involving social, mathematical, statistical, and computer sciences (see Burt, Minor, & Associates, 1983, for application in diverse social environments; in the latter sciences, see Wassermann & Faust, 1994, and especially for the field of economics, see Dutta & Jackson, 2003). It has its own parameters and methodological tools. In this book, we intend to show how graph-theoretic and statistical techniques can be used to study some important parameters of global social networks and illustrate their use in social science studies with some examples of real-life survey data. We hope our illustrations will provide ideas to researchers in various other fields as well.

1.2 CONCEPT OF A SOCIAL NETWORK

The term *social network* refers to the articulation of a social relationship, ascribed or achieved, among individuals, families, households, villages, communities, regions, and so on. Each of them can play dual roles, acting both as a unit or node of a social network as well as a social actor (cf. Laumann

& Pappi, 1976). Kinship is a very common example of an ascribed relationship, while some common examples of an achieved relationship are those that are established in the course of regular interaction in the processes of daily life and living, cultural activities, and so on, such as one household requesting help, support, or advice from another; ties of friendship or choice of individuals to spend leisure time together; and preferences in marriage. Incidentally, a relationship can also be *negative*—for instance, hostility or conflict as opposed to friendship or alliance and alienation versus mutuality or integration. In this book, we will focus on *positive relationships*. Again, much of what we will discuss is based on sociological data, but it can also be used to study demographic and economic processes such as migration from one region to another, value of any type of economic (e.g., postal money order or trade) exchange between regions, volume of flow of goods between countries, flow of traffic between different places, and so on.

Thus, the units of a "social network" can be different, no doubt, such as individuals, families, households, and rural or urban areas, according to the relationship under consideration. But there is a common feature—namely, whatever the type of units we study, a specific dyadic relationship exists or does not exist between the members of any pair of them.

Furthermore, if the relationship exists between a pair of units, it is also quite pertinent to ask whether it flows in both directions or only in one direction and, in the latter case, from which direction to the other, because a social relationship is not necessarily symmetric. Asymmetric relations, such as the following examples, are as common as symmetric ones. For instance, A prefers B, A invites B to a household festival, or A goes to B for help or advice. But B may or may not prefer, invite, or approach A.

We should mention, however, that only because of the presence of such pairwise ties, a *social network* should not be equated with *social group*. There are two concepts of a social group: realist and nominalist. The realist concept is most commonly used in sociological parlance. According to this concept, it is an entity consisting of social actors such as individuals, families, and so on and is set apart from the rest. A social group retains a multidimensional system of somewhat durable contacts or interactions within the group: psychic, emotional, verbal, and behavioral. Thus, there is an element of a feeling of awareness or consciousness shared by its members. Besides, a social group generates its own boundary within which its members obey certain rules, norms, and functional roles toward each other as well as toward its common goal. (For a detailed discussion of different characteristics of social groups, see Homans et al., 1968.) However, moving outside the realist concept of social group, a researcher also enjoys the option to impose his or her own definition of the boundary of group membership to identify a group for a study. This is the nominalist concept of a social group. For example, compare the Marxian concept of class as a "class for itself," a realist concept, and a class as "class in itself," the nominalist view (Laumann, Marsden, & Prensky, 1983). Wasserman and Faust (1994) have followed the nominalist concept of a social group for an illustration of methods. Thus, while a social group can be both realist and nominalist, a social network cannot be a realist one. A social network is a category of actors bound by a process of interaction among themselves. It is thus a nominalist category. However, a social network or its parts are endowed with the potential of being transformed into a social group in a realist sense provided that there is enough interaction.

For analytical purposes, a social network is conceptualized as a *digraph* (or a *graph* if the relationship has no direction). Digraph diagrams may be drawn to instantly provide direct mapping of ties showing their clustering as well as scatteredness. In a digraph, we call a unit—whether an individual, a family, a household, or a village—a *vertex* or *node*. A tie between two nodes indicates the presence of the relationship connecting them. Absence of a tie indicates absence of the relationship. A tie with a direction is called an *arc*, and a tie without direction is called an *edge*. One could also note the value or volume of flow as the weight of a tie and thus obtain a network that would then be a *weighted digraph*. More precise definitions of the graph-theoretic terms will be given in Chapter 2. Since the structure of the same network can be visually perceived differently depending on the manner in which a diagram is drawn, it is necessary to eliminate the bias in visual perception in order to draw an inference about the structure of a network from a digraph diagram (McGrath, Blythe, & Krackhardt, 1997). This visual bias is eliminated if we take recourse to numerically measure some of the selected important characteristics of a network and draw inference from there (see Chapter 6 for illustration).

For the sake of simplicity, we will concentrate on social networks showing only the presence (1) or absence (0) of the relationship. We also assume that ties have directions. Later, in Chapter 6, we will indicate, citing reciprocity as an illustration, how social network analysis can be extended to the case when the 0–1 restriction is dropped and there are nonnegative weights associated with the ties.

Networks are usually represented by diagrams where the vertices are represented by points, arcs by lines with arrowheads, and edges by lines without arrowheads. When two nodes are connected by ties in both directions, we often represent the two ties together by an edge, omitting the arrowheads.

1.3 SOCIAL NETWORK ANALYSIS

Search for a Theoretical Base in Sociological Theories of Generalized Social Exchange Behavior—A Brief Interlude Social network analysis (SNA) means analyzing various characteristics of the pattern of distribution of relational ties as mentioned above and drawing inferences about the network as a whole or about those belonging to it considered individually or in groups.

Beginning its journey as a descriptive metaphor, social network, in the course of the past few decades, has, as a parallel to the theories of market exchange, carved out a position for itself in the realm of theories and methodology for the study of society (Collins, 1988). Although its theoretical premise seems to be very close to market theories, it does not consist of looking for a best bargain in the case of an utilitarian exchange of goods and services. Rather, as a matter of generalized social exchange, it conceptualizes exchange not only in terms of economic interest but also of reciprocal role expectations as well as value orientations, social norms, and obligations. (See Homans, 1961, and Blau, 1964, for explication of the basic ideas relevant to understanding the rationale of the workings of social network, and see Turner, 1987, for a comprehensive discussion of social exchange and exchange network theories.) These attributes have made network theory more comprehensive and flexible enough to accommodate both asymmetric and symmetric relations as its natural elements. Hence, while social network theory does not deny the role of traditionally used a priori structural-functional concepts and categories in social research such as family, kinship, caste and ethnic groups, status groups, class, strata, and organization, it sees the actors and their roles and positions in a real-life situation rather in the light of the crystallization of patterns of interactions among individuals (Laumann, 1966; Wellman, 1988). This has also been discussed in detail in the context of Indian society (Srinivas & Beteille, 1964).

Social network theories do not consider individuals as forming a mechanical aggregate but as an organic whole where the constituent elements are connected among themselves as well as with the others through a mosaic of ties based on interactions, directly or indirectly, at various domains such as social, economic, political, and the like. This enables a social network to be quite flexible to include the ties of the relationship of a social actor, which exist in ground reality even if those fall outside the boundaries of traditional social categories and derive appropriate ways to incorporate them in theoretical and methodological structure befitting the dynamics in social reality. Thus, SNA, unlike conventional social science methodologies, is rooted in the fact that the social universe does not consist of an aggregate of mutually independent social actors. On the contrary, they exist in a system of interlinkages and interdependence, creating and structuring ties among themselves. (Incidentally, Berkowitz, 1982, has encapsulated the concept of SNA in the wider perspective of structural analysis.)

The methodology of SNA has also contributed to the formulation of precise quantitative measures of many qualitative concepts that have long been in use in the study of society but have remained vague often due to the degree of separation between the concept and the measure (Adhikari, 1960). Power, cohesion, fragmentation, reciprocity, hierarchy, cliques, and alliances are some examples. Dissatisfaction with prevalent macro theories of society, such as those of structural functionalism, therefore has led to an alternative in social network theories, particularly with respect to studying the lack of social cohesion and conflicting situations, steep asymmetry, and fragmentation in society.

Furthermore, SNA also serves as a powerful tool for the identification of changes in a pattern of group structure, whether it is the case of data obtained on participation in a small group; survey research with large communities such as villages, towns, and so on; or flows of population, trade, traffic, and so on among different regions.

The mainstream of social network studies in the past has been the study of personal networks, even though the central thrust is oriented toward "looking for community," "to discover it," in various areas of life and living of individuals (Wellman, 1997). The aim of this book is to supplement this by showing how one may obtain the social network of a community by undertaking a survey, how one may derive measures of various sociological parameters from SNA, and how combined with contextual data it can provide deep insight into the changing pattern of a society, its dynamicity. We will illustrate these at the end of this chapter with a quick comparison of the social networks of a large village community before and after various official measures aimed at rural progress have been implemented during the past two decades, although a detailed analysis of the measures and comparison of various parameters is deferred until Chapter 6.

In this chapter, we also state the preliminaries of SNA along with its general features and some specificities, including different types of measures derived from it. In the following chapters, we discuss different mathematical and statistical models leading to the derivation of various measures and inference about them. With the help of analysis of live data derived from some cross-sectional and longitudinal case studies, we then illustrate in Chapter 6 (the chapter on case studies) the use of the techniques developed.

1.4 PRELIMINARIES

At the outset, we should point out that, as yet, there does not exist any set of standard methods of data analysis and inference for SNA as it exists in the case of commonly used economic or demographic variables in social science research. Methods of SNA, in fact, have evolved in an ad hoc manner according to the needs of the topic (Mitchell, 1969). Even then, the methodology of SNA shows a pattern on the whole. It is largely bifocal in the sense that we can broadly classify the methods as leading to *local measures*, which analyze the network attributes with respect to individual units or dyads, and the *global measures*, which study the characteristics of the network considered as a whole. The two types of measures are not unrelated. Rather, the latter can be obtained from the former in a few instances by some sort of aggregation, as in the case of density or reciprocity. It may also be noted that the usual statistical methods of data analysis and inference, such as measures of central tendency and dispersion, are applicable mainly in case of the former derived from personal attributes. In contrast, analysis of the global measures generally remains problematic as we will see later in the case of fragmentation, level of hierarchy, reachability, and so on. By their very nature, for such characteristics of a network, either there is no local measure or the global measure cannot be obtained by aggregation of the local measures.

Vertices and arcs and their counts are the basic data used for analysis of a social network. These are used to obtain the values of various parameters of the network. We now give a few such parameters of a social network, discuss their social meaning and significance, and show how one can apply them in not only describing a social situation but also studying its dynamicity. Last, we conclude by describing, with the help of digraphs, how SNA, applied to actual data on a village community at two points of time, provides insight into its structural dynamicity. In fact, the findings from this study (especially the changes in the parameters over time) have emboldened us to ponder over questions such as the following: Is what we observe to be happening in the village community today a matter of random drift, or does it indicate that it is standing on the threshold of a social transformation in the society?

Before we proceed to the study of specific characteristics of a social network, we make a few general observations.

We emphasize that in social network analysis, we study *dyadic relation* (which involves a pair of nodes), whereas in the usual statistical or socio-economic surveys, one studies one or more attributes of a *single* node such as income, educational status, age, family size, and so on, which are assumed to be statistically independent. But the data of social network blatantly violate this assumption. For this reason, the usual statistical techniques may not always be applicable to SNA. Moreover, whereas the analytical forms of the first few theoretical moments give a reasonably good picture of a statistical distribution, there seems to be a large number of features of a social network, each of which can vary independently of the others and may not be amenable to statistical study only through their moments. Even if the measures are amenable to statistical analysis, it requires an extremely complex exercise to derive exact statistical formulae for estimation of these measures, especially when one is considering global measures. Besides, a whole social network is a unique case and, as such, has not been drawn at random from a pool of social networks. Hence, the usual mode of drawing statistical inference is also not valid. Again, global characteristics of a social network, even its out-degree and in-degree sequences, cannot be assumed to be necessarily normally distributed; they follow exponential or power law, mostly in a finite range. Hence, it requires selection of appropriate nonparametric statistical tools for SNA data.

In Figure 1.1, we give five hypothetical social networks involving a small number of nodes to illustrate some of the wide variety of networks possible.

For example, the first network involving 5 nodes in Figure 1.1 is close to the situation where everybody goes to everybody else. In the second network involving 10 nodes, the ties are all reciprocated, but the network is highly fragmented. The third network, comprising 5 nodes, is connected but shows

Figure 1.1

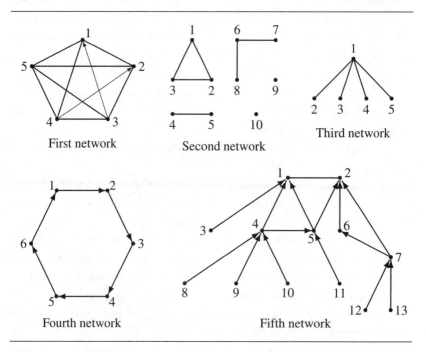

First network   Second network

Third network

Fourth network   Fifth network

concentration of power. It is held together by a single node (number 1) whose disappearance will cause the disintegration of the network. The fourth network involving six nodes is also connected in the sense that everybody can go to everybody else but through a large number of intermediaries. The fifth, involving 13 nodes, displays a strong hierarchy, and although it is connected, the ties flow only in one direction.

Vertices and arcs provide the primary constituent data set in a network. Even if these are fixed, the distribution of the ties among the vertices and the structure of the network can vary significantly. We illustrate this with the hypothetical example of six households in a neighborhood connected as in the fourth network in Figure 1.1 through six ties. Note that in this network, each of the households goes to exactly one among the remaining five, and only one of the remaining five comes to each household. Even if we impose this further condition, there are three other patterns possible besides those shown in Figure 1.1, which are presented in Figure 1.2.

Figure 1.2

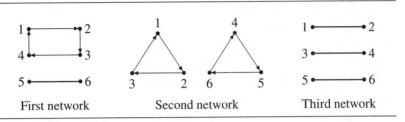

| First network | Second network | Third network |

Need for Standardization

For the purpose of comparing different social networks, one has to carefully standardize the parameter in question to get a measure. To illustrate this, consider two social networks N_1 and N_2. Suppose the vertices represent persons, and a tie from u to v indicates that u goes to v to spend (some of) his or her leisure time. How do we find the answer to the following question: Which of the networks is more cohesive? By cohesion, we mean that the actors in a network are bound closely by ties of interaction. For example, suppose N_1 is a network with 10 vertices and 20 ties, and N_2 is a network with 100 vertices and 200 ties. Which network is more cohesive, or are they equally cohesive? Even though the second network has a larger number of ties, we cannot conclude that it is more closely tied up. Let us look at another network to illustrate this better. Suppose N_3 that has 5 vertices and 20 ties. Clearly, N_3 is more cohesive than N_1 since everybody goes to everybody else in N_3, whereas in N_1, on average, a person goes to only 2 out of the other 9. Thus, one has to standardize the number of ties in terms of the number of vertices properly before using it to compare two networks. How do we do this? The *density* of the network, defined as $m/n(n-1)$, provides a natural measure (Berkowitz, 1982, pp. 45–46). Here, and in what follows, n and m denote, respectively, the number of vertices and the number of ties in the network. Note that $n(n-1)$ is the maximum possible number of ties given that n is the number of vertices. Hence, the measure is $m/n(n-1)$. Density lies in the range of 0 to 1, irrespective of the number of vertices, and can be used to compare two networks. Clearly, the density is $20/90 = 22.2\%$, $200/9,900 = 2.02\%$, and $20/20 = 100\%$ in N_1, N_2, and N_3, respectively.

Although density as defined above is a good measure of cohesion (i.e., how closely the vertices are tied up in the network), what about its valid-ity when n is large as in the network N_2? The implicit assumption in the above-mentioned standardization is that every vertex *can* interact with all the others. Is it realistic in a real-life situation to hold that, in order to spend leisure time, each person potentially visits 99 others as a matter of regular practice? Perhaps one has to think of a *potential set* for each vertex u from which u makes its *actual* choices or one has to at least assume something about the size of this potential set. For example, if we assume that nobody can go to more than 10 others to spend leisure time, then the maximum possible number of ties in the network with 100 persons would be 1,000, and the density in N_2 would be revised to $200/1,000 = 20\%$, which perhaps gives a more realistic picture.

The main difficulty with the approach using potential sets is in determining them or their sizes because there is no unique way to decide what would be the potential set of a vertex. One researcher might decide in favor of asking the respondent directly to find out who belongs to his or her potential set, while another might hesitate since there would be no way to check data reliability. One might opt for a structural approach such as considering those who belong to the same ethnic category (e.g., caste, community, or locality) as constituting the potential set. However, that approach could make a potential set too large to be realistic. Again, one could come up with a solution such as the following example: The potential set for a vertex consists of those vertices that are reachable from the former, if needed, in a few, say two or three, steps (in forward or backward direction) in the network. However, one needs to verify whether the assumption that ties can easily be used in the reverse direction hold. Moreover, when the approach of potential sets is used, perhaps one should report the potential sets used along with the value of the measure. In view of these problems, one usually falls back on the density as defined earlier. However, But one needs to be cautious about the way data are standardized and in interpreting the values of the measures in general.

1.5 A FEW BASIC PARAMETERS

The two most basic parameters of a social network are the *number of vertices* n and the *number of arcs* m. We have already discussed how m can be standardized to get the *density* $m/n(n-1)$, a global measure of cohesion.

Since the arcs in the network may not be distributed uniformly over the vertices, one may be interested in the corresponding local measure that we call the *local density*. What is the counterpart of m for the ith vertex? It is the number of ties d_i going out from it and is called the *out-degree* of the ith vertex. How do we standardize d_i? Since the minimum and maximum values d_i can take are 0 and $n - 1$, we take $d_i/(n - 1)$ to be the local density of the ith vertex.

There is another possible counterpart of m for the ith vertex: the number of ties e_i coming to it, known as the *in-degree* of the ith vertex. The corresponding local measure of density is $e_i/(n - 1)$. We show that d_i and e_i signify entirely different things. However, it is easy to see that the sum of the d_is, as well as the sum of the e_is, is m. Hence, the global density is the average of the local densities of the vertices, whether they are based on the out-degrees or in-degrees. However, one traditionally takes $d_i/(n - 1)$, rather than $e_i/(n - 1)$, as the local measure, particularly when the network represents a sociological choice relation.

What is the sociological significance of the out-degree and the in-degree of a vertex? If it is a network of individual choice or preference (i.e., if a tie uv means that u chooses or prefers v), then the in-degrees of the vertices in the network indicate respective status by popularity, potential for influence or leadership, and so on. Out-degree of a vertex will then indicate its capacity for sociability.

On the other hand, suppose it is a matter of giving assistance or help and support, whether financial, material, or physical, or by counseling and providing advice at critical times when it is urgently requested (i.e., a tie uv means that u takes help from v). Then the in-degree of a vertex suggests its status in the network in terms of resource potential or the potential to lead someone to another who is resourceful. In-degree thus becomes a measure of potential power or influence as well. Out-degree, on the other hand, can be an indicator of buffer against vulnerability of the resource poor in the community. It can also bring out the extent of dependency. From the assessment of the ground situation based on available contextual data, appropriate interpretation of the finding (i.e., whether it is a matter of dependency or buffer against vulnerabilities) can be ascertained. In a general sense, out-degree denotes expansiveness.

Last, if both in-degree and out-degree of a vertex are zero, it is an isolate without any interaction with others in the social network being studied. Its interpretation again depends on contextual data. It may indicate a situation of self-contained self-sufficiency arising out of resourcefulness or, on the contrary, a state of atomization by fragmentedness where one does not care for the other as if in a state of anomie or alienation from the others in the society (see Simmel translated and edited by Wolff, 1964).

The third basic parameter of a social network is the *number of reciprocal* (also called *symmetric* or *mutual*) *pairs* in it. This is the number s of unordered pairs of vertices $\{u, v\}$ such that both uv and vu are ties in the network. As a matter of sociological concept, reciprocity is not defined as an instantaneous phenomenon. It "does not mean equivalence of return on every occasion; equivalence is usually achieved over a long period of time" (Srinivas, 1952). As an illustration, we quote Mayer's (1975) idea of "balanced reciprocity," which we believe adds another dimension to broaden the meaning of the concept: "I had come to study and write a book; they had helped me to gather the material to do so; and I had returned with the book which was the result of our joint efforts . . . a reciprocally balanced relation between myself and Ram Kheri over the years."

How do we standardize s to get a measure of reciprocity so that it can be used to compare different networks? It is not difficult to see that in a network with n vertices, s can take all integer values from 0 to $n(n - 1)/2$, so we may take $2s/n(n - 1)$ as a standardized *measure of reciprocity*. However, this measure again implicitly assumes that everybody can interact and reciprocate with everybody else in the network. Thus, in a sense, it is a combined measure of reciprocity and cohesion. One may rather want a measure of the extent to which the arcs present in the network (whether they are small or large in number) are reciprocated. Then one fixes both the number of vertices n and the number of arcs m and standardizes s. It can be shown that the corresponding standardized measure of reciprocity is $2s/m$ provided $m \leq n(n - 1)/2$. (Actually, the denominator in the measure should be reduced by 1 in case it is odd.) Following Rao and Bandyopadhyay (1987), the derivation of this and other measures of reciprocity is discussed in detail in Chapter 5. We have refrained ourselves from further studies of reciprocity using boundary specifications such as class, caste, kinship, and so on. The interested reader is referred to the work by Chatterjee, Bandyopadhyay, and Rao (1993).

Just as in the case of density, there may be wide variation in the degree of reciprocity displayed by different vertices in the network. Thus, one would like to have a measure of *local reciprocity* for a vertex. The counterpart of s for the ith vertex is the number s_i of other vertices with which it is tied up reciprocally. By dividing s_i by $n - 1$, we get the standardized measure of local reciprocity of the ith vertex to be $s_i/(n - 1)$. Since the sum of all s_is equals

$2s$ (recall that the definition of s involves unordered pairs), the global measure $2s/n(n-1)$ is the average of the local measures of all the vertices.

What is the local measure of reciprocity of the ith vertex corresponding to the global measure $2s/m$? We may take it to be s_i/d_i, where d_i is the out-degree of the ith vertex. Notice that now the global measure is a weighted average of the local measures, the weight of s_i/d_i is d_i. One may again wonder why not use the in-degree e_i instead of the out-degree d_i. The reason is that, usually, the out-degree is what is in the control of the ith vertex. Sometimes, instead of asking an open question, the out-degrees are determined by the investigator such as when he or she asks following the "fixed-choice" technique of the name generator, "Who are your three best friends?"

Reciprocity in a social network indicates some sort of balance or harmony, which can nullify the negative effects of social stratification. Local reciprocity of a vertex in the network of a social choice relation is an indicator of its social congeniality or level of being integrated with others in the network. Global reciprocity, on the other hand, is a measure of integration of its vertices among themselves. Hence, it becomes a measure of social solidarity of a group or community. In fact, global reciprocity was pointed out to be a distinctive characteristic of a community in the past. (See, for example, the writings of classical sociologists such as Durkheim or Tonnies.) The roots of theoretical properties of reciprocity have been researched in the sociological literature from various theoretical positions as a matter of a cultural norm of the society as well as functional explanation of its persistence (Gouldner, 1960), on one hand, and as a model of social exchange of resources, services, products, knowledge, and expertise, on the other hand (Collins, 1988).

We now give the values of the above measures for the networks in Figures 1.1 and 1.2. We start with the fifth network in Figure 1.1. It has 13 vertices and 16 arcs. Hence, its density is 0.103. It can be checked that the out-degrees and the in-degrees of the vertices are $1, 1, 1, 2, 2, 1, 2, 1, 1, 1, 1, 1, 1$ and $4, 4, 0, 3, 2, 1, 2, 0, 0, 0, 0, 0, 0$. Thus, the local density based on out-degree is 0.167 for the fourth, fifth, and seventh vertices and 0.0833 for the others. The local density based on in-degree is 0.333 for the first and second vertices, 0.25 for the fourth, 0.167 for the fifth and seventh, 0.0833 for the sixth, and 0 for the remaining vertices. It can be checked that the densities of the first four networks in Figure 1.1 are 0.90, 0.121, 0.40, and 0.20, respectively. For each of the networks in Figure 1.2, the density as well as the local density of each vertex is 0.20.

The last network in Figure 1.1 has only one reciprocal pair, so its measure of reciprocity, $2s/n(n-1)$, is 0.013. It can be checked that the measure is 0.80 for the first network, 1.00 for the second and third networks, and 0 for the fourth. It is 0.067, 0, and 1.00 for the three networks in Figure 1.2. The measure $2s/m$ is not applicable to the first network in Figure 1.1 since m is too close to $n(n-1)$. It is 1.00 for the second and third networks, 0 for the fourth, and 0.125 for the last. It is 0.333, 0, and 1.00 for the three networks in Figure 1.2.

We have indicated here only some of the important commonly used basic parameters of a social network. More detailed discussion—both graph theoretic and statistical—of these and some other complex parameters that can be used to study various aspects of a social network such as fragmentation, reachability, centrality, cliques, hierarchy, and structural equivalence will be given in Chapter 5.

As already stated, since theoretical probability distributions of the measures of global parameters as described above, as well as their estimation by drawing a sample of nodes, remain problematic, statistical tests for differences between networks with respect to them could not be performed unless one invoked a superpopulation setup or used computer simulation to estimate the distributions.

1.6 A COMPARATIVE STUDY OF THE SOCIAL NETWORKS OF A VILLAGE AT TWO TIME PERIODS

Objectives of the Study

Our illustration of social network analysis came out of a study undertaken first during 1971–1972 and later in 1997–1998. The fact that the economic structure of rural society in West Bengal is not egalitarian but stratified by sharp inequality in income distribution was argued a long time ago, supported by an extensive sample survey of households in a large number of villages (Mukherjee, 1957). The subject matter of our study is, rather, to explore the structural pattern of social relations in rural areas. Our concern was with how the "community" could survive in villages despite steep economic stratification.

For this purpose, we decided to scan the empirically derived structure that arises out of the pattern of interactions in rural society, especially in the course of the processes of help and support that people provide to one another at the time of a crisis or emergency in daily life. The structure constitutes a major binding block of a social mosaic of a community. A study of its pattern can certainly shed light on many other parameters of dynamics in the society as well, which operate independently or jointly with economic or traditional sociocultural parameters.

Since a system of sharp socioeconomic stratification pervades the rural social structure and the social positions and functional roles correspond to it, one is required to look for an appropriate answer outside the orbit of structural functionalism. Again, neither the theory of general systems nor the organic theory of society provides any satisfactory concept to grasp its nuances. Conflict theory, on the other hand, argues coercion and hence aggressive behavior as the basic motif. While the former cannot explain fragmentation and polarization or conflict in society, its focus being to look for a symbiotic balance that implicitly binds the components of its structure to maintain a stable equilibrium, the latter, on the other hand, has no room for equality or symmetry except as a temporary or passing feature in the society. Network theory can capture both.

Background of the Survey

The sources of our social network data are two longitudinal studies undertaken in a typical rain-fed traditional rice-based economy in central West Bengal in India covering 2,697 households in 21 villages in the Md. Bazar Community Development Block of Birbhum district. Since our study was explanatory, we had to go beyond the boundaries of only a survey of these households (HHs). We had included appropriate qualitative methods for collection of supplementary qualitative data, such as case history collection and group discussion as and when required. One study, which may be considered as a sort of baseline study for the purpose, was conducted during 1971–1972 and the other, its follow-up after about 25 years, during 1997–1998. We start by briefly stating the pertinent findings of the 1971–1972 study (for details, see Bandyopadhyay & von Eschen, 1981, 1991).

The majority of the villagers in the study area belonged to Hindu caste (like the Bagdi) or non-Hindu tribal ethnic groups (like the Santal), which were traditionally ascribed low ritual status according to orthodox religious hierarchy. They were occupationally small or marginal farmers, agricultural and other day laborers, sharecroppers, daily workers in roadside tea stalls or garages, hawkers, and so on. The agro-economic situation of the study area at that time was marked by scarcity of irrigated cultivable land and lack of credit facilities for poor cultivators. Inadequate and irregular supply of agricultural inputs, such as water for irrigation, fertilizers, and high-yield value (HYV) seeds for rice, forced the farmers to remain "resource poor" and rain fed. Lack of road and transport facilities restricted the access to the outside labor market, which in turn pushed down the level of job availability and compelled the laborers to accept quite low wage rates and inimical terms and conditions of employment. Earning by appropriation rather than by production was the thrust of the large land-owning upper-class elite families that dominated these villages at that time. Acute poverty did not permit a considerable section of the villagers to provide for even a meager "two meals a day" for their families throughout the year. Bureaucratic apathy and bias against ordinary villagers, as well as "red tapism" in redressing their grievances, all taken together had further aggravated the condition of their life and living (Bandyopadhyay & von Eschen, 1995).

The negative experiences created a cultural setup of "amoral familism" (Banfield, 1958). Scarcity of access to resources for the villagers except for a few large land-owning elite families of Hindu castes of high ritual status, coupled with the feeling of helplessness about any possibility of changing the course of life and living in the near future, created a "zero-sum" situation. This, in turn, had generated during the past few decades a covert attitude of jealousy and distrust among the villagers, which continued to dampen the motivation for organizing extensive help and cooperation among the common villagers (Bandyopadhyay & von Eschen, 1988). While the upper-class elites were economically resourceful, socially enjoyed high ritual status, and organized mostly in a few large cliques, the commoners in the lower rung in the village remained economically weak, resourceless and dependent on the elites, socially low in status, and among themselves highly fragmented into a large number of small groups or isolates and hence utterly disorganized. Thus, the local power structure was marked by acute polarization in terms of a highly unequal power base in the community. (For a detailed discussion of power bases and potentials of power, see Wrong, 1988.)

Subsequently, since around the mid-1980s, several important official measures of rural development have been implemented. These measures were aimed particularly at the redistribution of resources and democratization of an administrative system facilitating the involvement of the rural poor in it (Bandyopadhyay & von Eschen, 1995). These include measures such as the redistribution of vested land (Patta); registration of sharecroppers and a Minimum Wages Act for agricultural and other laborers; development of schemes of minor irrigation; easily available bank loans; establishment of *Panchayats*, which looked after the implementation of these measures; development of a total literacy campaign; extension of road and transport connections; implementation of schemes of rural electrification; and so on. Findings of empirical studies undertaken in the district in general as well as in and around our study villages corroborate that these measures have not only ameliorated the economic condition of the rural poor in a noteworthy way but also catalyzed their socio-administrative participatory role (Rao & Bandyopadhyay, 1998).

Central Query

In the context of the above-mentioned changes in the socioeconomic and administrative scenario in the villages, we asked the following question: Evidence indicates that the economic condition of the rural poor has improved, but with the economic and administrative changes, what has happened to the pattern of articulating ties of social relations such as help and support among the villagers? Does it indicate empowerment of the rural poor or at least a sign of alteration in the power structure within the village due to a decrease in its social dependency on those who are at the top of the structure? And that way, can one make a conjecture of an upcoming change in the structure of social power relations in the villages? In this chapter, we show only in a preliminary way how one can infer in that regard from the distribution of ties in social networks. Detailed analysis of analytical measures will be discussed in the subsequent chapter of case studies.

We have chosen to undertake analysis of a social network formed through help and cooperation in the daily life of the villagers because this constitutes an important element in organizing informal social insurance against vulnerabilities faced by the lower rung of the village community in daily life and living. This query thus becomes directly rooted in the theory of social exchange— in the structure of "resource dependencies," imposing an "unequal flow of resources" in social exchanges among different sets of actors (Cook, 1982).

Morphological Characteristics of Ties of Social Networks

We briefly refer to relevant data of one village (e.g., Kabilpur, occasionally abbreviated as *K*) among the 21 villages studied by Bandyopadhyay and von Eschen. A detailed discussion in this regard is given in Chapters 6 and 7 after

Table 1.1   Distribution of Ties by Purpose

Purpose	Frequency	Number of Ties as %
Related to medical treatment	289	28.7
Food/related to food	203	20.1
Family rites	161	16.0
Production (mostly farming)	86	8.5
Family crisis (counseling, mediation, or general suggestions)	84	8.3
Miscellaneous	185	18.4
Total	1,008	100.0

Table 1.2   Distribution of Ties by Type of Request

Type	Frequency	Number of Ties as %
Financial	517	51.29
Material	261	25.89
Physical	230	22.82
Advice/recommendations	173	17.17
Total	1,008	100.00

the mathematical and statistical issues of SNA are discussed in the intervening chapters.

Requests for help, cooperation, and assistance during emergencies in daily life and living still occur in the village despite implementation of various measures of rural development. Informal help and support to meet the urgencies of daily life and living still play an important role in daily village life mostly because the effects of the measures taken for economic development are not yet strong enough for villagers to be able to cope with all kinds of urgent requirements. The data on the distribution of ties of requests for various purposes and types of help made by one household to another in 1997–1998 are given in Tables 1.1 to 1.6.

About half of the requests for help were made in connection with medical treatment and arranging for food in an emergency (Table 1.1). Financial help was the major thrust, although need for material and physical help were also considerable (Table 1.2). The observation that requests for help were also often repeated by one household to another indicated the stability of a behavioral pattern (Table 1.3).

Table 1.3   Number of Times a Household Made Requests to Another During the Past Year

Number	Frequency	Number of Requests as %
1	537	53.27
2	238	23.61
3	119	11.81
4	39	3.87
5	22	2.18
6	53	5.26
Total	1,008	100.00

Mean $= 1.94$, standard deviation $= 1.36$.

Villagers seek help both in cash and in kind. Requests for help in kind are made mostly for rice. The extent of help sought by a household over the year is moderate, but it varies from quite a small amount to a moderately large one, depending on the nature of the problem. Data in this regard are given in Tables 1.4 and 1.5.

Table 1.4   Distribution of Ties by Amount of Monetary Help

Amount (Rs. in a Year)	Number of Ties	Number of Ties as %
Below 100	142	25.7
100 to 250	136	24.6
250 to 500	151	27.3
500 to 1,000	69	12.5
Above 1,000	55	9.9
Total	553	100.0

Mean $=$ Rs. 346.46 and standard deviation $= 31.99$.

Content of Network Ties

Data on sources of informal help show that these have become more diversified than before. Employers and political elements have been added to kin and friends (the latter dominated the earlier scenario), as shown in Table 1.6. Knowledge and experience have also become objects of sharing

Table 1.5 Distribution of Ties by Quantity of Rice Borrowed

Quantity (kg in a Year)	Number of Ties	Number of Ties as %
Below 20	59	26.6
20 to 60	51	23.0
60 to 200	62	27.9
200 to 500	38	17.1
Above 500	12	5.4
Total	222	100.0

Mean = 79.81 kg and standard deviation = 22.03.

as and when needed. Nowadays, the villagers interact at many more different levels in their ordinary daily life, which has led to the diversification of social relationships along which the ties of request flow. Providing alternative sources of support in case of a crisis or emergency faced in the course of everyday life has no doubt added to the strength of the buffer against vulnerabilities.

An in-depth exploration of meanings attached by actors to the ties of these social relationships, as if untying the knots of a discourse, unfolds a social reality in transition.

The underlying rationale of the bulk of the requests (59.2%) is instrumentally oriented to secure personal gratifications of the partners at both ends. From one end, the sender of the request does it explicitly for financial, material, or physical support at the time of an urgent need. At the other end, the potential giver calculates in terms of the expectation of some sort of future reward in the form of uninterrupted labor supply as in case of an employer (30.2%), creating confidence or extending a support base among the villagers by a political figure (5.0%), or gaining the obligation of the neighbor to provide help in return as and when such a need occurs (24.0%). Incidence of goal-oriented instrumental requests such as to share experience and knowledge whether in social life or material production in exchange of social respectability is low (6.0%). But what is most relevant for the conjecture made earlier concerning social reality is that fulfillment of traditional customs or duties or moral bindings motivates "the other end" to act only in a moderate-size stratum (29.8%) unlike three decades earlier. In other words, on the whole, social relationships now operate much more instrumentally, or perhaps "unrurally."

Table 1.6   Distribution of Ties by Relationship

Relation	*Number of Ties*	*Number of Ties as %*
Employer	304	30.2
Neighbor	243	24.0
Political	51	5.0
Kin	300	29.8
Friend	50	5.0
Knowledgeable/ experienced	60	6.0
Total	1,008	100.0

Findings From SNA of the Village *K*

A significant finding of the SNA is that on average, the number of HHs one can depend on and approach for help of any type at the time of an emergency was 3.6 in 1971–1972, and this later became even smaller at 1.7 during 1998 in village *K*, considering that there were 239 and 472 HHs in the village during the two time periods, respectively.

The second feature is that the pattern of the articulation of ties was predominantly reciprocal earlier but not any longer. The number of reciprocal pairs has decreased sharply from 387 to 46, although the number of HHs has more than doubled. But one can now reach many more households for help indirectly (i.e., through intermediaries). That is, on other considerations, the role of intermediaries has become more important for the villagers to cope with the "crisis situation" and survive. This is evident from the increase in the percentage of reachable pairs from 2.5% to 15.1%. But this seems to have been achieved at a price: The average distance to the reachable household has increased from 1.2 to 5.8 (see Table 1.7).

Note that in Table 1.7, we have used some common graph-theoretic terms as such since their connotations are quite appropriate sociologically. To illustrate: If an HH *y* can be requested directly (i.e., in one step) by another HH *x*, then in the pair of HHs *xy*, *y* is reachable from *x*, and the distance of *y* from *x* is 1. Again, if *x* has to go through two or more intermediaries to request *y*, then also reachable *y* is from *x*, but this time the distance of *y* from *x* is greater than 1. In fact, if there are different sets of intermediary HHs through whom HH *x* can approach another HH *y*, then the smallest number of such steps (i.e.,

Table 1.7   Summary of Data on Some Measures of the Social Networks in 1972 and 1998

Measure	1972	1998
Number of households	239	432
Number of ties		
within castes	800	366
between castes within village	71	368
going out of village	0	274
Total number of ties	871	1,008
Average out-degree (within village)	3.6	1.7
Number of reciprocal pairs	387	46
Number of isolates (within village ties)	94	40
Number of isolates (all ties)	94	3
Percentage of reachable pairs (directed)	2.5	15.1
Average finite distance (directed)	1.2	5.8
Maximum finite distance (directed)	4	16
Percentage of reachable pairs (undirected)	7.7	78.2
Average finite distance (undirected)	2.3	4.4
Maximum finite distance (undirected)	6	10

the number of steps in the shortest "distance chain") is regarded as a measure of distance of y from x. In short, a "reachable pair" of HHs xy means x can place a request to y, and the "distance" means the minimum number of steps x needs to reach y with the request. Note that in a directed social network the, distance of y from x can be quite different from that of x from y.

The boundaries of ties of help and assistance have also extended in two important dimensions between the two time periods. Requests now cut across caste and village boundaries much more than in the past. A summary of data on some of the measures for social networks in 1972 and 1998 is presented in Table 1.7.

Two Poor Communities in the Village and Changes in Their Networks

In the village K, the Bagdi and the Santal households constitute the bulk of the village poor. Even within this bottom rung of village society, signs of upward occupational mobility under the impact of land reforms and related measures can clearly be discerned. The occupational class composition of these

Table 1.8   Principal Sources of Livelihood of Bagdi and Santal Households

| Year | Farm and Nonfarm Laborer | | Factory Laborer | Small or Marginal Farmer or Share-cropper | Total |
	Employed at the Beck and Call of the Employer	Working on the Basis of Contract (Per Day/Week/ Month or Job, etc.)			
		Bagdi community			
1997–1998	16	89	38	60	203
	(7.88%)	(43.84%)	(18.72%)	(29.56%)	(100.00%)
1971–1972	67	25	0	4	96
	(69.79%)	(26.04%)	(0.00%)	(4.17%)	(100.00%)
		Santal community			
1997–1998	1	35	9	36	81
	(1.24%)	(43.21%)	(11.11%)	(44.44%)	(100.00%)
1971–1972	33	17	0	3	53
	(62.26%)	(32.08%)	(0.00%)	(5.66%)	(100.00%)

two communities has notably changed between the two time periods, as shown in Table 1.8. Households belonging to these communities have become mostly small or marginal farmers, agricultural/factory laborers, and sharecroppers. Since minimum daily wage rates and terms and conditions of employment have improved in these occupations, their economic condition has now become better than what it was earlier when they were largely employed as "attached laborers" hired on the basis of terms and conditions that amounted almost to being a bonded laborer of the land owner. We will not go into these aspects since those have been discussed in detail in Bandyopadhyay and von Eschen (1981). Here we only indicate changes in local power centers and in the overall social relational pattern as a result of economic changes using diagrams of social networks for the village as well as for the two communities separately. Comparison of the networks using measures based on different features will be discussed later in Chapter 6.

In Diagram 1 at the end of the book, we show the social network of the Kabilpur village during the 1971–1972 time period. The numbers in the diagram are the serial numbers of the households. To avoid cluttering, the ties in a clique (where everybody is tied both ways with almost everybody else) are not shown. The flow of out-degrees for the village network is listed in a table at the end of this chapter for ready reference and for use by the interested readers for any reanalysis.

As one can see, the major component of structural configuration in Kabilpur was a hierarchically organized pyramid: one-way ties from a large number of households going upwards to a small clique of seven households who belonged to the large land-owning Hindu Sadgope caste of high ritual status in the village. There were also two other large cliques of high-caste (Sadgope) large- and medium-sized farmers. These two cliques did not have any tie with the others in the village. Factional conflicts in the past pushed them to continue to live like two isolated groups. The rest of the households in the village were fragmented into small connected groups. There were a large number of isolates as well.

In Diagram 2 at the end of the book, we give the networks of the Sadgope households in the 1997–1998 time period. These show how the cliques of high-caste (Sadgope) landed elites of the earlier period got dispersed later into egocentric fragments, connected through intermediaries.

On the other hand, the trend is different for the Bagdis and Santals. Their networks in 1971–1972 and in 1997–1998 are given in Diagrams 3 through 6 at the end of the book. The networks of the earlier period show the predominance of a reciprocally tied but highly fragmented structure of the two communities. How this apparently paradoxical situation, reciprocity with fragmentation, has come to exist is described later in Chapter 6 on case studies.

In the networks of the Bagdi and Santal communities in 1997–1998, one finds how the social network structures of these communities have become connected through asymmetric ties. These are also marked by a few households, forming mini-hubs, with large in-degrees indicating emergence of egocentric power centers. Small in size but vertically tied up mini-pyramid-like structures have appeared among them, showing the rise of power elites from among them.

The alteration in power structure in the village is further substantiated by an examination of the changes in the distribution of in-degrees. If the in-degrees are arranged in decreasing order, all 21 households at the top chunk of the distribution during 1971–1972 were high-caste landed elites (large farmer Sadgopes). By households at the top of the in-degree distribution, we refer to those whose in-degrees exceeded the mean by more than twice the standard deviation. During 1997–1998, there were 16 households at the top of the in-degree distribution. Among them, two belonged to the Bagdi and one each to the Santal and the Barber (Napit) communities. Three of these four are only marginal farmers-cum-agricultural laborers, and one—the Barber (Napit)—is a small grocery shop owner who was originally a roadside barber. Recent official measures have increased their income and enabled them to save money. At that stage, with the support of the local Panchayat, they secured financial support from the local bank and have been able to purchase land, a pump set for irrigation, and so on and earn more from agriculture. Two of them were among the important organizers of the local peasants movement as well. One was elected vice-president of the local Panchayat. In times of crises, villagers nowadays depend on them for help and support instead of depending on the high-caste landed elites as they used to do earlier.

The findings of SNA raise a critical question for consideration as a matter of future perspective of social transformation. The mini-pyramids and new power centers from within the lower rungs of society and the disintegration of the cliques at the top are certainly a structural shift away from unequal distribution of power in the society. But is it a move toward an egalitarian society? Is this likely to be a truncated shift and the trend to be rather an instance of substitution of old elites by new ones? Or will it continue to move further ahead through some socially conscious goal-oriented checks to transform the society? Only further studies can enable us to answer these questions.

We close this introduction with a display of the flow of out-degrees of the HHs in the entire village of Kabilpur (1971–1972) in case the reader becomes interested in doing any further analysis of SNA data for this village. Serial numbers of the HHs are shown in ascending order and for each such HH, and we indicate the detailed listing of all other HHs at the receiving end of the ties originating at the initial HH. We separate the HH that originates such tie(s) by a colon(:).

Kabilpur (1971–1972) Village Network:
Flow of Out-Degrees of the HHs in the Village

[7 : 218, 219]; [8 : 218, 219]; [9 : 218, 219]; [10 : 218, 219]; [11 : 218, 219]; [12 : 218, 219];
[13 : 218, 219]; [14 : 12, 15, 20]; [15 : 12, 14, 20]; [20 : 24, 25, 218, 219], [24 : 2025];
[25 : 20, 24]; [26 : 13, 17, 30, 218]; [27 : 218, 219]; [28 : 49, 210]; [29 : 32, 33, 36];
[32 : 29, 33, 36]; [33 : 29, 32, 36]; [34 : 132]; [36 : 29, 32, 33]; [37 : 218]; [38 : 42, 69];
[40 : 41, 54, 55, 63, 80]; [41 : 54, 55, 63, 80]; [42 : 38, 69]; [49 : 169, 170, 210]; [52 : 56];
[56 : 52]; [57 : 65, 79, 83]; [58 : 83]; [63 : 40, 41, 80]; [64 : 122, 145]; [65 : 57, 79, 83];

[69 : 38, 42]; [70 : 75]; [72 : 78]; [75 : 70, 218]; [76 : 218]; [78 : 72]; [79 : 57, 65, 83];
[80 : 40, 63, 218]; [83 : 57, 65, 79]; [84 : 88, 137]; [88 : 84, 137]; [94 : 99, 112, 168];
[95 : 102]; [96 : 218]; [97 : 218]; [99 : 94]; [102 : 95]; [109 : 210, 218, 219]; [110 : 111];
[111 : 110]; [113 : 104]; [114 : 115, 117, 118, 119]; [115 : 114, 117, 118, 119]; [116 : 218];
[117 : 114, 115, 118, 119]; [118 : 114, 115, 117, 119]; [119 : 114, 115, 117, 118];
[122 : 64, 145]; [127 : 129]; [129 : 127]; [132 : 34, 218]; [137 : 84, 88]; [142 : 143];
[143 : 142]; [145 : 64, 122]; [147 : 148, 149, 150, 151, 152];
[148 : 147, 149, 150, 151, 152]; [149 : 147, 148, 150, 151, 152];
[150 : 147, 148, 149, 151, 152]; [151 : 147, 148, 149, 150, 152];
[152 : 147, 148, 149, 150, 151]; [169 : 49, 170, 210, 218]; [170 : 49, 169, 210]; [172 : 218];
[174 : 175, 177, 179, 180, 181, 182, 183, 184, 185, 186, 187, 189, 190, 194, 195, 196, 197, 200];
[175 : 174, 177, 179, 180, 181, 182, 183, 184, 185, 186, 187, 189, 190, 194, 195, 196, 197, 200];
[176 : 178, 191, 193, 206, 208, 229, 230, 231, 232, 233, 234, 235, 236, 237];
[177 : 174, 175, 179, 180, 181, 182, 183, 184, 185, 186, 187, 189, 190, 194, 195, 196, 197, 200];
[178 : 176, 191, 193, 206, 208, 229, 230, 231, 232, 233, 234, 235, 236, 237];
[179 : 174, 175, 177, 180, 181, 182, 183, 184, 185, 186, 187, 188, 189, 190, 194,
195, 196, 197, 200];
[180 : 174, 175, 177, 179, 181, 182, 183, 184, 185, 186, 187, 188, 189, 190, 194,
195, 196, 197, 200];
[181 : 174, 175, 177, 179, 180, 182, 183, 184, 185, 186, 187, 188, 189, 190, 194,
195, 196, 197, 200];
[182 : 174, 175, 177, 179, 180, 181, 183, 184, 185, 186, 187, 189, 190, 194, 195,
196, 197, 200];
[183 : 174, 175, 177, 179, 181, 182, 184, 185, 186, 187, 188, 189, 190, 194, 195, 196, 197, 200];
[184 : 174, 175, 177, 179, 180, 181, 182, 183, 185, 186, 187, 188, 189, 190, 194,
195, 196, 197, 200];
[185 : 174, 175, 177, 179, 180, 181, 182, 183, 184, 186, 187, 188, 189, 190, 194,
195, 196, 197, 200];
[186 : 174, 175, 177, 179, 180, 181, 182, 183, 184, 185, 187, 188, 189, 190, 194,
195, 196, 197, 200];
[187 : 174, 175, 177, 179, 180, 181, 182, 183, 184, 185, 186, 188, 189, 190, 194,
195, 196, 197, 200];
[188 : 174, 175, 177, 179, 180, 181, 182, 183, 184, 185, 186, 187, 189, 190, 194,
195, 196, 197, 200];
[189 : 174, 175, 177, 179, 180, 181, 182, 183, 184, 185, 186, 187, 188, 190, 194,
195, 196, 197, 200];
[190 : 174, 175, 177, 179, 180, 181, 182, 183, 184, 185, 186, 187, 188, 189, 194,
195, 196, 197, 200];
[191 : 176, 178, 193, 206, 208, 229, 230, 231, 232, 233, 234, 235, 236, 237];
[193 : 176, 178, 191, 206, 208, 229, 230, 231, 232, 233, 234, 235, 236, 237];
[194 : 174, 175, 179, 180, 181, 182, 183, 184, 185, 186, 187, 188, 189, 190, 195, 196, 197, 200];
[195 : 174, 175, 179, 180, 181, 182, 183, 184, 185, 186, 187, 188, 189, 190, 194, 196, 197, 200];

[196 : 174, 175, 179, 180, 181, 182, 183, 184, 185, 186, 187, 188, 189, 190, 194, 195, 197, 200];
[197 : 174, 175, 179, 180, 181, 182, 183, 184, 185, 186, 187, 188, 189, 190, 194, 195, 196, 200];
[198 : 199, 201, 203, 207, 215, 218, 226]; [199 : 198, 201, 203, 207, 215, 218, 226];
[200 : 174, 175, 179, 180, 181, 182, 183, 184, 185, 186, 187, 188, 189, 190, 194, 195, 196];
[201 : 198, 199, 203, 207, 215, 226]; [202 : 204, 205, 211, 212, 218, 219];
[203 : 198, 199, 201, 207, 215, 226]; [204 : 202, 205, 211, 212, 218, 219, 220];
[205 : 202, 204, 211, 212, 218, 219, 220];
[206 : 176, 178, 191, 193, 208, 229, 230, 231, 232, 233, 234, 235, 236, 237];
[207 : 198, 199, 201, 203, 215, 226];
[208 : 176, 178, 191, 193, 206, 229, 230, 231, 232, 233, 234, 235, 236, 237];
[209 : 213]; [210 : 49, 169, 170, 202]; [211 : 204, 205, 212]; [212 : 202, 204, 205, 211];
[213 : 209]; [214 : 215]; [215 : 198, 199, 201, 203, 207, 214, 218, 226];
[217 : 218, 219, 220, 223, 227, 228]; [218 : 217, 219, 220, 223, 227, 228];
[219 : 217, 218, 220, 223, 227, 228]; [220 : 217, 218, 219, 223, 227, 228];
[221 : 222]; [222 : 221]; [223 : 217, 218, 219, 220, 227, 228];
[226 : 198, 199, 201, 203, 207]; [227 : 217, 218, 219, 220, 223, 228];
[228 : 217, 218, 219, 220, 223, 227];
[230 : 176, 178, 191, 193, 206, 229, 231, 232, 233, 234, 235, 236, 237];
[231 : 176, 178, 191, 193, 206, 229, 230, 232, 233, 234, 235, 236, 237];
[232 : 176, 178, 191, 193, 206, 229, 230, 231, 233, 234, 235, 236, 237];
[233 : 176, 178, 191, 193, 206, 229, 230, 231, 232, 234, 235, 236, 237];
[234 : 176, 178, 191, 193, 206, 229, 230, 231, 232, 233, 235, 236, 237];
[235 : 176, 178, 191, 193, 206, 229, 230, 231, 232, 233, 234, 236, 237];
[236 : 176, 178, 191, 193, 206, 229, 230, 231, 232, 233, 234, 235, 237];
[237 : 176, 178, 191, 193, 206, 229, 230, 231, 232, 233, 234, 235, 236]; [238 : 218, 219, 220]

REFERENCES

Adhikari, B. P. (1960). Construction of socio-economic models for planning. *Eastern Anthropologist, India*, pp. 84–94.

Bandyopadhyay, S., & von Eschen, D. (1981). *The conditions of rural progress in India*. Submitted as a report to the Canadian International Development Agency.

Bandyopadhyay, S., & von Eschen, D. (1988). Villager failure to cooperate: Some evidence. In D. W. Attwood & B. S. Baviskar (Eds.), *Who shares cooperatives and rural development?* (pp. 112–145). Oxford, UK: Oxford University Press.

Bandyopadhyay, S., & von Eschen, D. (1991). Agricultural failure: Caste, class and power in rural West Bengal. In D. Gupta (Ed.), *Social stratification* (pp. 353–368). Oxford, UK: Oxford University Press.

Bandyopadhyay, S., & von Eschen, D. (1995). Electoral communism and destruction of cooperation in West Bengal. In B. S. Baviskar & D. W. Attwood (Eds.), *Finding the middle path* (pp. 293–322). Boulder, CO: Westview.

Banfield, E. C. (1958). *Moral basis of a backward society*. Glencoe, IL: Free Press.

Berkowitz, S. D. (1982). *An introduction to structural analysis*. Toronto: Butterworths.

Blau, P. M. (1964). *Exchange and power in social life*. New York: John Wiley.

Burt, R. S., Minor, M. J., & Associates. (1983). *Applied network analysis*. Beverly Hills, CA: Sage.

Chatterjee, A. K., Bandyopadhyay, S., & Rao, A. R. (1993). Relative importance of different factors for boundary of reciprocity. *Connections: Bulletin of the INSNA, 16*, 15–22.

Collins, R. (1988). *Theoretical sociology*. New York: Harcourt Brace Jovanovich.

Cook, K. S. (1982). Network structures from an exchange perspective. In P. V. Marsden & N. Lin (Eds.), *Social structure and network analysis* (pp. 177–199). Beverly Hills, CA: Sage.

Dutta, B., & Jackson, M. (Eds.). (2003). *Networks and groups: Models of strategic formation*. Berlin: Springer Verlag.

Gouldner, A. V. (1960). The norm of reciprocity: A preliminary statement. *American Sociological Review, 25*, 161–177.

Homans, G. C. (1961). *Social behaviour: Its elementary forms*. London: Routledge and Kegan Paul.

Homans, G. C., Deutsch, M., Sherif, M., Sherif, C. W., Hare, A. P., & Raven, B. H. (1968). Groups: The study of groups, group behavior, group formation, role structure and group performance. In D. C. Sills (Ed.), *International encyclopedia of the social sciences* (pp. 259–293). New York: Macmillan/Free Press.

Laumann, E. O. (1966). *Prestige and association in urban community*. Indianapolis, IN: Bobbs-Merrill.

Laumann, E. O., Marsden, P. V., & Prensky, D. (1983). The boundary specification problem. In R. S. Burt & M. J. Minor (Eds.), *Applied network analysis* (pp. 18–34). Beverly Hills, CA: Sage.

Laumann, E. O., & Pappi, F. U. (1976). *Networks of collective action: A perspective on community influence system*. New York: Academic Press.

Mayer, A. C. (1975). On becoming a participant-observer. In A. Beteille & T. N. Madan (Eds.), *Encounter and experience* (pp. 40–41). Delhi, India: Vikas Publishing House Pvt. Ltd.

McGrath, C., Blythe, J., & Krackhardt, D. (1997). The effect of spatial arrangement on judgments and errors in interpreting graphs. *Social Networks, 19*, 223–242.

Mitchell, J. (1969). The concept and use of social networks. In J. Mitchell (Ed.), *Social networks in urban situations*. Manchester, UK: Manchester University Press.

Mukherjee, R. (1957). *The dynamics of a rural society*. Berlin: Academic Verlag.

Rao, A. R., & Bandyopadhyay, S. (1987). Measures of reciprocity in a social network. *Sankhyā Series A, 49*, 141–188.

Rao, A. R., & Bandyopadhyay, S. (1998). Project on "*A study of changing social relations—Social network approach*." Funded by Survey Research and Data Analysis Centre, Indian Statistical Institute.

Srinivas, M. N. (1952). *Religion and society among the Coorghs of South India*. Oxford, UK: Clarendon.

Srinivas, M. N., & Beteille, A. (1964). Networks in Indian social structure. *Man, 122*, 165–168.

Turner, J. H. (1987). *The structure of sociology theory.* Jaipur, India: Dorsey.

Wassermann, S., & Faust, K. (1994). *Social network analysis: Methods and applications.* Cambridge, UK: Cambridge University Press.

Wellman, B. (1988). Thinking structurally. In B. Wellman & S. D. Berkowitz (Eds.), *Social structures: A network approach* (pp. 15–19). Cambridge, UK: Cambridge University Press.

Wellman, B. (Ed.). (1997). *Networks in the global village.* Boulder, CO: Westview.

Wolff, K. H. (Ed.). (1964). *The sociology of Georg Simmel.* New York: Free Press.

Wrong, D. H. (1988). *Power, its forms, bases and uses.* Chicago: University of Chicago Press.

TWO

INTRODUCTION TO DIGRAPHS

————◦•◆•◦————

2.1 INTRODUCTION

As noted in Chapter 1, a social network may be considered, with some oversimplification, to be a digraph. In this chapter, we formally define digraphs and study them, concentrating mainly on the aspects that are relevant to the study of social networks. However, we will occasionally be giving some concepts and results whose relevance to social networks may not immediately be clear but will be needed in a concept, proof, or procedure in connection with social networks.

In regard to references, most books on graph theory have a chapter on digraphs. Harary, Norman, and Cartwright (1965) wrote an excellent book devoted to digraphs, but some of the terminology used in it differs slightly from ours. Most books on social network analysis also give an introduction to digraphs (see the references at the end of this chapter).

A *directed graph* (abbreviated *digraph*) is a pair (V, A), where V is a finite nonempty set and A is a set of ordered pairs of distinct elements of V. Elements of V are called *vertices, nodes,* and so on, and elements of A are called *arcs, links, ties,* and so on. For simplicity of notation, we will denote the arc (i.e., ordered pair) (u, v) simply by uv. Note that arc uv is different from arc vu, assuming both are arcs. Clearly, for any two distinct vertices u and v, there are four possibilities: (1) neither uv nor vu is an arc, (2) uv is an arc but not vu, (3) vu is an arc but not uv, and (4) both uv and vu are arcs.

As already mentioned, in applications, the vertices of the digraph may be persons, households, organizations, regions, and so forth, and the arcs may represent any particular binary (dyadic) relation R on the set of vertices, such as going for help, disliking friendship/companionship, having a specified type of connection, and so on. The ordered pair uv will be an arc if and only if u is related to v according to R.

We use G to denote a digraph. We will denote the vertex set of G by $V(G)$ and the arc set of G by $A(G)$.

Usually, a digraph is represented diagrammatically by taking vertices to be points in the plane and drawing an arrow from vertex u to vertex v if uv is an arc. In such a representation, the positions of the points representing the vertices have no significance and may be chosen based on convenience, and the arrows need not be straight. *If, in a digraph, both* uv *and* vu *are arcs, we sometimes represent these two together by a line without arrowheads joining* u *and* v.

We give an example of a digraph G in Figure 2.1.

Figure 2.1

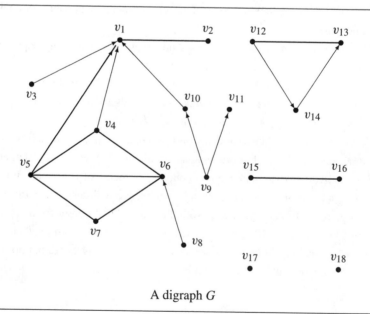

A digraph G

The vertex set of the digraph is $V = \{v_1, v_2, \ldots, v_{18}\}$. Note that $v_1 v_2$, $v_2 v_1$, $v_3 v_1$, $v_4 v_1$, $v_4 v_5$, and so on are arcs, and $v_1 v_3$ and $v_2 v_3$ are not arcs of G.

We now define several graph-theoretic concepts that are of importance in social networks. Note that it is not difficult to remember most of these since the terminology is natural and/or borrowed from everyday use.

2.2 A FEW BASIC DEFINITIONS

Probably the most important parameter of a network (i.e., a digraph) is the number of vertices, which we denote by n. Next comes the number of arcs, which we denote by m. Some people call n the *order* and m the *size* of the digraph. We say that the arc uv is *from u to v*. u is the *initial vertex* and v the *terminal vertex* of the arc uv. If uv is an arc, we say that u is *adjacent to* v, and v is *adjacent from u*. Sometimes we loosely say u and v are adjacent if at least one of uv and vu is an arc. The arc uv *joins u to v* and is *incident* with both of them. u and v are the two *end vertices* of the arc uv.

A digraph $G = (V, A)$ with $V = \{v_1, v_2, \ldots, v_n\}$ can conveniently be represented by its *adjacency matrix* **A**. This is the $n \times n$ matrix $((a_{ij}))$ where a_{ij} is 1 or 0 according to whether $v_i v_j$ is an arc. Note that $a_{ii} = 0$ for all i.

2.3 SUBDIGRAPH, CONVERSE, AND COMPLEMENT

When do we say that (V_1, A_1) is a *subdigraph* of a digraph $G = (V, A)$? Naturally, we want $V_1 \subseteq V$ and $A_1 \subseteq A$. But these are not enough because if uv is an element of A_1, then u and v must belong to V_1. We thus define a subdigraph of G to be (V_1, A_1), where $V_1 \subseteq V$, $A_1 \subseteq A$, and if uv is an element of A_1, then u and v belong to V_1. For any $V_0 \subseteq V$, the *subdigraph* G_0 *of* $G = (V, A)$ *induced by* V_0 is the subdigraph (V_0, A_0), where A_0 is the set of *all* arcs uv of G such that both u and v belong to V_0. G_0 is the network formed by the elements of V_0. The adjacency matrix of the subdigraph of G induced by $\{v_{i_1}, v_{i_2}, \ldots, v_{i_k}\}$ is the principal submatrix of the adjacency matrix of G formed by the rows and columns numbered $i_1, i_2, \ldots, i_k$. This is a $k \times k$ submatrix.

Note that $(\{v_1, v_2, v_3, v_5, v_{15}, v_{17}\}, \{v_1 v_2, v_5 v_1\})$ is a subdigraph of G in Figure 2.1. But the subdigraph of G induced by the vertex set $\{v_1, v_2, v_3, v_5, v_{15}, v_{17}\}$ is $(\{v_1, v_2, v_3, v_5, v_{15}, v_{17}\}, \{v_1 v_2, v_2 v_1, v_3 v_1, v_5 v_1\})$.

The *converse* of a digraph $G = (V, A)$ is the digraph H with the same vertex set V, with uv being an arc in H if and only if vu is an arc of G. We obtain the converse of G by reversing the direction of each arc of G. If both uv and vu are arcs of G, they remain arcs of H. Note that the adjacency matrix of the converse of G is the transpose $\mathbf{A}^\mathsf{T}$ of the adjacency matrix $\mathbf{A}$ of G. An example of the converse of a digraph is given in Figure 2.2.

For any digraph $G = (V, A)$, we define the *complement* $\bar{G}$ to be the digraph with the same vertex set V, with uv being an arc of $\bar{G}$ if and only if $u \neq v$ and uv is not an arc of G. If G is the digraph representing a relation R, then $\bar{G}$ represents the negation of R (for pairs of distinct elements). If G has n vertices and m arcs, then $\bar{G}$ has $n(n-1) - m$ arcs. The adjacency matrix of $\bar{G}$ is $\mathbf{J} - \mathbf{I} - \mathbf{A}$, where $\mathbf{J}$ is the $n \times n$ matrix with all elements as 1s, $\mathbf{I}$ is the $n \times n$ identity matrix with 1 along the diagonal and 0 elsewhere, and $\mathbf{A}$ is the adjacency matrix of G. Note that if both uv and vu are arcs of G, none of them is an arc of $\bar{G}$. We give an example of the complement of a digraph in Figure 2.2.

Figure 2.2

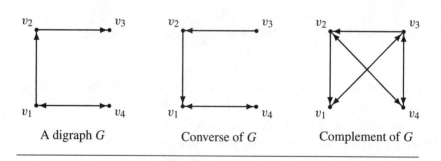

A digraph G Converse of G Complement of G

2.4 NULL DIGRAPH AND COMPLETE DIGRAPH

A digraph G is said to be *null* if no two vertices of G are adjacent. G is said to be *complete* if, for any two distinct vertices u and v, *at least one of uv and vu* is an arc. Clearly, the null digraph on n vertices has no arcs, and any complete digraph on n vertices has at least $\binom{n}{2} = n(n-1)/2$ arcs.

Figure 2.3

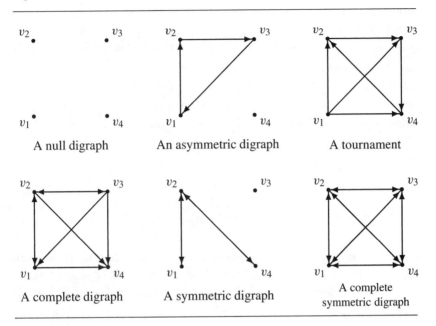

| A null digraph | An asymmetric digraph | A tournament |

| A complete digraph | A symmetric digraph | A complete symmetric digraph |

2.5 SYMMETRY IN A DIGRAPH

A digraph G is said to be *symmetric* if vu is an arc whenever uv is an arc. Note that G is symmetric if and only if its adjacency matrix is a symmetric matrix. G is said to be *asymmetric* (or *antisymmetric*) if vu is *not* an arc *whenever uv* is an arc. Note that "G is asymmetric" is much stronger than "G is not symmetric." In social networks, symmetry is also referred to as *reciprocity* or *mutuality*. Note that the digraph G of Figure 2.1 is neither symmetric nor asymmetric. A complete asymmetric digraph is called a *tournament* (because it can represent the result of a round-robin tournament where no draws are possible, with $v_i v_j$ being an arc if v_i beats v_j). A digraph G with vertex set V is asymmetric if and only if it is contained in a tournament with the same vertex set V. Note that a tournament on n vertices has exactly $\binom{n}{2}$ arcs, but the converse is not true, and the complete symmetric digraph on n vertices has the maximum possible number of arcs—namely, $n(n-1)$.

The subdigraph of G in Figure 2.1 induced by the vertex set $\{v_{12}, v_{13}, v_{14}\}$ becomes a tournament if any one of the arcs $v_{12}v_{13}$ and $v_{13}v_{12}$ is dropped. The subdigraph of G induced by $\{v_2, v_4, v_7, v_{15}, v_{18}\}$ is null and that induced by

$\{v_{12}, v_{13}, v_{14}\}$ is complete. The subdigraph of G induced by $\{v_4, v_5, v_6, v_7\}$ is symmetric. Figure 2.3 (p. 35) illustrates some of the above concepts.

We will call an unordered pair of vertices $\{u, v\}$ in a digraph a *symmetric pair* (or *reciprocal pair*) if both uv and vu are arcs. We will use $s(G)$ to denote the number of symmetric pairs in G. Clearly, the number of symmetric pairs in G equals that in the converse of G. Also, $0 \leq s \leq \lfloor m/2 \rfloor$, where $\lfloor x \rfloor$ denotes the integer part of x, and m is the number of arcs in G. If $\mathbf{A}$ is the adjacency matrix of a digraph G, $s(G) = \sum_{i<j} \min(a_{ij}, a_{ji}) = \sum_{i<j} a_{ij}a_{ji}$. Note that $s(G) = 8$, $\{v_1, v_2\}$ is a symmetric pair, and $\{v_1, v_3\}$ and $\{v_1, v_6\}$ are not symmetric pairs for the digraph G of Figure 2.1.

2.6 OUT-DEGREES AND IN-DEGREES

The arcs in a digraph G may not be evenly distributed at the different vertices. So one considers the *out-degree* $d_G^+(u)$ of a vertex u in G, defined as the number of vertices v such that uv is an arc. It may be noted that $d_G^+(u)$ is the number of vertices u is joined to and does not tell which are those vertices. In a social network, $d_G^+(u)$ usually indicates the *expansiveness* of u. The *out-degree sequence* of a digraph with vertex set $V = \{v_1, v_2, \ldots, v_n\}$ is $(d_1, d_2, \ldots, d_n)$, where $d_i = d^+(v_i)$ for all i. For the digraph in Figure 2.1, $d^+(v_1) = 1$, $d^+(v_4) = 3$, and $d^+(v_{11}) = 0$.

Two natural questions arise here. First, what are the conditions a given sequence $(d_1, d_2, \ldots, d_n)$ with integer entries has to satisfy so that it is the out-degree sequence of some digraph? Second, given the out-degree sequence of a digraph, can we reconstruct the digraph uniquely from it? The answer to the first question is simple. It is easy to see that necessary and sufficient conditions for $(d_1, d_2, \ldots, d_n)$ to be an out-degree sequence are $0 \leq d_i \leq n-1$ for $i = 1, 2, \ldots, n$. The answer to the second question is no in general. For example, every vertex has out-degree 1 in all three digraphs in Figure 2.4.

But these three digraphs are obviously very different. In fact, one can find many more digraphs with the same out-degree sequence.

Although the first two digraphs in Figure 2.4 have the same out-degree sequence, their in-degree sequences are different, where the *in-degree* $d_G^-(u)$ of u is defined as the number of vertices w such that wu is an arc. In a social network, $d_G^-(u)$ usually indicates the *popularity* or *power* of u. Clearly, the out-degree (respectively, the in-degree) of u in G is the in-degree

Figure 2.4

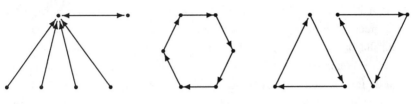

Three digraphs with out-degrees 1

(respectively, the out-degree) of u in the converse of G. When the digraph is clear from the context, we write $d^+(u)$ for $d_G^+(u)$ and $d^-(u)$ for $d_G^-(u)$. The *in-degree sequence* of a digraph G with vertex set $V(G) = \{v_1, v_2, \ldots, v_n\}$ is $(e_1, e_2, \ldots, e_n)$, where $e_i = d^-(v_i)$ for all i. We will denote $\max\{d^+(v_i) : 1 \leq i \leq n\}$ by $d_{\max}$ and $\max\{d^-(v_i) : 1 \leq i \leq n\}$ by $e_{\max}$.

The out-degree sequence and the in-degree sequence of G in Figure 2.1, with the vertices in the natural order, are

$$(1, 1, 1, 3, 4, 3, 2, 1, 2, 1, 0, 2, 1, 1, 1, 1, 0, 0),$$
$$(5, 1, 0, 2, 3, 4, 2, 0, 0, 1, 1, 1, 2, 1, 1, 1, 0, 0).$$

Note that G has 18 vertices and 25 arcs.

It is easy to see that, for a digraph, $\sum d_i = m$ since each arc is counted once (at its initial vertex) when the out-degrees of the vertices are added. Similarly, $\sum e_i = m$ for a digraph (now each arc is counted once at its terminal vertex). Note that the out-degree and the in-degree of the ith vertex of a digraph G are, respectively, the ith row sum and the ith column sum of the adjacency matrix $\mathbf{A}$ of G, and the grand total of all the entries in the adjacency matrix is the number of arcs m. Note also that the out-degree and the in-degree of the ith vertex are the ith components of the vectors $\mathbf{A1}$ and $\mathbf{1}^T\mathbf{A}$, where $\mathbf{1}$ is an $n \times 1$ vector with all entries 1 and the superscript T denotes transpose.

It is easy to see that a given sequence $(e_1, e_2, \ldots, e_n)$ with integer entries is the in-degree sequence of some digraph if and only if $0 \leq e_i \leq n - 1$ for $i = 1, 2, \ldots, n$. Also, the in-degree sequence does not determine the digraph uniquely. What happens if we fix both out-degree and in-degree sequences? The conditions $0 \leq d_i \leq n - 1$ and $0 \leq e_i \leq n - 1$ for $i = 1, 2, \ldots, n$ and $\sum d_i = \sum e_i$ are not sufficient for a digraph to exist with $\mathbf{d} = (d_1, d_2, \ldots, d_n)$ and $\mathbf{e} = (e_1, e_2, \ldots, e_n)$ as the out-degree and in-degree sequences. For example, suppose $\mathbf{d} = (4, 3, 2, 2, 1)$ and $\mathbf{e} = (4, 4, 1, 2, 1)$ for a digraph G. Then we see from the out-degrees of the first two vertices that there should be at least five arcs from these to the last three vertices, whereas from the in-degrees of the last three vertices, we see that there are at most four arcs from the first two vertices to the last three, a contradiction. Necessary and sufficient conditions for $\mathbf{d}$ and $\mathbf{e}$ to be the out-degree and in-degree sequences of a digraph were found by Ryser and Fulkerson (see Berge, 1973). Do the out-degree and in-degree sequences together determine the digraph uniquely? The answer is again no in general. For example, the last two digraphs in Figure 2.4 have both the out-degree and the in-degree of every vertex equal to 1 but are clearly different.

A vertex of a digraph with out-degree 0 is called a *sink*, and a vertex with in-degree 0 is called a *source*. A vertex with both out-degree and in-degree 0 is called an *isolated vertex*. Note that a vertex v is a source (respectively, sink) of G if and only if v is a sink (respectively, source) of the converse of G.

In the digraph G of Figure 2.1, vertices v_{17} and v_{18} are isolates, v_3 and v_9 are sources (v_{17} is also a source according to the above definition), and v_{11} is a sink.

2.7 CONNECTEDNESS AND COMPONENTS

We now turn to *connectedness*. A *directed walk* (we often omit the word *directed*) from vertex u to vertex v in a digraph is a finite sequence of vertices $[u = u_1, u_2, \ldots, u_k = v]$ such that $u_i u_{i+1}$ is an arc for $i = 1, 2, \ldots, k - 1$. Its *length* is $k - 1$. (We allow, as a matter of convention, $k = 1$ and say that $[u]$ is a walk of length 0.) We say that u is the *initial vertex* and v the *terminal* vertex of the walk. A *(directed) trail* is a walk in which no arc is repeated (vertices may be repeated) as one travels along the walk. A *(directed) path* is a walk in which the vertices are all distinct (i.e., a walk that does not cross itself). A *directed cycle* (or a *circuit*) in a digraph is a directed walk $[u_1, u_2, \ldots, u_k]$ such that $k \geq 3$, $u_1, u_2, \ldots, u_{k-1}$ are all distinct and $u_k = u_1$. Its *length* is $k - 1$. Note that no arc is repeated as one goes around a circuit. If both uv and vu are arcs, then $[u, v, u]$ is a circuit. A digraph is said to be *acyclic* if it has no circuit.

In the digraph G of Figure 2.1, $[v_8, v_6, v_4, v_5, v_4]$ is a (directed) walk from v_8 to v_4, which is not a path; $[v_8, v_6, v_4]$ is a path from v_8 to v_4, and $[v_8, v_6, v_5, v_4, v_1]$ is a path from v_8 to v_1. $[v_1, v_2, v_1]$ and $[v_{13}, v_{12}, v_{14}, v_{13}]$

Figure 2.5

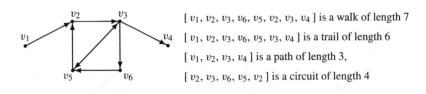

[$v_1, v_2, v_3, v_6, v_5, v_2, v_3, v_4$] is a walk of length 7

[$v_1, v_2, v_3, v_6, v_5, v_3, v_4$] is a trail of length 6

[v_1, v_2, v_3, v_4] is a path of length 3,

[v_2, v_3, v_6, v_5, v_2] is a circuit of length 4

are circuits. The subdigraph of G induced by the vertex set $\{v_{12}, v_{13}, v_{14}\}$ becomes acyclic if the arc $v_{13}v_{12}$ is dropped. Figure 2.5 explains some of these concepts.

In a digraph, vertex v is said to be *reachable* from vertex u if there is a (directed) walk from u to v. It is easy to see that any walk from u to v contains a path from u to v, so v is reachable from u if and only if there is a path from u to v. In the digraph G of Figure 2.1, the vertices reachable from v_7 are v_1, v_2, v_4, v_5, v_6, and v_7 itself. The only vertex reachable from v_{11} is v_{11}.

A digraph G is said to be *transitive* if uw is an arc whenever uv and vw are arcs and $u \neq w$. Note that, in a transitive digraph, uw is an arc whenever there is a path from u to w and $u \neq w$. The set of all reachable pairs in a digraph G forms what is known as the *transitive closure* H of G. More precisely, H has the same vertex set as G, and uw is an arc in H if and only if u and w are distinct and w is reachable from u in G. Clearly, H is transitive (see Figure 2.6 for an illustration).

A digraph G is said to be *strongly connected* (or *strong* for short) if, for any two vertices u and v, v is reachable from u and u is reachable from v. The vertices of a strongly connected social network form a single group in the sense that every vertex can communicate with or reach every other vertex by using the ties of the network and passing through intermediaries if necessary.

For any digraph G (strongly connected or not), consider the relation $\sim$ defined on V by $u \sim v$ if and only if each of u and v is reachable from the other. This is an equivalence relation on V. The equivalence classes with respect to this relation are called the *strong components* of G, and they form a partition of V. Clearly, a strong component of G is a maximal set of vertices in G that induces a strongly connected subdigraph. If $C \subseteq V$ forms a strong component of G, the subdigraph of G induced by C is also referred to as the strong component C. By definition, two vertices belong to the same strong component if and only if each of them is reachable from the other.

Figure 2.6

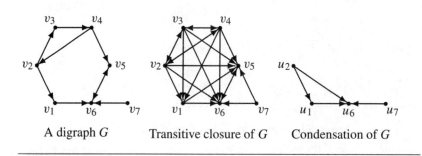

A digraph G Transitive closure of G Condensation of G

If C_1 and C_2 are two strong components of a digraph G and if there is an arc from (some vertex of) C_1 to (some vertex of) C_2, then there cannot be any arc from C_2 to C_1 since if there is such an arc, then C_1 and C_2 will be part of a single strong component. More generally, we have the following. Suppose $C_1, C_2, \ldots, C_k$ are the strong components of G. We define the *condensation* H of G to be the digraph with vertex set $\{C_1, C_2, \ldots, C_k\}$, where we draw an arc from C_i to C_j in H if and only if there is at least one arc from C_i to C_j in G. Then it is easy to see that H is always acyclic. Note that the condensation of G is obtained by "contracting" each strong component to a single vertex.

The digraph G of Figure 2.1 has 11 strong components, their vertex sets being $\{v_1, v_2\}$, $\{v_3\}$, $\{v_4, v_5, v_6, v_7\}$, $\{v_8\}$, $\{v_9\}$, $\{v_{10}\}$, $\{v_{11}\}$, $\{v_{12}, v_{13}, v_{14}\}$, $\{v_{15}, v_{16}\}$, $\{v_{17}\}$, and $\{v_{18}\}$. Denoting these by $C_1, C_2, \ldots, C_{11}$, we note that although there are two arcs in G from C_3 to C_1, the condensation of G is a digraph and has only one arc from the vertex corresponding to C_3 to the vertex corresponding to C_1.

In the definition of strong connectedness, we insist that there should be a (directed) walk from every vertex to every other vertex. Sometimes we relax the definition of a walk given above by insisting only that at least one of $u_i u_{i+1}$ and $u_{i+1} u_i$ is an arc for each i. The idea is that perhaps the link between u_i and u_{i+1} can be used in either direction (for each i) to ultimately establish a connection between u_1 and u_k. Such a "walk" is called a *semi-walk*, an *undirected walk*, or a *chain*. A *semi-path* and a *semi-cycle* are defined similarly. Note that a semi-walk in a digraph G may be thought of as a walk in the *symmetrization of G* (i.e., the symmetric digraph H obtained from G

by introducing the arc vu, whenever it is not already present, for every arc
uv). We say that G is *weakly connected* (or *weak* for short) if H is strongly
connected. More generally, the strong components of H are called the *weak*
components or simply *components* of G. Since every directed path in G is also
a directed path in H, it follows that every strongly connected digraph is weakly
connected and, more generally, every weak component of a digraph is a union
of one or more strong components. We will call a digraph *disconnected* if it is
not even weakly connected.

Figure 2.7

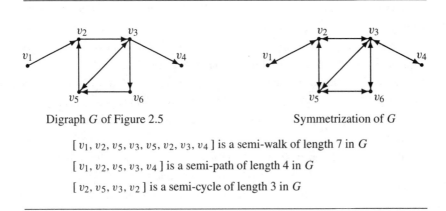

Digraph G of Figure 2.5   Symmetrization of G

$[\,v_1, v_2, v_5, v_3, v_5, v_2, v_3, v_4\,]$ is a semi-walk of length 7 in G

$[\,v_1, v_2, v_5, v_3, v_4\,]$ is a semi-path of length 4 in G

$[\,v_2, v_5, v_3, v_2\,]$ is a semi-cycle of length 3 in G

Figure 2.8

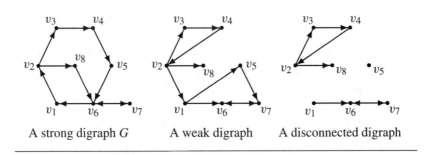

A strong digraph G A weak digraph   A disconnected digraph

   In the digraph G of Figure 2.1, $[v_3, v_1, v_4, v_6, v_8]$ is a semi-path that is not
a path. $[v_{12}, v_{13}, v_{14}, v_{12}]$ is a semi-cycle. G has exactly five weak components
with vertex sets $\{v_1, v_2, \ldots, v_{11}\}$, $\{v_{12}, v_{13}, v_{14}\}$, $\{v_{15}, v_{16}\}$, $\{v_{17}\}$, and $\{v_{18}\}$.

A procedure for finding the strong and weak components from the adjacency matrix will be given in the next section.

2.8 DISTANCE BETWEEN VERTICES

Reachability of vertex v from vertex u does not take into account the number of intermediaries through which u has to go to reach v. To remedy this problem, we now define the distance between two vertices. As already mentioned, $k - 1$ is called the *length* of the walk $[u_1, u_2, \ldots, u_k]$ in a digraph. Thus, length is the number of steps taken (i.e., arcs used) when one travels along the walk from u_1 to u_k. The *length* of the circuit $[u_1, u_2, \ldots, u_k]$ with $u_k = u_1$ is $k - 1$. Note that the length of a circuit equals the number of distinct vertices on it as well as the number of arcs used when one travels around it.

In the digraph G of Figure 2.1, $[v_8, v_6, v_4, v_5, v_4, v_1]$ is a walk of length 5 from v_8 to v_1. $[v_8, v_6, v_5, v_4, v_1]$ is a path of length 4 from v_8 to v_1. $[v_1, v_2, v_1]$ and $[v_{13}, v_{12}, v_{14}, v_{13}]$ are circuits of lengths 2 and 3, respectively.

The *distance $d(u, v)$ from a vertex u to a vertex v* in a digraph G is the smallest length of a path from u to v. $d(u, v)$ is defined to be infinity (∞) if there is no path from u to v. This distance function in a digraph has the following properties: (i) $d(u, v) \geq 0$, (ii) $d(u, v) = 0$ if and only if $u = v$, and (iii) $d(u, w) \leq d(u, v) + d(v, w)$ for any u, v and w. Properties (i) and (ii) are obvious. To prove (iii), note that if P is a path from u to v with length k, and Q is a path from v to w with length ℓ, then P followed by Q gives a walk from u to w with length $k + \ell$, so $d(u, w) \leq k + \ell$. This proves (iii). But $d(u, v) \neq d(v, u)$ in general. It may be noted that in a digraph with n vertices, $d(u, v)$ is either ∞ or less than n.

A path from u to v with length $d(u, v)$ (in other words, the shortest path from u to v) is called a *geodesic* from u to v. Suppose $[u_1, u_2, \ldots, u_k]$ is a geodesic from u_1 to u_k. If $1 \leq i < j \leq k$, then $d(u_i, u_j) = j - i$, and $[u_i, u_{i+1}, \ldots, u_j]$ is a geodesic from u_i to u_j. It also follows that $u_i u_j$ cannot be an arc if $j \geq i + 2$. In a digraph, a vertex v is said to be *reachable from a vertex u in k steps* if $d(u, v) \leq k$.

In the digraph G of Figure 2.1, $d(v_8, v_1) = 3$, $d(v_1, v_8) = \infty$, $d(v_{13}, v_{14}) = 2$ and $d(v_{14}, v_{13}) = 1$. The vertices reachable from v_7 in two steps are v_1, v_4, v_5, v_6, and v_7. Another illustration is given in Figure 2.9 (diameter and radius will be defined in Section 2.11).

Figure 2.9

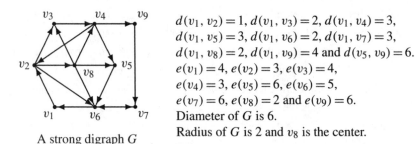

$d(v_1, v_2) = 1, d(v_1, v_3) = 2, d(v_1, v_4) = 3,$
$d(v_1, v_5) = 3, d(v_1, v_6) = 2, d(v_1, v_7) = 3,$
$d(v_1, v_8) = 2, d(v_1, v_9) = 4$ and $d(v_5, v_9) = 6.$
$e(v_1) = 4, e(v_2) = 3, e(v_3) = 4,$
$e(v_4) = 3, e(v_5) = 6, e(v_6) = 5,$
$e(v_7) = 6, e(v_8) = 2$ and $e(v_9) = 6.$
Diameter of G is 6.
Radius of G is 2 and v_8 is the center.

A strong digraph G

Given a vertex, say v_1 of a digraph, it is sometimes convenient to partition the vertex set V into $V_0 = \{v_1\}$, V_1, $V_2, \ldots$ and V_∞, where $V_i = \{v : d(v_1, v) = i\}$. Then note that there cannot be any arc from V_i to V_j with $j \geq i + 2$. The digraph of Figure 2.9 is redrawn in this way in Figure 2.10.

Figure 2.10

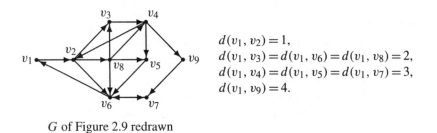

$d(v_1, v_2) = 1,$
$d(v_1, v_3) = d(v_1, v_6) = d(v_1, v_8) = 2,$
$d(v_1, v_4) = d(v_1, v_5) = d(v_1, v_7) = 3,$
$d(v_1, v_9) = 4.$

G of Figure 2.9 redrawn

Let **A** be the adjacency matrix of a digraph G with vertex set $\{v_1, v_2, \ldots, v_n\}$. Then we claim that the (i, k)th element of $\mathbf{A}^p$ is the number of walks of length p from v_i to v_k in G. This is trivial for $p = 1$. Assume it for p, and let $\mathbf{A}^p = ((a_{ij}^{(p)}))$. Then the the (i, k)th element of $\mathbf{A}^{p+1}$ is $\sum_{j=1}^n a_{ij}^{(p)} a_{jk}$. Since the jth summand in this sum is precisely the number of walks of length $p + 1$ from v_i to v_k with v_j as the penultimate vertex, it follows that the sum is the total number of walks of length $p + 1$ from v_i to v_k. This proves the claim. Hence, using powers of **A**, we can find the distance from v_i to v_k, and thus $d(v_i, v_k)$ is the smallest p such that the (i, k)th element of $\mathbf{A}^p$ is nonzero (note that $\mathbf{A}^p$ is a matrix with nonnegative integer entries). However, there are better algorithms for finding shortest paths in digraphs (see Deo, 1980).

The adjacency matrix can also be used to find strong and weak components of a digraph G as follows. If there is a path from a vertex v_i to a vertex v_k, then there is such a path of length at most $n - 1$. So v_k is reachable from v_i if and only if the (i, k)th entry in $\mathbf{I} + \mathbf{A} + \cdots + \mathbf{A}^{n-1}$ is a (strictly) positive integer. We can thus determine all reachable pairs. Then we find the strong component C_1 containing v_1: It is the set of all vertices v such that v and v_1 are reachable from each other. If $C_1 \neq V$, we take a vertex not in C_1 and find the strong component C_2 containing it. If $C_1 \cup C_2 \neq V$, we take a vertex not in $C_1 \cup C_2$ and find the strong component C_3 containing it. Proceeding in this manner, we find all the strong components. To find the weak components of digraph G, we first find the adjacency matrix $\mathbf{B}$ of the symmetrization H of G thus: $b_{ij} = \max(a_{ij}, a_{ji})$ for all i and j. Now the weak components of G are simply the strong components of H.

2.9 UNDIRECTED GRAPHS

Sometimes a symmetric digraph is viewed as what is known as a graph (or an undirected graph). A *graph* is a pair (V, E) where V is the set of vertices and E is a set of unordered pairs of distinct vertices called *edges*. The edge $\{u, v\}$ is usually represented in a diagram by a line joining the points u and v, as shown in Figure 2.11. A symmetric digraph (V, A) can be viewed as the graph (V, E) and vice versa, where $\{u, v\} \in E$ if and only if uv and $vu \in A$. Many of the concepts we defined for digraphs have obvious analogs for graphs, but we will not discuss them except to note that a cycle in a graph has length of at least 3, whereas in a digraph, there can be circuits of length 2. The graph corresponding to the symmetrization of a digraph G is sometimes called the *graph underlying* G.

A vertex u of a connected graph (V, E) is said to be a *cut vertex* if the subgraph induced by $V - \{u\}$ is disconnected. Such a vertex plays a critical role in keeping the network connected. This concept can be generalized by calling a vertex u of a graph a cut vertex if the component containing u splits into two or more components when u is dropped. Note that a graph may or may not have a cut vertex. The cycle on n vertices does not have any cut vertex, whereas a path on n vertices has $n - 2$ cut vertices. Similarly, a *cut edge* of a

Figure 2.11

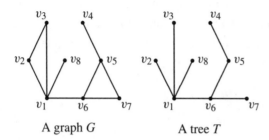

In G, v_1, v_5 and v_6 are the cut vertices and v_1v_6, v_1v_8 and v_4v_5 are the cut edges.

Note that T is a spanning tree of G.

A graph G A tree T

graph may be defined as an edge $\{u, v\}$ such that if that edge is removed, then u and v will belong to different components. It can be proved that an edge $\{u, v\}$ of a graph G is a cut edge if and only if it does not belong to any cycle of G. Cut vertices and cut edges of digraphs can be considered by applying the concepts to the underlying graphs. In the underlying graph of the digraph G of Figure 2.1, the vertices v_1, v_6, v_9, and v_{10} are cut vertices, and the rest are not. Also, edges v_1v_2, v_1v_3, v_1v_{10}, v_6v_8, v_9v_{10}, v_9v_{11}, and $v_{15}v_{16}$ are cut edges, and the others are not.

A connected graph without cycles is called a *tree*. A weakly connected digraph that has no circuits of length 2 and no semi-cycles is also called a *tree*. It can be shown that any tree on n vertices has exactly $n - 1$ edges (arcs if the tree is a digraph). Every connected graph has a *spanning tree* (i.e., a subgraph that is a tree on the same set of vertices), obtained by sequentially removing an edge belonging to a cycle in the current graph if a cycle exists.

2.10 CLIQUES AND INDEPENDENT SETS

A *clique* in a digraph is a maximal set of vertices that induces a complete symmetric digraph. Clearly, all the vertices of a clique belong to a single strong component. While it is easy to determine the strong and weak components of any digraph, the determination of all the cliques is not easy in general. Whereas the components form a partition of the vertex set, the cliques do not and can overlap. Even determining the maximum number, known as the *clique number*, of vertices that form a clique in a given graph is difficult for large graphs and is known to be an "NP-hard" problem. (All known algorithms take time, which is exponential in the number of vertices.) Note that the largest clique may not contain a vertex of the maximum out-degree or the maximum in-degree (see Figure 2.12). In the digraph G of Figure 2.1, the vertex sets $\{v_1, v_2\}$, $\{v_3\}$, $\{v_4, v_5, v_6\}$, $\{v_5, v_6, v_7\}$, $\{v_8\}$, $\{v_9\}$, $\{v_{10}\}$, $\{v_{11}\}$, $\{v_{12}, v_{13}\}$, $\{v_{14}\}$, $\{v_{15}, v_{16}\}$, $\{v_{17}\}$, and $\{v_{18}\}$ form cliques.

Figure 2.12

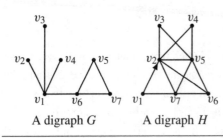

A digraph G A digraph H

In G, the clique with 3 vertices does not contain the maximum degree vertex.
In H, $\{v_1, v_7\}$, $\{v_2, v_3, v_5\}$, $\{v_2, v_4, v_5\}$, $\{v_2, v_5, v_6, v_7\}$ are all cliques.

A set W of vertices in a digraph is said to form an *independent set* if W induces a null digraph. Note that W is a maximal independent set of vertices in G if and only if W forms a clique in $\bar{G}$. In the digraph H of Figure 2.12, $\{v_2\}$, $\{v_1, v_5\}$, and $\{v_1, v_3, v_4, v_6\}$ are all maximal independent sets of vertices.

A method for finding the clique number of a digraph G is the following: By checking (if necessary, all) sets of vertices with size 2, find if there is a complete symmetric subdigraph on two vertices (i.e., a symmetric pair of vertices). If there is none, the clique number is 1. If there is, then by checking (if necessary, all) sets of vertices with size 3, find if there is a complete symmetric subdigraph on three vertices. If there is none, the clique number is 2. Proceeding in this manner, we can find the clique number, although this takes exponential time.

Sometimes the following method can be used to reduce the amount of computation. Suppose we have a partition of the vertex set V into disjoint nonempty sets $V_1, V_2, \ldots, V_k$. (Incidentally, the minimum k for which such a partition exists is called the *chromatic number* of G.) Then the clique number cannot exceed k. Moreover, any set W of vertices forming a complete subdigraph can contain at most one vertex from each V_i, so any subset of V containing more than one vertex from any V_i need not be considered while looking for complete symmetric subdigraphs. This can reduce the amount of checking substantially. Figures 2.7 and 2.8 (p. 41) depict the above concepts.

2.11 CENTRALITY, RADIUS, AND DIAMETER

We now study centrality briefly. The *eccentricity* $e(u)$ of a vertex u in a (di)graph G with vertex set V is $\max\{d(u, v) : v \in V\}$. If $d(u, v) = \infty$ for at least one vertex v, we define $e(u) = \infty$. The *diameter* $d(G)$ of G is $\max\{e(u) : u \in V\} = \max\{d(u, v) : u, v \in V\}$. Clearly, every vertex of G is reachable from every other vertex in at most $d(G)$ steps, and some pair needs $d(G)$ steps (assuming $d(G)$ is finite).

Another aspect that can be studied through distance is centrality and radius. The *radius* $r(G)$ of G is $\min\{e(u) : u \in V\}$, and any vertex v such that $e(v) = r(G)$ is called a *center* (or a central vertex) of G. Thus, from a central vertex, every other vertex can be reached in $r(G)$ steps, and this is the best possible in the sense of least distance.

For the subdigraph of G of Figure 2.1 induced by $\{v_1, v_2, v_4, v_5, v_6, v_7\}$, the diameter is ∞, the radius is 2, and v_4 and v_5 are centers (see Figure 2.9 for another example).

It follows trivially from definitions that $d(G) \geq r(G)$. Moreover, for a symmetric digraph G, we have $d(G) \leq 2r(G)$. To illustrate this, let v be a center. Then, for any two vertices u and w, $d(u, w) \leq d(u, v) + d(v, w) = d(v, u) + d(v, w) \leq 2r(G)$, so $d(G) \leq 2r(G)$. However, in a general digraph, $d(G)$ may even be infinity when $r(G)$ is finite as seen above. Even when both $r(G)$ and $d(G)$ are finite, $d(G)$ may be much larger than $r(G)$. For example, if G consists of a circuit $[v_1, v_2, \ldots, v_n, v_1]$ together with the arcs $v_1 v_j$ for $j = 3, 4, \ldots, n$, then $r(G) = 1$ and $d(G) = n - 1$ since $d(v_2, v_1) = n - 1$. It can also happen that every vertex in a digraph is a center: consider a circuit.

The radius r' of the converse of a digraph G is of interest sometimes, although there is no standard name for this. Note that here we are interested in the least number of steps in which all the vertices can reach a single vertex.

We will also use the following definition, although it is not standard in the literature: We call a vertex v *peripheral* if $e(v) = \max\{e(u) : u \in V\}$.

It may be noted that the concepts of central and peripheral vertices, as defined above, do not have any importance for disconnected digraphs since, for such a digraph, the radius is infinity, and every vertex is both central and peripheral. However, we may modify the definitions in a couple of ways to make these concepts somewhat meaningful for such digraphs. One modification is to define the eccentricity $e(u)$ of u to be $\max\{d(u, v) : v \in V$ and $d(u, v)$ is finite$\}$, and identify central vertices accordingly. Another is the following. For any positive integer k and vertex u of G, let $r(k, u)$ be the number of vertices reachable from u in at most k steps. We will say that a vertex v belongs to the k-core of G if $r(k, v) = \max_u r(k, u)$. The idea is that if the connection between two vertices established by a path of length more than k is considered to be too tenuous because of too many intermediaries, then v is the vertex that can reach the maximum number of vertices in paths that are short enough to be of use.

2.12 ISOMORPHISM

We now briefly study isomorphism of digraphs. An *isomorphism* from $G_1 = (V_1, A_1)$ to $G_2 = (V_2, A_2)$ is a one-to-one map φ from V_1 onto V_2 such that $uv \in A_1$ if and only if $\varphi(u)\varphi(v) \in A_2$. An isomorphism of a digraph G with itself is called an *automorphism* of G.

Two digraphs G_1 and G_2 are said to be *isomorphic* if there is an isomorphism between them. Isomorphic digraphs have the same structure, although the labels of the vertices may differ. In general, finding out whether two digraphs are isomorphic is difficult in theoretical terms. If an isomorphism is given, it is relatively easy to verify that the map is indeed an isomorphism, and hence the digraphs are isomorphic. The difficulty lies in finding the isomorphism. If some simple parameter (like out-degree sequence, number of symmetric pairs, number of strong components, etc.) is given, which takes different values for two digraphs, then this can be verified, proving that the digraphs are not isomorphic. Again, the theoretical difficulty is in identifying such a simple parameter. To verify from the definition that two digraphs with n vertices are not isomorphic, one has to check that each of the n one-to-one onto maps from the vertex set of one to the vertex set of the other is not an isomorphism. From an application point of view, computational complexity could be a major issue for large complex networks, although the availability of computer programs might prove useful on some occasions.

The diagrams of two isomorphic digraphs may *look* very different. We leave it to the reader to verify that the first digraph in Figure 2.13 is isomorphic to the third but not to the second (all three digraphs are symmetric, and the out-degree as well as the in-degree of each vertex is 3 in all of them).

Figure 2.13

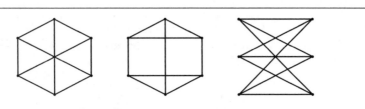

It can be seen easily that the set of all automorphisms of G forms a *group* under composition (i.e., the resultant of two automorphisms is an automorphism; there is an identity element that is an automorphism—namely, the identity map—and every automorphism has an inverse, which is an automorphism). Clearly every permutation of V is an automorphism for the complete symmetric digraph and the null digraph on V. In general, the size of the automorphism group of G is an indicator of how "symmetric" the digraph G is. Here, by *symmetry*, we mean similarity of various vertices and similarity of various arcs in the digraph. We note that the digraph consisting of a (directed) path has only one automorphism since an automorphism takes a source to a source and so forth. However, the symmetrization of the path $[v_1, v_2, \ldots, v_5]$ has two automorphisms: the identity map and the map taking v_i to v_{6-i} for $i = 1, 2, \ldots, 5$. If we add the arcs v_1v_4, v_4v_1, v_2v_5, and v_5v_2 to this digraph, then any map that fixes v_1, permutes v_2 and v_4 among themselves, and permutes v_1 and v_5 among themselves is an automorphism.

If there is an automorphism of a digraph taking v_i to v_j, then v_i and v_j are similar (e.g., they have the same out-degree, same in-degree, same eccentricity, etc.) and play similar roles in the digraph.

2.13 MULTIDIGRAPHS

Until now, we have discussed digraphs where either there is an arc or there is no arc from any vertex to any other vertex. But often in a social network, one may not have a 0–1 situation. For example, u may be going to both v and w for help, but he or she may go to v five times in a year and to w only once a year.

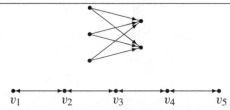

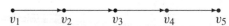

$$v_1 \qquad v_2 \qquad v_3 \qquad v_4 \qquad v_5$$

The only automorphisms are identity and ψ taking
v_1 to v_5, v_2 to v_4, v_3 to v_3, v_4 to v_2 and v_5 to v_1

$$v_1 \qquad v_2 \qquad v_3 \qquad v_4 \qquad v_5$$

The only automorphism is identity taking v_i to v_i for all i

Or, u may be getting a more important type of help from v than from w. To take care of such situations, we may consider what are known as multidigraphs. We take a cursory look at these now.

A *multidigraph* consists of a finite nonempty set V whose elements are called vertices and a *multiplicity function* that associates a nonnegative integer $m(u, v)$ with every ordered pair (u, v) of distinct vertices. For convenience, we will define $m(u, u) = 0$ for all $u \in V$. Note that a digraph can be viewed as a multidigraph with $m(u, v) = 1$ or 0 according to whether uv is an arc. In a diagrammatic representation of a multidigraph, we may either draw $m(u, v)$ arrows from u to v or draw one arrow and indicate $m(u, v)$ alongside. In the former case, the arrows from u to v are said to be multiple arcs provided $m(u, v) > 1$. Multiplicity may indicate frequency, strength, weight, and so on and is taken to be a nonnegative integer for convenience. Multidigraphs may also be thought of as weighted digraphs.

Clearly, the analog of the total number of arcs for a multidigraph is $\sum_u \sum_v m(u, v)$. If the vertex set is $\{v_1, v_2, \ldots, v_n\}$, the matrix $((m(v_i, v_j)))$ may be taken to be the adjacency matrix. The converse of a multidigraph is obtained by transposing the adjacency matrix. However, we do not define the complement of a multidigraph since there is no upper bound for the multiplicity of an arc. A multidigraph is symmetric if $m(v_i, v_j) = m(v_j, v_i)$ for all i and j. The analog of the number of symmetric pairs is $\sum_{i<j} \min(m(v_i, v_j), m(v_j, v_i))$. The out-degree of v_i is $\sum_j m(v_i, v_j)$, and the in-degree is defined in an obvious way. Concepts

related to connectedness can be studied by replacing all nonzero multiplicities by 1. However, this destroys the essence of multidigraphs, so a clustering-type approach is probably better.

The notion discussed above is different from another prevalent notion of a multipurpose digraph. From the very description, the latter is relevant when different types of arrows are generated between two vertices, based on very different purposes. In that sense, multidigraphs are essentially multivisit (same purpose) digraphs.

The notion of multigraphs, as introduced above, was mentioned in Chapter 1 and will be further exemplified in Chapter 6.

REFERENCES

Berge, C. (1973). *Graphs and hypergraphs*. Amsterdam: North-Holland.

Deo, N. (1980). *Graph theory with applications to engineering and computer science*. New Delhi: Prentice Hall of India.

Harary, F., Norman, R. Z., & Cartwright, D. (1965). *Structural models: An introduction to the theory of directed graphs*. New York: John Wiley.

THREE

GRAPH-THEORETIC AND STATISTICAL MODELS

3.1 INTRODUCTION

In this chapter, we consider several graph-theoretic and probabilistic models for a social network, which we do under different assumptions related to two basic parameters stated earlier in Chapter 1—namely, the number of vertices (n) and the number of arcs (m). We will take a social network to be a digraph. Models analogous to some of these can also be considered for graphs and weighted digraphs, although we will not discuss them in detail.

At the outset, we mention that when we talk of models in this chapter, we do not imply that any of them is a typical realistic representation of the situation in real life. We are not trying to build or present such models. Rather, the models we present can be used as a sort of *null model* with which one can standardize some of the parameters or statistics in the underlying social networks.

Each model generally stipulates in some way the set of all possible digraphs of which the observed digraph is an element. A *statistical model*, moreover, assigns a probability distribution, depending on some parameters, over the class of all possible digraphs. For some purposes, one may use a probability model that does not completely specify the probability of each possible digraph. By a *graph-theoretic model*, we simply mean a model that uses some digraph parameters and is not probabilistic.

The general procedure we adopt for obtaining a standardized measure of any characteristic of a social network is as follows. We start with an initial simple real valued measure X, which is a function of the observed network, for the characteristic under consideration. We then choose an appropriate model and standardize X as follows.

If the model is statistical, we take $P(X \leq x)$ to be the standardized measure, where x is the value of X for the particular network observed. This measure lies between 0 and 1 and can be converted to a percentage by multiplying by 100. In case the distribution of X is not known, one can still use $(x - E(X))/\sigma(X)$ as a measure and can get some idea about the tail probability from Chebychev's inequality.

If the model is graphical, we find the minimum x_{min} and the maximum x_{max} of the values X takes. Then we scale the observed value x in its range and take

$$\frac{x - x_{min}}{x_{max} - x_{min}} \tag{3.1}$$

as the standardized measure. The situation is sometimes complicated by the fact that not all (integer) values between x_{min} and x_{max} are attained by X. Then, perhaps one can choose one of the following alternatives: (1) use the above measure regardless of whether X takes all values between x_{min} and x_{max} and (2) use the probabilistic measure assuming that the distribution of X gives equal probabilities to each of the values taken by X.

Thus, under each of the graphical models, we want to find the range (or at least the minimum and the maximum values) of the crude measure X. Under each of the probabilistic models, we want to find the distribution of X, either exactly or at least approximately, and, if this is not possible, then the mean and the variance of X. We consider the following variables X, some of which will be used in the next chapter to construct measures of various characteristics of a social network:

- the number of arcs;

- the out-degree and the in-degree of a vertex;

- the maximum out-degree and the maximum in-degree in the digraph;

- the numbers of sources, sinks, and isolates;

- the number of symmetric pairs;

- the diameter;

- the radius;

- the number of reachable pairs;

- the number of pairs reachable in k steps ($k = 2$ or 3);

- the numbers p and q of strong and weak components, $p - q$;

- the number of arcs within strong components;

- the number h of arcs between strong components;

- the number of arcs uv such that $d(v, u) \leq 2$; and

- the clique number.

Under the probabilistic models, we will also look at the following, where G denotes a random digraph.

- P(G is symmetric),

- P(G is asymmetric),

- P(G is complete asymmetric),

- P(G is a tree),

- P(G is acyclic),

- P(G is strongly connected), and

- P(G is weakly connected).

To avoid trivialities, we will assume that $n \geq 2$ in all the models considered below, although we allow m to be 0. Also note that the probability distribution of the sources, sinks, and isolates has received special attention as these immediately reveal some important features of social structures. This is discussed later in Chapter 5.

It is perhaps worth mentioning that, in applying these to actual social networks, one has to modify some of the above variables X for various reasons. First, X may not precisely measure the characteristic it is intended to measure (often the latter has different versions or nuances, all of which cannot be captured by a single variable). Then, the value of X itself may be very difficult to find even for the observed network, not to mention the distribution of X, especially if the number of vertices is large, although sometimes, using various computational and theoretical techniques, it may be possible to compute the value for reasonably sized networks. For many of the variables, the exact range or even the values of x_{min} and x_{max} and the distribution or even the mean and variance of X are not known exactly, and only occasionally some theoretical approximations or bounds are known. Sometimes it may be possible to use iterative methods or simulation to get approximations, and one has to be satisfied with them. Finally, many of the definitions or properties of graph-theoretic variables are too stringent to be of use in real-life situations, and one has to either modify the variable or use some sort of cutoff to decide whether one can consider a network to have the particular property.

It may not be out of context to also mention that discussions on specific graph parameters such as sinks, sources, and isolates may be overemphasized in the later parts of this chapter. These terms have natural sociological inter-pretations, as discussed in Chapter 5. The theoretical study of such parame-ters requires probabilistic arguments, and we thought it proper to derive some results and present them hereinafter along with the description of other more useful parameters such as out-degree, in-degree, and reciprocity.

The basic assumptions underlying different models that will be considered in this chapter are summarized in the following table. We have conceptualized four categories of models (I–IV), penetrating step-by-step according to four different levels of available information related to the formation of the social network. Minimally, since the level of information available is that of only the size of a network (i.e., the number of actors (n)), we begin with n as given. Therefore, the possible digraphs are all digraphs with vertex set $v_1, v_2, \ldots \ldots, v_n$ with no additional assumptions. Models I.1 to I.3 fall under this category. At the next level, the quantum of interaction among the n actors (i.e., total number of ties of interaction or arcs (m)) is also assumed to be known. Models II.1 to II.2 fall in this category. Information available on the out-degrees of the actors—that is, $(d_1, d_2, \ldots \ldots, d_n)$—gives us the third level of modeling, and III.1 to III.3 deal with this aspect. Models IV.1 to IV.2 deal with the situation when both the out-degree and in-degree sequences are known. For each of the four categories, we have considered graph-theoretic (deterministic) and statistical (probabilistic) versions along with appropriate special cases, if any. The remaining models (V–VII) are known probabilistic models that can be related to those stated in Categories II and III above.

Model assumptions

Model no.	Assumptions
I.1	None
I.2	All digraphs are equally likely
I.3	$P(v_i v_j$ is an arc$) = p$ for $i \neq j$, distinct pairs being independent
II.1	The number of edges is m
II.2	The number of edges is m and all possible digraphs are equally likely
III.1	$d^+(v_i) = d_i$ for $i = 1, 2, \ldots, n$
III.2	$d^+(v_i) = d_i$ for $i = 1, 2, \ldots, n$ and all possible digraphs are equally likely
III.3	$|N(v_i)| = d_i$, $N(v_i) \subseteq P_i$ for $i = 1, 2, \ldots, n$ and all possible digraphs are equally likely
IV.1	$d^+(v_i) = d_i$ and $d^-(v_i) = e_i$ for $i = 1, 2, \ldots, n$
IV.2	$d^+(v_i) = d_i$ and $d^-(v_i) = e_i$ for $i = 1, 2, \ldots, n$ and all possible digraphs are equally likely
V	$P(v_j v_i \in A \mid v_i v_j \in A) = P(v_j v_i \in A) + \tau P(v_j v_i \notin A)$ and $P(v_i v_j \in A) = d_i / (n-1)$ whenever $i \neq j$
VI	$P((0,0)) = \exp(\lambda_{ij})$; $P((1,0)) = \exp(\lambda_{ij} + \theta + \alpha_i + \beta_j)$; $P((0,1)) = \exp(\lambda_{ij} + \theta + \alpha_j + \beta_i)$; $P((1,1)) = \exp(\lambda_{ij} + 2\theta + \alpha_i + \beta_j + \alpha_j + \beta_i + \rho)$; for an ordered pair of vertices (i, j) in a digraph G with the scores for dyadic movements expressed by $2^2 = 4$ combinations of 0s and 1s; $\sum \alpha_i = 0$ and $\sum \beta_i = 0$
VII	$P(G) = \text{const.} \exp(\theta m + \rho s + \sum \alpha_i d_i + \sum \beta_i e_i)$ for any digraph G; $\sum \alpha_i = 0$ and $\sum \beta_i = 0$

3.2 MODELS FIXING THE TOTAL NUMBER OF VERTICES

Model I.1

This is the simplest graphical model one can consider and takes the vertex set $V = \{v_1, v_2, \ldots, v_n\}$ comprising n vertices as fixed and assumes that all the $2^{n(n-1)}$ digraphs on V are *actually* possible.

Clearly, the range of the number m of arcs is $\{0, 1, \ldots, n(n-1)\}$.

The range of the out-degree d_i (as well as the in-degree e_i) of the ith vertex is $\{0, 1, \ldots, n-1\}$ for each i. The range of d_{max}, defined as $\max(d_1, d_2, \ldots, d_n)$, as well as that of e_{max}, defined as $\max(e_1, e_2, \ldots, e_n)$, is also $\{0, 1, \ldots, n-1\}$.

The range of the number of sources (as well as the number of sinks) is $\{0, 1, \ldots, n\}$. However, the range of the number of isolates is $\{0, 1, \ldots, n-2, n\}$ (note that if $n-1$ of the vertices are isolates, the remaining vertex is automatically an isolate).

The range of the number s of symmetric pairs is $\{0, 1, \ldots, n(n-1)/2\}$.

The range of the diameter is $\{1, 2, \ldots, n-1, \infty\}$. (To get a digraph with diameter $k < \infty$, take a complete symmetric digraph on $n-k+1$ vertices and attach a symmetric path on k vertices at some vertex.) The range of the radius is $\{1, 2, \ldots, n-1, \infty\}$. (To get a digraph with radius $k < \infty$, take a directed path on $k+1$ vertices and join the first vertex *to* the remaining $n-k-1$ vertices; then, the first vertex of the path is a center, and the radius is k.)

Next we study R, the number of reachable pairs of *distinct* vertices. (Note that we are leaving out pairs of the type (u, u), even though u is reachable from u in a trivial sense.) Clearly, the minimum and maximum values of R are 0 and $n(n-1)$, but the range S_n of R is not continuous. It can be shown by induction on n that $S_n \subseteq T_n$, where

$$T_n = \{0, 1, \ldots, n^2 - 3n + 4\} \cup \{n^2 - 2n + 1, n^2 - n\}. \tag{3.2}$$

We give S_n below for n up to 15 for ready reference.

$$
\begin{aligned}
S_1 &= \{0\} \subseteq T_1, \\
S_2 &= \{0, 1, 2\} = T_2, \\
S_3 &= \{0, 1, 2, 3, 4, 6\} = T_3, \\
S_4 &= \{0, 1, \ldots, 9, 12\} = T_4, \\
S_5 &= \{0, 1, \ldots, 14, 16, 20\} = T_5, \\
S_6 &= \{0, 1, \ldots, 22, 25, 30\} = T_6, \\
S_7 &= \{0, 1, \ldots, 28, 30, 31, 32, 36, 42\} = T_7 - \{29\}, \\
S_8 &= \{0, 1, \ldots, 44, 49, 56\} = T_8, \\
S_9 &= \{0, 1, \ldots, 52, 54, 56, 57, 58, 64, 72\} = T_9 - \{53, 55\}, \\
S_{10} &= \{0, 1, \ldots, 67, 69, 72, 73, 74, 81, 90\} = T_{10} - \{68, 70, 71\}, \\
S_{11} &= \{0, 1, \ldots, 84, 86, 90, 91, 92, 100, 110\} = T_{11} - \{85, 87, 88, 89\}, \\
S_{12} &= \{0, 1, \ldots, 97, 99, \ldots, 103, 105, 110, 111, 112, 121, 132\}, \\
S_{13} &= \{0, 1, \ldots, 117, 120, \ldots, 124, 126, 132, 133, 134, 144, 156\}, \\
S_{14} &= \{0, 1, \ldots, 139, 142, \ldots, 147, 149, 156, 157, 158, 169, 182\}, \\
S_{15} &= \{0, 1, \ldots, 163, 166, 168, \ldots, 172, 174, 182, 183, 184, 196, 210\}.
\end{aligned}
$$

Moreover, Rao (2002) has shown that for $n \leq 208$,

$$x \in S_n \text{ if and only if } x - k(n-1) \in S_{n-k} \text{ for some } k \text{ with } 1 \leq k \leq n-1, \quad (3.3)$$

using which S_n can be determined for $n \leq 208$. He also showed that if $f(n)$ is defined by $\{0, 1, \ldots, f(n)\} \subseteq S_n$ and $f(n) + 1 \notin S_n$, then $f(n) \geq (n - \lfloor n^{0.57} \rfloor)(n-1)$ and that this bound is fairly good. It has also been found empirically that the number of elements in S_n is close to $(n - \lfloor n^{0.45} \rfloor)(n-1)$ at least for $n \leq 208$.

Until now, we considered the number of pairs reachable in an arbitrary number of steps. Let $R^{(k)}(G)$ denote the number of pairs (u, v) of distinct vertices in G such that v is reachable in k or fewer steps from u, and let $S_n^{(k)}$ be the range of $R^{(k)}(G)$ as G varies over all networks on n vertices. Rao (2002) has shown that $S_n^{(2)} = S_n$ for $n = 1, 2, 3$ and $S_n^{(2)} = \{0, 1, \ldots, n(n-1)\}$ whenever $n \geq 4$; $S_n^{(3)} = S_n$ for $n = 1, 2, 3, 4$ and $S_n^{(3)} = \{0, 1, \ldots, n(n-1)\}$ whenever $n \geq 5$. He has also shown that for every $k \geq 2$, $S_n^{(k)} = \{0, 1, \ldots, n(n-1)\}$ provided, $n \geq k + \lfloor (k+1)^{0.57} \rfloor + 2$.

The range is $\{1, 2, \ldots, n\}$ for the number of strong components, the number of weak components, and the clique number.

It is easy to see that the range of the difference $p - q$ between the number of strong components p and the number of weak components q is also $\{0, 1, \ldots, n-1\}$. The range of the number h of arcs between strong components is $\{0, 1, \ldots, \binom{n}{2}\}$. This is because such arcs cannot be reciprocated. The range of the minimum number P of paths, formed with arcs joining different strong components of G and covering the vertex set, is clearly $\{1, 2, \ldots, n\}$.

Model I.2

Model I.2 is a probabilistic version of Model I.1, and takes the vertex set as fixed (e.g., $V = \{v_1, v_2, \ldots, v_n\}$) and assumes that all the $2^{n(n-1)}$ possible digraphs on V are equally likely.

Let X_{ij} be the random variable taking value 1 if $v_i v_j$ is an arc and 0 otherwise. Then under the present model, $P(X_{ij} = 1) = 1/2$ since there are $2^{n(n-1)-1}$ digraphs with $v_i v_j$ as an arc. Also, it is easy to see that the $n(n-1)$ random variables X_{ij} $(1 \leq i \neq j \leq n)$ are mutually independent. Thus, the model is equivalent to $v_i v_j$, which is an arc with probability $1/2$, and the ordered pairs are all mutually independent. Hence, a random digraph G under the model can be generated by making $v_i v_j$ an arc with probability $1/2$ for each ordered pair (i, j), with distinct ordered pairs being independent. Repeating this, one can generate any given number of random digraphs and estimate the distribution of any statistic under the model by simulation.

It is easy to see that under the present model, the number of arcs m has the binomial distribution $B(n(n-1), 1/2)$ since m is the sum of the $n(n-1)$ independent Bernoulli random variables X_{ij}. The notation $B(..)$ will be used for a binomial distribution without any further explanation.

Since the out-degree d_i of v_i is $\sum_{j \neq i} X_{ij}$, it follows that d_i has the binomial distribution $B(n-1, 1/2)$. Hence, $E(d_i) = (n-1)/2$ and $V(d_i) = (n-1)/4$. Since the d_is are independent, the distribution of $d_{\max} : = \max(d_1, d_2, \dots, d_n)$ can be computed easily, although one cannot give a closed formula for it. Note that $P(d_{\max} \leq k) = (P(d_1 \leq k))^n$. It is easy to see that the in-degree e_i of v_i also has the distribution $B(n-1, 1/2)$, and $d_{\max}$ and $e_{\max}$ have the same distribution.

To give an example, let $n = 3$. Then each d_i takes values 0, 1, and 2 with probabilities $1/4$, $1/2$, and $1/4$. Hence, we have $P(d_{\max} = 0) = (1/4)^3 = 1/64$. Also, $P(d_{\max} \leq 1) = (3/4)^3 = 27/64$, so $P(d_{\max} = 1) = 13/32$ and $P(d_{\max} = 2) = 37/64$. When $n = 4$, it can be checked that $d_{\max}$ takes values 0, 1, 2, and 3 with probabilities $1/4,096$, $255/4,096$, $2,145/4,096$, and $1,695/4,096$, respectively.

The probability that v_i is a source is $1/2^{n-1}$. Also, different v_is being sources are independent events, so the number of sources has the distribution $B(n, 1/2^{n-1})$. It follows similarly that the probability that v_i is a sink is also $1/2^{n-1}$, and the number of sinks has the distribution $B(n, 1/2^{n-1})$.

The probability that v_i is an isolated vertex is $1/2^{2n-2}$. But the events in which different vertices are isolates are not independent. For example, if any $n-1$ vertices are isolates, it follows that the remaining vertex is also an isolate. So, to find the distribution of the number of isolates, we use the following formulae (see Feller, 1968). The probability that exactly k of the events $A_1, A_2, \dots, A_n$ occurs is

$$S_k - \binom{k+1}{k} S_{k+1} + \binom{k+2}{k} S_{k+2} - + \cdots + (-1)^{n-k} \binom{n}{k} S_n, \qquad (3.4)$$

and the probability that at least k of $A_1, A_2, \dots, A_n$ occurs is

$$S_k - \binom{k}{k-1} S_{k+1} + \binom{k+1}{k-1} S_{k+2} - + \cdots + (-1)^{n-k} \binom{n-1}{k-1} S_n, \qquad (3.5)$$

where S_k denotes $\sum P(A_{i_1} \cap A_{i_2} \cap \cdots \cap A_{i_k})$, with the sum being taken over all $i_1, i_2, \ldots, i_k$ such that $1 \leq i_1 < i_2 < \cdots < i_k \leq n$. Clearly, now the probability that k given vertices are isolates is

$$\frac{1}{2^{k(k-1)+2k(n-k)}} = \frac{1}{2^{k(2n-k-1)}}.$$

Hence, taking A_i to be the event that the ith vertex is an isolate, we see that the probability that there are exactly k isolates is

$$\binom{n}{k}\frac{1}{2^{k(2n-k-1)}} - \binom{k+1}{k}\binom{n}{k+1}\frac{1}{2^{(k+1)(2n-k-2)}} + \binom{k+2}{k}$$

$$+ \binom{n}{k+2}\frac{1}{2^{(k+2)(2n-k-3)}} - + \cdots + (-1)^{n-k}\binom{n}{k}\frac{1}{2^{n(n-1)}}. \quad (3.6)$$

The probability that there are at least k isolates can be found by using (3.2). Taking the events that different vertices are isolates to be nearly independent, we see that the distribution of the number of isolates is approximately $B(n, 1/2^{2n-2})$. However, this is not of much importance as the probability that there is no isolate is more than 0.999 for all $n \geq 10$.

By definition, the probability that G is any particular digraph (including the null digraph and the complete symmetric digraph) is $1/2^{n(n-1)}$.

The probability that G is symmetric is $1/2^{n(n-1)/2}$ since, for G to be symmetric, either none or both of $v_i v_j$ and $v_j v_i$ should be arcs for each unordered pair $\{i, j\}$ with $i \neq j$.

The probability that G is asymmetric and the probability that G is complete are both $(3/4)^{n(n-1)/2}$ since, for G to be asymmetric, at most one of $v_i v_j$ and $v_j v_i$ should be an arc, and for G to be complete, at least one of $v_i v_j$ and $v_j v_i$ should be an arc, for each unordered pair $\{i, j\}$, with $i \neq j$.

The number of symmetric pairs $s(G)$ has the distribution $B(n(n-1)/2, 1/4)$ since $s(G)$ is the sum of the $n(n-1)/2$ independent Bernoulli variables Y_{ij}, where $Y_{ij} = X_{ij} X_{ji}$ for any unordered pair $\{i, j\}$ with $i \neq j$.

It is much more difficult to deal with probabilities of events depending on the distance between vertices because $d(v_i, v_j)$ depends not only on what happens at v_i and v_j but also on what happens in other parts of the digraph.

For example, to find the probability that G is strongly connected, we have to find the number $f(n)$ of strongly connected digraphs on the vertex set $\{v_1, v_2, \ldots, v_n\}$. A method for computing this number $f(n)$ for any n is known (see Harary, 1988). (The problem is usually referred to as enumeration

Figure 3.1

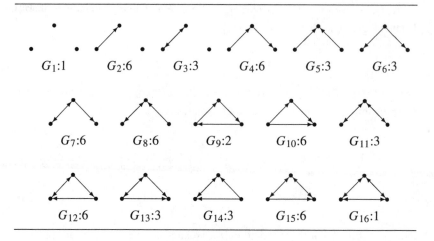

G_1:1 G_2:6 G_3:3 G_4:6 G_5:3 G_6:3

G_7:6 G_8:6 G_9:2 G_{10}:6 G_{11}:3

G_{12}:6 G_{13}:3 G_{14}:3 G_{15}:6 G_{16}:1

of strongly connected labeled digraphs on n vertices, with the word *labeled* signifying that the vertex set is fixed and we are not counting nonisomorphic digraphs.) However, this involves generating functions, and no closed formula is known for $f(n)$. Thus, even finding the probability that G is strongly connected is difficult. When $n = 2$, this probability is $1/4$. If $n = 3$, out of the 64 possible digraphs, 18 are strongly connected, so the probability is $9/32$. Here, the strongly connected digraphs consist of one digraph with six arcs; six digraphs with five arcs; three digraphs with four arcs forming two reciprocal pairs; six digraphs with four arcs, two of which form a reciprocal pair; and two digraphs with three arcs forming a circuit (see Figure 3.1). When $n = 4$, it can be checked that out of 4,096 possible digraphs, 1,606 are strongly connected, so the probability that G is strongly connected is $1,606/4,096 = 0.392$.

When $n = 2$, the probability that G is weakly connected is $3/4$. When $n = 3$, 54 out of the 64 possible digraphs are weakly connected, so the probability is $54/64 = 0.844$. When $n = 4$, it can be checked that out of 4,096 possible digraphs, 3,834 are weakly connected, so the probability is $3,834/4,096 = 0.936$.

In Figure 3.2, we give the 16 nonisomorphic digraphs on three vertices. Along with each of these, we also give the number of digraphs on $\{v_1, v_2, v_3\}$ isomorphic to it.

The probability that G has diameter 1 is clearly $1/2^{n(n-1)}$. When $n = 3$, it is easy to check from Figure 3.2 that the probability that G has diameter 2 is $17/64$, and the probability that G has diameter ∞ is $23/32$.

Figure 3.2

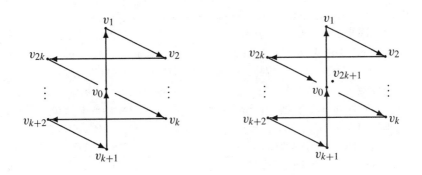

Let $n = 3$. Then $P(r(G) = 1) = P(d_{max} = 2) = 37/64$, where $r(G)$ is the radius of G. It can be checked that 14 digraphs have radius 2 and 13 digraphs have radius ∞, so $P(r(G) = 2) = 7/32$ and $P(r(G)) = \infty) = 13/64$.

We mention that for general n and k, even expressions such as (3.3) are difficult to find for $P(r(G) = k)$ and $P(d(G) = k)$. However, it is easy to prove that $P(d(G) = 2) \rightarrow 1$ as $n \rightarrow \infty$. To see this, let A_i be the event that at least one of $v_1 v_i$ and $v_i v_2$ is not an arc. Then $P(A_i) = 3/4$ for all $i \neq 1, 2$. Since $P(v_1 v_2$ is not an arc$) = 1/2$, it follows that $P(d(v_1, v_2) > 2) = (3/4)^{n-2}/2$. Since $P(d(v_i, v_j) > 2) = P(d(v_1, v_2) > 2)$, whenever $i \neq j$, we have $P(d(G) > 2) = P(d(v_i, v_j) > 2$ for at least one pair $(i, j)) \leq n(n-1)(3/4)^{n-2}/2 \rightarrow 0$ as $n \rightarrow \infty$. Since $P(d(G) = 1) = 1/2^{n(n-1)} \rightarrow 0$, we have $P(d(G) = 2) \rightarrow 1$ as $n \rightarrow \infty$.

Since $P(d(G) = 2) \rightarrow 1$, we also have $P(r(G) \leq 2) \rightarrow 1$ as $n \rightarrow \infty$. Now we show that $P(r(G) = 1) \rightarrow 0$ as $n \rightarrow \infty$. For any fixed i, let E_i be the event that $v_i v_j$ is an arc for all $j \neq i$. Then $P(E_i) = 1/2^{n-1}$. Also, E_is are independent, so

$$P(r(G) = 1) = P(E_1 \cup E_2 \cup \cdots \cup E_n) = 1 - P(\bar{E}_1 \cap \bar{E}_2 \cap \cdots \cap \bar{E}_n)$$
$$= 1 - \left(1 - \frac{1}{2^{n-1}}\right)^n = \sum_{k=1}^{n} (-1)^{k-1} \frac{\binom{n}{k}}{2^{k(n-1)}} \leq \frac{n}{2^{n-1}} \rightarrow 0 \qquad (3.7)$$

as $n \rightarrow \infty$. Here the inequality follows from the fact that $|a_k|/|a_{k+1}| > 1$ for all k, where a_k denotes the kth term in the sum (it also follows from the fact that $P(\cup E_i) \leq \sum P(E_i)$). Hence, $P(r(G) = 1) \rightarrow 0$, and $P(r(G) = 2) \rightarrow 1$ as $n \rightarrow \infty$.

The distribution of the clique number $\omega(G)$ is difficult to find for general n, although it can be worked out for small n using (3.2). It may be noted that, for any n, $P(\omega(G)=1)=P(G \text{ is asymmetric})=(3/4)^{n(n-1)/2}$ and $P(\omega(G)=n)=1/2^{n(n-1)}$. Hence, when $n=3$, the clique number takes values 1, 2, and 3 with probabilities 27/64, 9/16, and 1/64. Next let $n=4$. Then $P(\omega(G)=1)=729/4{,}096$, so $P(\omega(G)\geq 2)=3{,}367/4{,}096$. To find $P(\omega(G)\geq 3)$, let A_1, A_2, A_3, A_4 be the events that $\{v_1, v_2, v_3\}$, $\{v_1, v_2, v_4\}$, $\{v_1, v_3, v_4\}$, and $\{v_2, v_3, v_4\}$ induce complete symmetric digraphs. Then $P(A_i)=1/2^6$, $P(A_i \cap A_j)=1/2^{10}$ whenever $i \neq j$, $P(A_i \cap A_j \cap A_k)=1/2^{12}$ whenever i, j, k are distinct, and $P(A_1 \cap A_2 \cap A_3 \cap A_4)=1/2^{12}$. So $P(\omega(G)\geq 3)=4/64-6/1{,}024+4/4{,}096-1/4{,}096=235/4{,}096$. Hence, $P(\omega(G)=2)=3{,}132/4{,}096$, $P(\omega(G)=3)=234/4{,}096$, and $P(\omega(G)=4)=1/4{,}096$. However, if we try to find $P(\omega(G)\geq 3)$ in the same way when $n=5$, we note that $P(A_i \cap A_j \cap A_k)$ depends on what i, j and k are. Thus, the formulae become more complicated as n increases.

Results of Simulation

It should be evident that for some of the statistics, the exact distributional properties are hard to derive. These are analytically intractable unless n is small. For ready reference, therefore, we give the distribution of various statistics considered above, for some values of n. These were obtained by simulation using 100,000 random digraphs (except for small values of n when the exact distribution can be computed). The error in the estimate of any probability should not exceed 0.005 and is expected to be much less (less than 0.001 when the probability is less than 0.01). We do not give the distributions of $m(G)$ and $s(G)$ as these are binomial distributions. Note that a dash in an entry in the table means that the probability is either 0 or is positive but less than 0.0005.

					Maximum Out-Degree					
	0	*1*	*2*	*3*	*4*	*5*	*6*	*7*	*8*	*9*
n										
2	.250	.750	–	–	–	–	–	–	–	–
3	.016	.406	.578	–	–	–	–	–	–	–
4	–	.062	.525	.413	–	–	–	–	–	–
5	–	–	.151	.572	.274	–	–	–	–	–
6	–	–	.015	.273	.537	.174	–	–	–	–
10	–	–	–	–	.001	.053	.337	.430	.159	.019

				Maximum Out-Degree (Continuation)				
	11	*12*	*13*	*14*	*15*	*16*	*17*	*18*
$n = 20$	.019	.155	.350	.301	.131	.036	.006	.001

					Maximum Out-Degree (Continuation)					
	22	*23*	*24*	*25*	*26*	*27*	*28*	*29*	*30*	*31*	*32*
$n = 40$	.001	.015	.095	.230	.281	.207	.106	.044	.015	.005	.001

	Sources					Isolates				
	0	*1*	*2*	*3*	*4*	*0*	*1*	*2*	*3*	*4*
n										
2	.250	.500	.250	–	–	.750	–	.250	–	–
3	.423	.421	.140	.016	–	.844	.140	–	.016	–
4	.586	.336	.071	.007	–	.943	.052	.005	–	–
5	.725	.240	.033	.002	–	.981	.019	.001	–	–
6	.826	.160	.013	.001	–	.994	.006	–	–	–
10	.981	.019	–	–	–	1	–	–	–	–
20	1	–	–	–	–	1	–	–	–	–
40	1	–	–	–	–	1	–	–	–	–

	Diameter						Radius					
	1	*2*	*3*	*4*	*5*	∞	*1*	*2*	*3*	*4*	*5*	∞
n												
2	.250	–	–	–	–	.750	.750	–	–	–	–	.250
3	.016	.267	–	–	–	.717	.578	.219	–	–	–	.203
4	–	.174	.219	–	–	.607	.413	.422	.047	–	–	.118
5	–	.131	.318	.093	–	.458	.274	.609	.054	.007	–	.055
6	–	.116	.413	.136	.020	.316	.174	.752	.045	.007	.001	.021
10	–	.124	.746	.086	.005	.039	.020	.974	.006	–	–	–
20	–	.475	.525	–	–	–	–	1	–	–	–	–
40	–	.987	.013	–	–	–	–	1	–	–	–	–

	Strong Components						Weak Components			
	1	2	3	4	5	6	1	2	3	4
n										
2	.250	.750	–	–	–	–	.750	.250	–	–
3	.283	.326	.391	–	–	–	.844	.140	.016	–
4	.393	.285	.188	.134	–	–	.936	.059	.005	–
5	.542	.257	.116	.057	.029	–	.979	.020	.001	–
6	.684	.213	.066	.023	.010	.004	.994	.006	–	–
10	.961	.037	.001	–	–	–	1	–	–	–
20	1	–	–	–	–	–	1	–	–	–

	Clique Number					
	1	2	3	4	5	6
n						
2	.750	.250	–	–	–	–
3	.422	.562	.016	–	–	–
4	.178	.765	.057	–	–	–
5	.057	.813	.129	.001	–	–
6	.014	.754	.229	.003	–	–
10	–	.263	.694	.043	–	–
20	–	–	.470	.517	.013	–
40	–	–	–	.648	.349	.003

Model I.3

Under Model I.2, the expected number of arcs is $n(n-1)/2$. So when m is very small or very large (close to $n(n-1)$), Model I.2 is not appropriate, and we consider Model I.3.

In this probabilistic model, we again take the vertex set to be fixed and assume that all the $2^{n(n-1)}$ digraphs on V are possible. But we stipulate that $v_i v_j$ is chosen as an arc with a fixed probability p $(0 < p < 1)$ and that the ordered pairs are all mutually independent. Note that Model I.2 is the special case of Model I.3 corresponding to $p = 1/2$.

Let X_{ij} be defined as before. Then, under the present model, we have $P(X_{ij} = 1) = p$, and X_{ij}s are independent. So the number of arcs m has the binomial distribution $B(n(n-1), p)$, and the out-degree d_i as well as the in-degree e_i of v_i has the same binomial distribution $B(n-1, p)$.

Clearly, the probability of getting any particular digraph G_0 on V is $p^m q^{n(n-1)-m}$, where m is the number of arcs in G_0 and $q = 1 - p$. Hence, any two digraphs with the same number of arcs are equally likely; in particular, $P(G = G_0) = P(G = G_0^c)$, where G_0^c denotes the converse of G_0.

Here, the probability that v_i is a source is q^{n-1}. Also, the number of sources has the distribution $B(n, q^{n-1})$. Similarly, the probability that v_i is a sink is q^{n-1}, and the number of sinks has the distribution $B(n, q^{n-1})$.

The probability that v_i is an isolated vertex is q^{2n-2}. The probability that k given vertices are isolates is $q^{k(2n-k-1)}$. Hence, the probability that there are exactly k isolates is

$$\binom{n}{k} q^{k(2n-k-1)} - \binom{k+1}{k}\binom{n}{k+1} q^{(k+1)(2n-k-2)}$$
$$+ \binom{k+2}{k}\binom{n}{k+2} q^{(k+2)(2n-k-3)} - + \cdots + (-1)^{n-k}\binom{n}{k} q^{n(n-1)}. \quad (3.8)$$

Again, an expression, similar to (3.2), for the probability that there are at least k isolates can be written down.

The probability that G is a null digraph is $q^{n(n-1)}$, and the probability that G is the complete symmetric digraph is $p^{n(n-1)}$.

The probability that G is symmetric is $(p^2 + q^2)^{n(n-1)/2}$, the probability that G is asymmetric is $(1 - p^2)^{n(n-1)/2}$, and the probability that G is complete is $(1 - q^2)^{n(n-1)/2}$.

The number of symmetric pairs $s(G)$ has the distribution $B(\binom{n}{2}, p^2)$.

When $n = 2$, the probability that G is strongly connected is p^2. If $n = 3$, the probability is $p^6 + 6p^5q + 9p^4q^2 + 2p^3q^3$. This can be seen easily from Figure 3.1.

Here also expressions for $P(r(G) = k)$ and $P(d(G) = k)$ cannot be found but, rather surprisingly, it is easy to prove that $P(d(G) = 2) \to 1$ and $P(r(G) = 2) \to 1$ as $n \to \infty$, provided only that $0 < p < 1$. To see this, let A_i be the event that at least one of $v_1 v_i$ and $v_i v_2$ is not an arc. Then $P(A_i) = 1 - p^2$ for all $i \neq 1, 2$. Since $P(v_1 v_2$ is not an arc$) = 1 - p$, we have $P(d(v_1, v_2) > 2) = (1 - p)(1 - p^2)^{n-2}$. It follows as before that $P(d(G) > 2) \leq n(n-1)(1-p)(1 - p^2)^{n-2} \to 0$ as $n \to \infty$. Since $P(d(G) = 1) = p^{n(n-1)} \to 0$, it follows that $P(d(G) = 2) \to 1$ as $n \to \infty$. Hence, we also have $P(r(G) \leq 2) \to 1$ as $n \to \infty$. Now we show that $P(r(G) = 1) \to 0$ as $n \to \infty$. For any fixed i, let E_i be the event that $v_i v_j$ is an arc for all $j \neq i$. Then $P(E_i) = p^{n-1}$. Also, E_is are independent, so

$$P(r(G) = 1) = P(E_1 \cup E_2 \cup \cdots \cup E_n)$$
$$= 1 - P(\bar{E}_1 \cap \bar{E}_2 \cap \cdots \cap \bar{E}_n) = 1 - (1 - p^{n-1})^n. \quad (3.9)$$

Moreover, $P(E_1 \cup E_2 \cup \cdots \cup E_n) \leq P(E_1) + P(E_2) + \cdots + P(E_n) = np^{n-1}$ $\to 0$. Hence, $P(r(G) = 1) \to 0$ and $P(r(G) = 2) \to 1$ as $n \to \infty$.

3.3 MODELS FIXING THE TOTAL NUMBER OF VERTICES AND THE TOTAL OF ALL ARCS

Model II.1

In Model I.1, we took only the number of vertices (n) as given and assumed that all values of m from 0 to $n(n-1)$ are actually possible. Often this is not realistic, particularly when n is large, so we introduce Model II.1.

This graphical (nonprobabilistic) model takes the vertex set $V = \{v_1, v_2, \ldots, v_n\}$ and the number of arcs m as fixed and assumes that all the $\binom{n(n-1)}{m}$ digraphs on V with m arcs are actually possible. Note that $0 \leq m \leq n(n-1)$, and m refers to the total of all out-degrees of the n vertices, and this is also the same as the total of all in-degrees.

Under the present model, the minimum value taken by the out-degree d_i (as well as the in-degree e_i) of the ith vertex is $\max(0, m - (n^2 - 2n + 1))$. To see this, it is enough to notice that the number of arcs left in the complete symmetric digraph, when all the arcs leaving v_i are dropped, is $n^2 - 2n + 1$. Trivially, the maximum value taken by the out-degree d_i (as well as e_i) is $\min(n-1, m)$, and every integer value between the minimum and the maximum can actually be attained by d_i (as well as by e_i).

We now show that the range of $d_{\max}$ is $\{\lceil \frac{m}{n} \rceil, \lceil \frac{m}{n} \rceil + 1, \ldots, \min(n-1, m)\}$. Here $\lceil a \rceil$ denotes the smallest integer greater than or equal to the number a. For example, $\lceil 2 \rceil = 2$ and $\lceil 2.1 \rceil = 3$. That the maximum value of $d_{\max}$ is $\min(n-1, m)$ is trivial to prove.

That $d_{\max}$ in any digraph on n vertices with m arcs is $\geq \lceil \frac{m}{n} \rceil$ follows from $\sum_{i=1}^{n} d_i = m$ since $\max(d_1, d_2, \ldots, d_n) \geq \sum d_i / n$. To construct a digraph G with $d_{\max} = \lceil \frac{m}{n} \rceil$, let $m = nq - r$, where $0 \leq r \leq n - 1$. We consider the cases n odd and n even separately. First suppose $n = 2k + 1$. Then we show how to partition the set A of arcs of the complete symmetric digraph on $V = \{v_0, v_1, \ldots, v_{2k}\}$ into $n - 1$ disjoint subsets of size n, each forming a single cycle (such a cycle is called a *Hamiltonian cycle*). Arrange the vertices $\{v_1, v_2, \ldots, v_{2k}\}$ regularly on a circle with center v_0. The first Hamiltonian cycle is $[v_0, v_1, v_2, v_{2k}, v_3, v_{2k-1}, v_4, \ldots, v_k, v_{k+2}, v_{k+1}, v_0]$. This is shown in the first diagram in Figure 3.2. For $i = 2, 3, \ldots, 2k$, the ith Hamiltonian cycle—namely, $[v_0, v_i, v_{i+1}, v_{i-1}, v_{i+2}, v_{i-2}, v_{i+3}, \ldots, v_{k+i-1}, v_{k+i}, v_0]$—is obtained by rotating the first cycle clockwise around v_0 by $i - 1$ steps. Now, we get G by taking the union of q of the Hamiltonian cycles and dropping r arcs of one cycle if $r > 0$. Next let $n = 2k + 2$. Then we replace the arc bypassing the central vertex v_0 by a path of length 2 with v_{2k+1} as the middle vertex, as shown in the second diagram in Figure 3.2 (imagine v_{2k+1} to be directly above v_0 in a different plane). As before, we get $2k$ Hamiltonian cycles here also. Now we also have another set of n arcs: the $2k$ arcs in the earlier digraph, which were replaced by paths of length 2 and the two arcs $v_0 v_{2k+1}$ and $v_{2k+1} v_0$. Note that every vertex has out-degree 1 w.r.t. the arcs in this last set also. Now, again, we get G by taking the union of q of the Hamiltonian cycles (including the last set if necessary) and dropping r arcs from one set if $r > 0$.

To give the minimum and maximum values taken by the number of sources, let p denote the number of sources. Then $\min p = \max(0, n - m)$. To see this, we note that p can be made 0 whenever $m \geq n$ by including a circuit on n vertices in the digraph. If $m \leq n - 1$, the m arcs can make at most m vertices nonsources, so $p \geq n - m$, and a digraph with $p = n - m$ is obtained by taking a directed path on $m + 1$ vertices together with $n - m - 1$ isolated vertices. We now show that $\max p = n - \lceil m/(n - 1) \rceil$. Denote the right-hand side (RHS) by k. If S is the set of sources in any digraph on n vertices with m arcs, then there is no arc entering any vertex in S, so $m \leq p(n - p) + (n - p)(n - p - 1) = (n - 1)(n - p)$, which gives $p \leq k$. A digraph G attaining $p = k$ is obtained as follows: Let H be a complete symmetric digraph with vertex set V, where $|V| = n$, and let S be a subset of V with $|S| = k$. Remove all the arcs within S and all the arcs from $V - S$ to S and a few more if necessary (so that exactly m arcs remain) to get G.

Since changing the position of an arc can change the number of sources by at most 1 and since any two digraphs on V with m arcs each can be obtained from each other by changing the position of one arc at a time, it follows that the number p of sources actually takes all integer values between the minimum and the maximum. Finally, it is easy to see that the range of the number of sources is the same as that of the number of sinks.

To give the minimum and maximum values taken by the number of isolates, let q denote the number of isolates. Then it is easy to see that $\min q = \max(0, n - 2m)$ since the number of distinct vertices that are end (initial or terminal) vertices of the m arcs is at most $2m$, and the remaining vertices are isolated. We next show that $\max q = \ell$, where $\ell = \max\{k : m \leq (n - k)$

$(n - k - 1)\}$. Clearly, we have $m \le (n - q)(n - q - 1)$ and so $q \le \ell$ for every digraph. To get a digraph attaining ℓ, all one has to do is to put the m arcs within $n - \ell$ vertices. Again, it is easy to see that all values between the minimum and the maximum are attained.

It is easy to see that the minimum and the maximum of the number s of symmetric pairs are $\max\left(0, m - \binom{n}{2}\right)$ and $\lfloor m/2 \rfloor$, respectively, and that every integral value between the minimum and the maximum is attained by s. If t is the number of arcs that are not reciprocated, we have (i) $2s + t = m$ and (ii) $s + t \le \binom{n}{2}$. Subtracting (ii) from (i), we get $s \ge m - \binom{n}{2}$. Since $t \ge 0$, (i) gives $s \le \lfloor m/2 \rfloor$.

The minimum and maximum values of the diameter were obtained by Goldberg and Ghouila-Houri, respectively (see Berge, 1973). If a digraph G is strongly connected, the out-degree as well as the in-degree of every vertex in G is at least 1, so $m \ge n$. Moreover, if $m = n$ in G, then G is a circuit, and the diameter is $n - 1$. Hence, the minimum and the maximum values of the diameter are ∞ if $m \le n - 1$. The minimum is $n - 1$ and the maximum is ∞ if $m = n$. Next we take $n < m \le n(n - 1)$. Let $n - 1 = (m - n + 1)q + r$ where $0 \le r < m - n + 1$. Then the minimum value of the diameter is

$$
\begin{cases}
2q & \text{if } r = 0 \\
2q + 1 & \text{if } r = 1 \\
2q + 2 & \text{otherwise}
\end{cases}
\tag{3.10}
$$

and the maximum value of the diameter is

$$
\begin{cases}
n - 1 & \text{if } m \le (n^2 + n - 2)/2 \\
\left\lfloor n + \frac{1}{2} - \sqrt{2m - n^2 - n + \frac{17}{4}} \right\rfloor & \text{otherwise}
\end{cases}
\tag{3.11}
$$

It is easy to see that the minimum and maximum values of the radius are ∞ if $m < n - 1$. If $m \ge n - 1$, the minimum radius is 1. For maximum radius, see Berge (1973).

We now prove that the minimum number θ of strong components is

$$
\theta =
\begin{cases}
n & \text{if } m = 0 \\
1 & \text{if } m \ge n \\
n - m + 1 & \text{otherwise}
\end{cases}
\tag{3.12}
$$

The result is trivial if $m \le 1$. If $m \ge n$, then we can get a strongly connected digraph on n vertices with m arcs by starting with a circuit on n vertices and adding $m - n$ arcs arbitrarily, so $\theta = 1$. So let $1 < m < n$. We first note that any strongly connected digraph on $t \geq 2$ vertices has at least t arcs since the out-degree of each vertex must be at least 1. Let G be any digraph on n vertices with m arcs. Suppose exactly ℓ of the p strong components of G are singletons. If $\ell = n$, then $p = n \geq n - m + 1$. If $\ell < n$, then $m \geq n - \ell$, so $p \geq \ell + 1 \geq n - m + 1$. To get a digraph with exactly $n - m + 1$ strong components, consider a circuit on m vertices together with $n - m$ isolated vertices.

We next prove that the maximum number Θ of strong components is

$$k_0 = \max \left\{ k : k \leq n \text{ and } m - \binom{n}{2} \leq \binom{n-k+1}{2} \right\},$$

which reduces to

$$\left\lfloor \frac{1}{2} \left(2n + 1 - \sqrt{8 \left(m - \frac{n(n-1)}{2} \right) + 1} \right) \right\rfloor \text{ if } m \geq \binom{n}{2}. \tag{3.13}$$

(Note that $\binom{1}{2} = 0$ by definition.) For this, suppose G is an arbitrary digraph on n vertices with m arcs. Let the strong components of G be $C_1, C_2, \ldots, C_p$, C_i containing n_i vertices. Then no arc between two C_is can be reciprocated, so the number of arcs between C_is is at most $\binom{n}{2}$. Hence,

$$m \leq \binom{n}{2} + \sum_{i=1}^{p} \binom{n_i}{2} \leq \binom{n}{2} + \binom{n-p+1}{2},$$

where the second inequality follows on observing that $\sum_{i=1}^{p} \binom{n_i}{2}$ is maximum when all but one of the n_is are 1 each. So $p \leq k_0$, and it follows that $\Theta \leq k_0$. To show equality, consider the digraph on the vertex set $\{v_1, v_2, \ldots, v_n\}$ obtained as follows: If $m \leq \binom{n}{2}$, put m arcs of the type $v_i v_j$ with $i < j$. If $m > \binom{n}{2}$, make $v_i v_j$ an arc whenever $1 \leq i < j \leq n$ and add $m - \binom{n}{2}$ arcs of the type $v_j v_i$ with $i < j$ within the first $n - k_0 + 1$ vertices. In this digraph, the last $k_0 - 1$ vertices form singleton strong components, so the digraph has at least k_0 and so exactly k_0 strong components.

We now prove that the minimum number ξ of weak components is $\max(1, n - m)$. The result is trivial if $m = 0$. If $m \geq n - 1$, then we can get a weakly connected digraph on n vertices with m arcs by starting with a path on n vertices and adding $m - n + 1$ arcs arbitrarily, so $\xi = 1$. Next let $0 < m < n - 1$. We first note that any weakly connected digraph on t vertices has at least $t - 1$ arcs (we omit the proof of this statement). Now let G be any digraph on n

vertices with m arcs. Suppose $C_1, C_2, \ldots, C_q$ are the weak components of G, with C_i having n_i vertices. Then $m \geq \sum_{i=1}^{q} (n_i - 1) = n - q$, so $q \geq n - m$. To get a digraph with exactly $n - m$ weak components, consider a path on $m + 1$ vertices together with $n - m - 1$ isolated vertices.

We next prove that the maximum number Ξ of weak components is

$$
\begin{aligned}
k^0 &= \max\{k : k \leq n \text{ and } m \leq (n - k + 1)(n - k)\} \\
&= \left\lfloor \tfrac{1}{2}\left(2n + 1 - \sqrt{4m + 1}\right) \right\rfloor .
\end{aligned}
\tag{3.14}
$$

The proof is similar to that for Θ. Suppose G is an arbitrary digraph with weak components $C_1, C_2, \ldots, C_q$, with C_i containing n_i vertices. Then there are no arcs between C_is, so

$$
m \leq \sum_{i=1}^{q} n_i (n_i - 1) \leq (n - q + 1)(n - q),
$$

where the second inequality follows as before. Hence, $q \leq k^0$ and $\Xi \leq k^0$. To show equality, consider a digraph with all the arcs belonging to one weak component with $n - k + 1$ vertices.

We now consider the difference $p - q$, where p and q denote the number of strong components and the number of weak components, respectively. We first note that $p \geq q$. If $m \geq 2$, then a digraph with a circuit on $\min(m, n)$ vertices has $p = q$. If $m = 1$, then $p = n$ and $q = n - 1$. If $m = 0$, then $p = q = n$. Hence, we have

$$
\min p - q = \begin{cases} 1 & \text{if } m = 1 \\ 0 & \text{otherwise} \end{cases} .
\tag{3.15}
$$

We next show that

$$
\max p - q = \begin{cases} m & \text{if } m \leq n - 1 \\ \Theta - 1 & \text{otherwise} \end{cases} ,
\tag{3.16}
$$

where Θ is the maximum number of strong components. For this, it is enough to observe that there is a digraph attaining the maximum number of strong components and the minimum number of weak components simultaneously.

We next consider the number h of arcs joining different strong components. The minimum value of h is 0 or 1 accordingly as $m \geq 2$ or $m = 1$. To see this, all one has to do is to include a circuit on $\min(m, n)$ vertices if $m \geq 2$. We next consider the maximum value of h. Clearly, $\max h = m$ if $m \leq \binom{n}{2}$. So let $m > \binom{n}{2}$. Let

$$t = \min\left\{\sum_{i=1}^{\ell}\binom{n_i}{2} : \quad \ell \geq 1, \ n_i \geq 1 \text{ for } i = 1, 2, \ldots, \ell, \right.$$

$$\left. \sum_{i=1}^{\ell} n_i = n \text{ and } m \leq \binom{n}{2} + \sum_{i=1}^{\ell}\binom{n_i}{2}\right\}.$$

Then we will show that $\max h = \binom{n}{2} - t$. Suppose G is a network on n vertices with m arcs, of which h is between strong components. Suppose G has ℓ strong components $C_1, C_2, \ldots, C_\ell$, with C_i containing n_i vertices. Then, for $i \neq j$, there cannot be arcs both from C_i to C_j and from C_j to C_i. Hence, $h \leq \binom{n}{2} - \sum_{i=1}^{\ell}\binom{n_i}{2} \leq \binom{n}{2} - t$. To prove that the bound is attained, consider a digraph with $v_i v_j$ an arc whenever $i < j$ and with the sizes of the strong components equal to $n_1, n_2, \ldots, n_\ell$ (it is easy to see that such a digraph exists). We mention that $t \geq m - \binom{n}{2}$, but the equality may not always hold. For example, if $n = 6$ and $m = 20$, then $t = 6$ attains when $\ell = 2$ and $n_1 = n_2 = 3$, whereas $m - \binom{n}{2} = 5$. Thus, $\max h$ is 9 here.

We finally come to clique number. It is easy to see that the maximum value for the clique number of a digraph on n vertices with m arcs is

$$\max\{k : m \geq k(k-1)\} = \left\lfloor \tfrac{1}{2}\left(1 + \sqrt{4m+1}\right)\right\rfloor. \tag{3.17}$$

It can be shown that the minimum value of the clique number is

$$\max\left\{k : m \leq n(n-1) - k\binom{q}{2} - rq \text{ where } q = \left\lfloor \frac{n}{k}\right\rfloor \text{ and } r = n - kq\right\}. \tag{3.18}$$

We omit the proof of this result. We mention that the corresponding result for (undirected) graphs is known as Turan's theorem. A digraph attaining the bound, which we denote by k, is obtained as follows: The vertex set is $V_1 \cup V_2 \cup \ldots \cup V_k$, where the V_is are pairwise disjoint, r of the V_is has size $q + 1$, and the rest have size q. The m arcs are adjusted in such a way that there is no symmetric pair within any V_i. The clique number of this digraph is k because any clique in it can contain only one vertex from each V_i.

Model II.2

This model is the probabilistic version of Model II.1. It takes the vertex set $V = \{v_1, v_2, \ldots, v_n\}$ and the number of arcs m ($0 \leq m \leq n(n-1)$) as fixed and assumes that all the $\binom{n(n-1)}{m}$ possible digraphs are equally likely. Note that a random digraph is now obtained by choosing m of the $n(n-1)$ ordered pairs $v_i v_j$, by simple random sampling without replacement, and making them arcs.

Since $n(n-1)$ occurs repeatedly, we will write M for $n(n-1)$ in what follows.

Let X_{ij} be defined as before. Then under the present model, $P(X_{ij}=1)=m/M$, but the X_{ij}s are not independent.

Since the out-degree d_i of v_i is the number of pairs chosen from $\{v_i v_j \ 1 \le j \le n, j \ne i\}$, it follows that d_i has the following hypergeometric distribution:

$$P(d_i = k) = \frac{\binom{n-1}{k}\binom{n^2-2n+1}{m-k}}{\binom{M}{m}}, \ \max(0, m-(n^2-2n+1)) \le k \le \min(n-1, m).$$

(3.19)

Hence, $E(d_i) = m/n$ and

$$V(d_i) = m\frac{1}{n}\left(1-\frac{1}{n}\right)\frac{M-m}{M-1}.$$

(3.20)

It may be noted that the distribution of d_i is approximately $B(m, 1/n)$ if $m \le n-1$ and $B(n-1, m/M)$ if $m \ge n-1$. The distribution can also be approximated by Poisson distribution with mean m/n when $m << n(n-1)$ and a normal distribution with mean and variance given above when m, M, and n are large subject to finite mean and variance in the limits. It is easy to see that the out-degree d_i and the in-degree e_i of v_i have the same distribution.

Now, different d_is are not independent. For example,

$$P(d_2 = k | d_1 = \ell) = \frac{\binom{n-1}{k}\binom{M-2(n-1)}{m-k-\ell}}{\binom{M-(n-1)}{m-\ell}}, \quad k = 0, 1, \ldots, \min(n-1, m-\ell).$$

So the distribution of $d_{\max}$ is not easy to compute now.

The probability that v_i is a source is

$$P(e_i = 0) = \frac{\binom{M-(n-1)}{m}}{\binom{M}{m}}.$$

(3.21)

Now, the events that different vertices are sources are not independent. However, the probability that k given vertices are sources is

$$\frac{\binom{(n-k)(n-1)}{m}}{\binom{M}{m}}.$$

(3.22)

So an expression similar to (3.1), for the probability that there are exactly k sources, can be written down. A simpler approximation to the distribution of the expected number of sources can be obtained as follows when n is large: We assume that the events that different vertices are sources are independent. Then the number of sources has the distribution $B(n, p)$, where p is given in (3.3). Now,

$$p = \prod_{i=0}^{n-2} \left(1 - \frac{m}{M-i}\right) \approx \left(1 - \frac{m}{M-2n/3}\right)^{n-1} \approx \exp\left(-\frac{m(n-1)}{M-2n/3}\right).$$

This approximation seems to be good if $m < n$. When $m \geq n$,

$$p = \prod_{i=0}^{m-1} \left(1 - \frac{n-1}{M-i}\right) \approx \left(1 - \frac{n-1}{M-2m/3}\right)^{m} \approx \exp\left(-\frac{m(n-1)}{M-2m/3}\right)$$

seems to be better. In both cases, the mean of the true distribution is quite close to the mean of the binomial distribution, but the variance of the true distribution is somewhat smaller than that of the binomial distribution.

The probability that v_i is a sink equals the probability that v_i is a source, and the number of sinks and the number of sources have the same distribution.

The probability that v_i is an isolated vertex is

$$P(d_i = 0 \text{ and } e_i = 0) = \frac{\binom{M-2(n-1)}{m}}{\binom{M}{m}}, \tag{3.23}$$

which is approximately $\exp(-2m(n-1)/(M-4n/3))$ if $m < 2n$. When $m \geq 2n$, $\exp(-2m(n-1)/(M-2m/3))$ is a better approximation. The events that different vertices are isolates are not independent. The probability that k given vertices are isolates is

$$\frac{\binom{(n-k)(n-k-1)}{m}}{\binom{M}{m}}. \tag{3.24}$$

So an expression similar to (3.1), for the probability that there are exactly k isolates, can be written down. However, again, the number of isolates is approximately $B(n, p)$, where p is given by (3.4).

By definition, any two digraphs with m arcs (in particular, any digraph and its converse) have the same probability—namely, $1/\binom{M}{m}$.

The probability that G is symmetric is $\binom{M/2}{m/2}/\binom{M}{m}$, provided that m is even (and 0 otherwise).

The probability that G is asymmetric is $\binom{M/2}{m}2^m/\binom{M}{m}$.

To find the probability that G is complete, we note that given k distinct unordered pairs $\{i_1, j_1\}, \{i_2, j_2\}, \ldots, \{i_k, j_k\}$, the probability that none of

$v_{i_1} v_{j_1}, v_{j_1} v_{i_1}, v_{i_2} v_{j_2}, v_{j_2} v_{i_2}, \ldots, v_{i_k} v_{j_k}, v_{j_k} v_{i_k}$ is an arc is $\binom{M-2k}{m} / \binom{M}{m}$. Hence, the probability that G is not complete is

$$\binom{n}{2} \frac{\binom{M-2}{m}}{\binom{M}{m}} - \binom{\binom{n}{2}}{2} \frac{\binom{M-4}{m}}{\binom{M}{m}} + \binom{\binom{n}{2}}{3} \frac{\binom{M-6}{m}}{\binom{M}{m}} - \cdots \qquad (3.25)$$

It is not difficult to see that

$$P(s(G) = k) = \frac{\binom{\binom{n}{2}}{k} \binom{\binom{n}{2} - k}{m - 2k} 2^{m-2k}}{\binom{n(n-1)}{m}}. \qquad (3.26)$$

From this it follows that

$$\frac{P(s(G) = k+1)}{P(s(G) = k)} = \frac{(m - 2k)(m - 2k + 1)}{4(k+1)(\binom{n}{2} - m + k + 1)}.$$

This ratio is greater than 1 or less than 1 accordingly as $k < x$ or $k > x$, where

$$x = \frac{(m + 4)(m - 1) - 2n(n - 1)}{2n(n - 1) + 6}. \qquad (3.27)$$

Hence, it follows that the distribution of $s(G)$ is unimodal with mode at $\lceil x \rceil$. (The maximum probability may be attained at most at two consecutive integers.) We can also find the mean and the variance since $s(G)$ is the sum of the $n(n - 1)/2$ variables Y_{ij}, where $Y_{ij} = X_{ij} X_{ji}$ for any unordered pair $\{i, j\}$ with $i \neq j$. Now

$$E(Y_{ij}) = P(Y_{ij} = 1) = \frac{\binom{M-2}{m-2}}{\binom{M}{m}} = \frac{m(m - 1)}{M(M - 1)}.$$

Let us denote $m(m - 1)/(M(M - 1))$ by p for convenience. Then

$$E(s(G)) = \frac{Mp}{2} = \frac{m(m - 1)}{2n(n - 1) - 2}. \qquad (3.28)$$

Now, $V(Y_{ij}) = p(1 - p)$. If $\{i, j\}$ and $\{k, \ell\}$ are distinct, then

$$\begin{aligned} \text{cov}(Y_{ij}, Y_{k\ell}) &= E(Y_{ij} Y_{k\ell}) - E(Y_{ij}) E(Y_{k\ell}) \\ &= \frac{m(m - 1)(m - 2)(m - 3)}{M(M - 1)(M - 2)(M - 3)} - p^2. \end{aligned}$$

Noting that $\binom{n}{2} = M/2$, we get

$$V(s(G)) = \frac{M}{2}p(1-p) + \frac{M}{2}\left(\frac{M}{2} - 1\right)p\left(\frac{(m-2)(m-3)}{(M-2)(M-3)} - p\right)$$

$$= E(s(G))\left(1 - E(s(G)) + \frac{(m-2)(m-3)}{2M-6}\right). \qquad (3.29)$$

If n is large ($n > 10$, say), $E(s(G)) \approx m^2/(2n^2)$ and $V(s(G)) \approx E(s(G)) \times (1 - m/M)^2$. Writing $\alpha = V(s(G))/E(s(G))$ and $\beta = (1 - m/M)^2$, we actually have

$$\alpha - \beta = \frac{(M-m)(3(M-m)(M-1) - mM)}{M^2(M-1)(M-3)},$$

so $|\alpha - \beta| \le 3/M$. Note that the range of $s(G)$ is $[\max(0, m - M/2), [m/2]]$.

It is now even more difficult than in Model I.2 to deal with probabilities of events depending on the distance between vertices.

For example, to find the probability that G is strongly connected, we have to find the number $g(n, m)$ of strongly connected digraphs on the vertex set $\{v_1, v_2, \ldots, v_n\}$ with m arcs. No method for computing this number $g(n, m)$ is known. Thus, even finding the probability that G is strongly connected is difficult. If $n = 3$ and $m \le 2$, the probability is 0. If $n = 3$ and $m = 3$, out of the 20 possible digraphs, only 2 are strongly connected, so the probability is $1/10$. If $n = 3$ and $m = 4$, out of the 15 possible digraphs, 9 are strongly connected, so the probability is $3/5$. If $n = 3$ and $m \ge 5$, then the probability is 1.

The probability that G has diameter 1 is clearly 1 or 0 according to whether $m = n(n - 1)$ or not. When $n = 3$ and $m = 5$, G has diameter 2 with probability 1. When $n = 3$ and $m = 4$, G has diameter 2 with probability $3/5$ and diameter ∞ with probability $2/5$. When $n = 3$ and $m = 3$, G has diameter 2 with probability $1/10$ and diameter ∞ with probability $9/10$. When $n = 3$ and $m \le 2$, G has diameter ∞ with probability 1.

When $n = 3$ and $m \ge 4$, G has radius 1 with probability 1. When $n = 3$ and $m = 3$, G has radius 1 with probability $3/10$ and radius 2 with probability $7/10$. When $n = 3$ and $m = 2$, G has radius 1 with probability $1/5$, radius 2 with probability $2/5$, and radius ∞ with probability $2/5$. When $n = 3$ and $m \le 1$, G has radius ∞ with probability 1.

Results of Simulation

To give an idea of the distributions of various statistics when both n and m are fixed, we give them for $n = 10$ and a few values of m. These were obtained by simulation using 100,000 random digraphs.

Maximum Out-Degree (Continuation)

	Maximum Out-Degree								
	1	2	3	4	5	6	7	8	9
m									
4	.538	.434	.027	.001	–	–	–	–	–
7	.076	.724	.184	.015	.001	–	–	–	–
10	.001	.478	.444	.071	.006	–	–	–	–
15	–	.055	.583	.305	.052	.005	–	–	–
20	–	–	.228	.546	.193	.030	.003	–	–
40	–	–	–	–	.122	.529	.291	.054	.004
60	–	–	–	–	–	–	.172	.630	.198
80	–	–	–	–	–	–	–	.001	.999

Sources

	0	1	2	3	4	5	6	7	8	9
m										
4	–	–	–	–	–	–	.538	.411	.050	.001
7	–	–	–	.076	.359	.412	.140	.013	–	–
10	.001	.024	.178	.392	.309	.088	.008	–	–	–
15	.075	.319	.394	.180	.030	.002	–	–	–	–
20	.323	.461	.189	.026	.001	–	–	–	–	–
40	.964	.036	–	–	–	–	–	–	–	–
60	1	–	–	–	–	–	–	–	–	–
80	1	–	–	–	–	–	–	–	–	–

Isolates

	0	1	2	3	4	5	6	7
m								
4	–	–	.029	.236	.450	.248	.036	.001
7	.046	.262	.414	.231	.044	.003	–	–
10	.312	.465	.195	.027	.001	–	–	–
15	.764	.221	.015	–	–	–	–	–
20	.940	.059	.001	–	–	–	–	–
40	1	–	–	–	–	–	–	–
60	1	–	–	–	–	–	–	–
80	1	–	–	–	–	–	–	–

	Symmetric Pairs							
	0	*1*	*2*	*3*	*4*	*5*	*6*	*7*
m								
4	.932	.067	.001					
7	.775	.212	.013	–	–	–	–	–
10	.571	.356	.069	.004	–	–	–	–
15	.247	.419	.254	.070	.009	.001	–	–
20	.065	.241	.337	.240	.094	.021	.002	–

	Symmetric Pairs (Continued)										
	4	*5*	*6*	*7*	*8*	*9*	*10*	*11*	*12*	*13*	*14*
$m = 40$	.004	.019	.062	.137	.213	.238	.181	.098	.037	.009	.002

	Symmetric Pairs (Continued)									
	16	*17*	*18*	*19*	*20*	*21*	*22*	*23*	*24*	*25*
$m = 60$	.008	.041	.126	.227	.261	.200	.097	.033	.006	.001

	Symmetric Pairs (Continued)			
	35	*36*	*37*	*38*
$m = 80$	.573	.356	.067	.004

	Diameter									
	1	2	3	4	5	6	7	8	9	∞
m										
4	–	–	–	–	–	–	–	–	–	1
7	–	–	–	–	–	–	–	–	–	1
10	–	–	–	–	–	–	–	–	–	1
15	–	–	–	–	–	.001	.001	.001	–	.997
20	–	–	–	.002	.028	.032	.015	.004	.001	.918
40	–	.001	.738	.181	.009	–	–	–	–	.071
60	–	.880	.119	–	–	–	–	–	–	.001
80	–	1	–	–	–	–	–	–	–	–

					Radius				
	1	2	3	4	5	6	7	8	∞
m									
4	–	–	–	–	–	–	–	–	1
7	–	–	–	–	–	–	–	–	1
10	–	–	.001	.002	.002	.002	.001	–	.992
15	–	.008	.092	.093	.054	.023	.007	.002	.721
20	–	.105	.389	.149	.057	.016	.004	.001	.279
40	.004	.987	.009	–	–	–	–	–	–
60	.199	.801	–	–	–	–	–	–	–
80	.999	.001	–	–	–	–	–	–	–

				Clique Number				
	1	2	3	4	5	6	7	8
m								
4	.932	.068	–	–	–	–	–	–
7	.775	.225	–	–	–	–	–	–
10	.571	.429	–	–	–	–	–	–
15	.247	.752	.001	–	–	–	–	–
20	.065	.928	.007	–	–	–	–	–
40	–	.492	.504	.004	–	–	–	–
60	–	–	.437	.544	.019	–	–	–
80	–	–	–	.001	.253	.645	.100	.001

					Strong Components					
	1	2	3	4	5	6	7	8	9	10
m										
4	–	–	–	–	–	–	–	.009	.067	.924
7	–	–	–	–	–	.004	.021	.074	.195	.706
10	–	–	–	.004	.018	.051	.104	.177	.251	.395
15	.003	.022	.069	.127	.166	.170	.158	.130	.095	.060
20	.082	.209	.250	.196	.126	.070	.037	.019	.008	.003
40	.929	.068	.003	–	–	–	–	–	–	–
60	1	–	–	–	–	–	–	–	–	–
80	1	–	–	–	–	–	–	–	–	–

					Weak Components				
	1	*2*	*3*	*4*	*5*	*6*	*7*	*8*	*9*	*10*
m										
4	–	–	–	–	–	.897	.102	.001	–	–
7	–	–	.444	.460	.092	.004	–	–	–	–
10	.197	.504	.262	.036	.001	–	–	–	–	–
15	.750	.234	.016	–	–	–	–	–	–	–
20	.939	.060	.001	–	–	–	–	–	–	–
40	1	–	–	–	–	–	–	–	–	–
60	1	–	–	–	–	–	–	–	–	–
80	1	–	–	- -	–	–	–	–	–	–

3.4 MODELS FIXING ALL OUT-DEGREES OF INDIVIDUAL VERTICES

Model III.1

Model II.1 leaves the possibility that all the m arcs are within a few vertices. This is often not realistic, and many of the vertices may have positive out-degree. In such a situation, as well as others in which the respondent is asked a question to name his or her three best friends, Model III.1 is more appropriate.

This model takes the vertex set $V = \{v_1, v_2, \ldots, v_n\}$ and the out-degree d_i of v_i as fixed for $i = 1, 2, \ldots, n$ and assumes that all the $\prod \binom{n-1}{d_i}$ digraphs on V with $d^+(v_i) = d_i$ for $i = 1, 2, \ldots, n$ are actually possible. Note that the d_is have to satisfy the following condition: $0 \le d_i \le n - 1$ for all i. For the sake of convenience, we will assume in the discussion of this model that $d_1 \ge d_2 \ge \cdots \ge d_n$. Moreover, G will denote a digraph with vertex set $\{v_1, v_2, \ldots, v_n\}$ and with $d^+(v_i) = d_i$ for all i.

Clearly, the present model fixes m since $m = \sum_{i=1}^{n} d_i$. The number of sinks is also fixed since v_i is a sink if and only if $d_i = 0$. We now show that the range of the in-degree e_j of v_j is $[\sum_{i \ne j} \max(0, d_i - n + 2), \sum_{i \ne j} \min(1, d_i)]$. Clearly, $e_j \ge \sum_{i \ne j} \max(0, d_i - n + 2)$ in every G since for all $i \ne j$ such that $d_i > n - 2$, $v_i v_j$ is an arc. It is easy to see that the bound is attained. Also, $e_j \le \sum_{i \ne j} \min(1, d_i)$ in every G since for all $i \ne j$, $v_i v_j$ can be an arc only if $d_i \ge 1$. Again it is easy to see that the bound is attained.

To give the minimum and maximum values taken by the number of sources, let p denote the number of sources. Then we show that min $p = \max(0, n - m)$. Suppose G has a source u and a vertex v with in-degree at least 2. We may then take an arc xv where $x \neq u$, drop the arc xv, and introduce the arc xu. This will give another digraph with the same out-degrees and with less number of sources. Now suppose $m \geq n$. If there is a source in G, then some vertex has in-degree at least 2, so we can reduce the number of sources. Repeating the process, we get a digraph with $p = 0$. Next let $m < n$. Then the m arcs can make at most m vertices nonsources, so $p \geq n - m$ in every G. By the argument given above, a digraph with the minimum number of sources has no vertex with in-degree larger than 2 and so has $n - m$ sources. Hence, min $p = n - m$.

To give the maximum value taken by p, let $k = d_1$. Then max $p = n - k$ if $d_{n-k+1} < k$ and $n - k - 1$ otherwise. To see this, we note that in any G, v_1 is joined to k vertices, so $p \leq n - k$. If $d_{n-k+1} < k$, then v_i can be joined to d_i of the last k vertices for $i = 1, 2, \ldots, n$, giving a digraph with $p = n - k$. Next let $d_{n-k+1} = k$. Then in any G, if W is the set of vertices to which v_1 is joined, the out-degree of at least one vertex in W is larger than $k - 1$, so at least one vertex outside W is not a source, and hence $p \leq n - k - 1$. It is easy to see that this bound is attained.

To give the minimum and maximum values taken by the number of isolates, let q denote the number of isolates. Let $d_1 = k$ and let ℓ be the number of d_is, which are 0. We show that min $q = \max(0, \ell - \sum_{i=1}^{n-\ell} d_i)$. In any G, at most $\sum_{i=1}^{n-\ell} d_i$ of the last ℓ vertices can have positive in-degree, and hence it follows that $q \geq \max(0, \ell - \sum_{i=1}^{n-\ell} d_i)$. A digraph attaining the bound is obtained by choosing a vertex among the last ℓ, which has not yet received any arc (if it exists) while choosing the vertices to which v_i is joined, $i = 1, 2, \ldots, n - \ell$.

We now give the maximum value taken by the number of isolates. If $k = 0$, then max $q = n$. So let $k \geq 1$. Then we show that max $q = \min(n - k - 1, \ell)$. Clearly, v_1 and the vertices to which it is joined as well as the $n - \ell$ vertices with positive out-degree are not isolates, so $q \leq \min(n - k - 1, \ell)$. Clearly, the bound is attained by the digraph obtained by joining v_i to d_i of the first $k + 1$ vertices for $i = 1, 2, \ldots, n - \ell$. It is easy to see that every value between the minimum and the maximum values of q is attained.

The range of $s(G)$ in the present model was determined by Achuthan, Rao, and Rao (1984). To give this range, let the d_is be arranged so that $d_1 \geq d_2 \geq \cdots \geq d_n$. For any t with $1 \leq t \leq n$, define

$$f(t) = \sum_{i=1}^{t} d_i - t(n - t) - \binom{t}{2}. \tag{3.30}$$

Then the minimum value of the number $s(G)$ of reciprocal pairs is $\max_t f(t)$. We show only that $\min s(G) \geq \max_t f(t)$. Fix any t and any digraph with vertex set $\{v_1, v_2, \ldots, v_n\}$ such that the out-degree of v_i is d_i for $i = 1, 2, \ldots, n$. Then the number of arcs $v_i v_j$ in G with $i \leq t$ is $\sum_{i=1}^{t} d_i$. Of these, at most $t(n - t)$ can have $j \geq t + 1$. So G has at least $\sum_{i=1}^{t} d_i - t(n - t)$ arcs within the first t vertices. Hence, G has at least $f(t)$ symmetric pairs (within the first t vertices). This proves $\min s(G) \geq \max_t f(t)$.

To give the maximum value of $s(G)$, define

$$g(t) = \sum_{i=1}^{t} d_i - t(t - 1) - \sum_{j=t+1}^{n} \min(t, d_j). \tag{3.31}$$

Then, $\max s(G) = (m - \max_t g(t))/2$, where $m = \sum_{i=1}^{n} d_i$. We only show that the left-hand side does not exceed the right-hand side. Fix t and G as in the preceding paragraph. Then the number of arcs $v_i v_j$ in G with $i \leq t$ is $\sum_{i=1}^{t} d_i$. Of these, at most $t(t - 1)$ can have $j \leq t$. So G has at least $\sum_{i=1}^{t} d_i - t(t - 1)$ arcs from the first t vertices to the last $n - t$ vertices. Now there are at most $\sum_{j=t+1}^{n} \min(t, d_j)$ arcs from the last $n - t$ vertices to the first t vertices. Hence, there are at least $g(t)$ arcs from the first t vertices to the last $n - t$ vertices, which are not reciprocated (i.e., do not form symmetric pairs). Hence, $s(G) \leq (m - g(t))/2$.

It is easy to see that every value between the minimum and the maximum values of $s(G)$ is attained.

Exact analytical determination of the range of the diameter seems to be a difficult problem when the out-degrees of the vertices are fixed.

We now give the minimum value ρ of the radius r. If $\sum_i d_i < n - 1$, clearly $\rho = \infty$. So let $\sum_i d_i \geq n - 1$. Let u be a center of G. Clearly, only $n_0 = 1$ vertex is at distance 0 from u. It is easy to see that at most, $n_1 : = n_0 + d_1$ vertices are at distance ≤ 1 from u, at most $n_2 : = n_1 + d_{n_0+1} + d_{n_0+2} + \cdots + d_{n_1}$ vertices are at distance ≤ 2 from u, at most $n_3 : = n_2 + d_{n_1+1} + d_{n_1+2} + \cdots + d_{n_2}$ vertices are at distance ≤ 3 from u, and so on. It follows easily that ρ is the smallest k such that $n_k \geq n$. To give an example, suppose the out-degrees are 3,2,2,1,1,1,1,1,1,0. Then, $n_0 = 1$, $n_1 = 4$, $n_2 = 9$, and $n_3 = 14$. Since $n = 10$, it follows that $\rho = 3$. We do not know the maximum value of the radius.

We now prove that the minimum number of strong components is min $(n, \ell + 1)$, where ℓ is the number of d_is, which are 0. Clearly, any G will have at least $\min(n, \ell + 1)$ strong components. We can get a digraph attaining this bound by including a circuit on the first $n - \ell$ vertices if $n - \ell \geq 2$.

We do not have a simple expression for the maximum number of strong components, but we will show that the digraph D with the property

$P : v_j$ is joined *to* the last d_j v_is (excluding v_j itself) for $j = 1, 2, \ldots, n$,

is extremal. We prove this by induction on n. The basis for induction is trivial. Assume the result for less than n vertices. Let G be any extremal digraph (i.e., a digraph with $d^+(v) = d_i$ for $i = 1, 2, \ldots, n$ and with the maximum number k of strong components). Then the strong components $C_1, C_2, \ldots, C_k$ in G can be numbered in such a way that (i) there is no arc from C_i to C_j if $i > j$. To see this, we note that the condensation H of G obtained by shrinking each C_i to a vertex has no circuits. Let P be an open (i.e., the first and last vertices are distinct) path of the maximum length in H. Then the first vertex of P is a source in H. Let C_1 be the strong component of G corresponding to this vertex. Now deleting C_1 and repeating the procedure, we can order the strong components so that (i) is satisfied. Now, if $u \in C_i$, $v \in C_j$, $i < j$, and $d^+(u) < d^+(v)$, then by interchanging u and v (note that condition (i) is easy to satisfy), we get another extremal digraph. Repeating this process, we get an extremal digraph G such that the last few (say, n_k) v_is form a strong component. Clearly, we may assume that each v_j belonging to C_k is joined *to* the last d_j v_is (excluding v_j itself). We may also assume that for all $i \leq n - n_k$, v_i is joined *to* the last $\min(d_i, n_k)$ v_is. Finally, the subdigraph induced by $C_1 \cup \cdots \cup C_{k-1}$ is also extremal and can be replaced by one satisfying P. Then G itself satisfies P. The number of strong components in such a digraph can easily be counted, although it is difficult to give a nice expression for it. For example, suppose the out-degree sequence is $(9, 8, 8, 5, 5, 5, 5, 3, 2, 0)$. Then the strong components in the extremal digraph obtained as above are $\{v_{10}\}$, $\{v_5, v_6, v_7, v_8, v_9\}$, $\{v_4\}$, $\{v_2, v_3\}$, and $\{v_1\}$ (note that it is convenient to determine the strong components starting at the right end).

Let p denote the number of weak components. Then we show that $\min p = \max(1, n - m)$. Suppose G has two weak components, C_1 and C_2, and C_1 is not a tree. Then C_1 has an arc uv such that C_1 remains weakly connected when arc uv is deleted. Now deleting the arc uv and joining u to a vertex of C_2 reduces the number of weak components. Thus, in a digraph attaining the minimum number of weak components, either there is only one weak component or there are at least two weak components, and all of them are trees. In the former case, $m \geq n - 1$, and in the latter case, $m = n - p \leq n - 2$. This proves that $\min p = \max(1, n - m)$.

We do not know the maximum value Ξ of the number of weak components precisely but have partial information on it. Let G be a maximal digraph (i.e., a digraph attaining Ξ). Let C_1 be the weak component containing v_1. If there is a vertex u other than v_1 in C_1 and a vertex v in another weak component such that the out-degree of u is less than the out-degree of v, then by interchanging u and v (note that this is possible since the out-degree of v is less than the size of C_1), we get another extremal digraph. Repeating this process, we get an extremal digraph such that the vertices in C_1 have the largest few out-degrees. Repeating the argument starting with the first vertex not in C_1, we ultimately get an extremal digraph in which the weak components are

$$\{1, 2, \ldots, n_1\}, \quad \{n_1 + 1, n_1 + 2, \ldots, n_2\}, \ldots, \{n_{p-1} + 1, n_{p-1} + 2, \ldots, n\}$$

for some $n_1, n_2, \ldots, n_p$ such that $1 \leq n_1 < n_2 < \cdots < n_p = n$ and $n_{i+1} - n_i \geq d_{n_i+1} + 1$ for $i = 0, 2, \ldots, p - 1$. It is also easy to see that Ξ is the maximum p such that such n_is exist. However, we cannot always take $n_1 = d_1 + 1$ and so forth. For example, if the d_is are $3, 3, 3, 2, 2, 2$, we have to take $n_1 = 6$ and $\Xi = 1$. Moreover, if the d_is are $3, 3, 3, 3, 3, 1, 1, 0$, taking $n_1 = 5, n_2 = 7$, and $n_3 = 8$ is better than taking $n_1 = 4$ and $n_2 = 8$.

We finally come to clique number ω. We show that $\max \omega = \max\{k : d_k \geq k - 1\}$. For this, it is enough to observe that k vertices can be made to induce a complete symmetric digraph if and only if their out-degrees are at least $k - 1$. The minimum value of $\emptyset$ is not known.

Model III.2

This model takes the vertex set $V = \{v_1, v_2, \ldots, v_n\}$ and the out-degree d_i $(0 \leq d_i \leq n - 1)$ of v_i as fixed for $i = 1, 2, \ldots, n$ and assumes that all the $\prod \binom{n-1}{d_i}$ possible digraphs are equally likely.

Note that now a random digraph is obtained by choosing, for each i, d_i of the $n - 1$ ordered pairs $v_i v_j$, $1 \leq j \leq n$, $j \neq i$, by simple random sampling without replacement and making them arcs. Note that different is are treated independently.

Let X_{ij} be defined as before. Then, under the present model, $P(X_{ij} = 1) = d_i/(n - 1)$. Also, X_{ij} and $X_{k\ell}$ are independent if $i \neq k$.

Clearly, now d_is and thus m are fixed. But the in-degrees are variable, and the distribution of e_j is not easy to compute. However, the mean and the variance of e_j can be computed as follows Since $e_j = \sum\{X_{ij} : 1 \leq i \leq n, i \neq j\}$, it follows that $E(e_j) = \sum_{i \neq j} E(X_{ij}) = \sum_{i \neq j} d_i/(n-1) = (m - d_j)/(n-1)$. Also, since X_{ij}s are independent for different is, we get

$$V(e_j) = \sum_{i \neq j} V(X_{ij}) = \sum_{i \neq j} \frac{d_i(n-1-d_i)}{(n-1)^2} = \frac{(n-1)(S_1 - d_j) - (S_2 - d_j^2)}{(n-1)^2},$$

(3.32)

where $S_1 : = \sum d_i = m$ and $S_2 : = \sum d_i^2$.

The probability that v_j is a source is

$$P(e_j = 0) = \prod_{i \,:\, i \neq j} \left(1 - \frac{d_i}{n-1}\right).$$

(3.33)

Even though one can, in principle, write an expression for any k-given vertices to be sources, this and the expression obtained from it for the probability that there are exactly k sources are not useful. Note that the e_js are not independent since their sum is a constant. So the distribution of $e_{\max}$ is also not easy to compute.

The probability that v_j is an isolated vertex is $P(e_i = 0)$ if $d_i = 0$ and 0 otherwise. The events that different vertices are isolates are not independent. The probability that k-given vertices are isolates and the probability that there are exactly k isolates are not easy to compute.

Now the probabilities that G is symmetric, asymmetric, complete, and so on are all difficult to find.

For any unordered pair $\{i, j\}$, the probability that none of $v_i v_j$ and $v_j v_i$ is an arc is

$$\frac{(n-1-d_i)(n-1-d_j)}{(n-1)^2}.$$

But given k distinct unordered pairs $i_1 j_1, i_2 j_2, \ldots, i_k j_k$, the probability that none of $v_{i_1} v_{j_1}, v_{j_1} v_{i_1}, v_{i_2} v_{j_2}, v_{j_2} v_{i_2}, \ldots, v_{i_k} v_{j_k}, v_{j_k} v_{i_k}$ is an arc is not easy to write down. Hence, the probability that G is not complete cannot be found easily.

The distribution of the number of symmetric pairs $s(G)$ is complicated, but its mean and variance were computed by Katz and Wilson (1956). To compute these, we write $s(G)$ as the sum of Y_{ij}s as before. Now $E(Y_{ij}) = d_i d_j/(n-1)^2$. Hence, writing $S_k = \sum d_i^k$ for $k = 1, 2, \ldots$, we get

$$E(s(G)) = \frac{S_1^2 - S_2}{2(n-1)^2}.$$

(3.34)

It can be proved similarly that

$$V(s(G)) \;=\; E(s(G)) + \frac{S_1^2 S_2 - S_2^2 - 2S_1 S_3 + 2S_4 - S_1^3 + 3S_1 S_2 - 2S_3}{(n-1)^3 (n-2)}$$

$$-\frac{2S_1^2 S_2 - S_2^2 - 4S_1 S_3 + 3S_4}{2(n-1)^4}. \tag{3.35}$$

If the d_is do not differ much, it can be seen that

$$E(s(G)) \approx \frac{n\bar{d}^2}{2(n-1)} \quad \text{and} \quad V(s(G)) \approx E(s(G))\left(1 - \frac{\bar{d}}{n-1}\right)^2,$$

where $\bar{d}$ denotes $\sum d_i / n$.

Model III.3

This model is a generalization of Model III.2. Here, again, we take the vertex set $V = \{v_1, v_2, \ldots, v_n\}$ and the out-degree d_i $(0 \le d_i \le n-1)$ of v_i as fixed for $i = 1, 2, \ldots, n$. But we now assume that for each i, there is a set $P_i \subseteq \{1, 2, \ldots, n\} - \{i\}$ and that the terminal vertices of the d_i arcs leaving v_i belong to P_i. Finally, the model assumes that the $\prod \binom{n_i}{d_i}$ possible digraphs are equally likely, where n_i denotes the size of P_i.

The set P_i may be called the *potential set* for v_i since v_i makes its choices from P_i. The need for considering this type of model has already been explained in Chapter 1. Model III.2 implicitly makes two important assumptions: (i) for any fixed i, the probability that v_j is chosen by v_i is the same for all j, and (ii) the choices of different v_is are statistically independent. Assumption (i) is perhaps unrealistic when d_i is much smaller than n. So we remove it in the present model while still retaining assumption (ii).

Let X_{ij} be defined as before. We take X_{ii} to be 0. Then, under the present model, $P(X_{ij} = 1)$ is d_i/n_i if $j \in P_i$ and 0 otherwise. Also, X_{ij} and $X_{k\ell}$ are independent if $i \ne k$.

Clearly, again, d_is and thus m are fixed. But the in-degrees are variable, and the distribution of e_j is not easy to compute. However, the mean and the variance of e_j can be computed as follows. Let us denote d_i/n_i by r_i. Then $E(X_{ij}) = r_i$ and $V(X_{ij}) = r_i(1 - r_i)$ if $j \in P_i$. If $j \notin P_i$, then $E(X_{ij}) = V(X_{ij}) = 0$. Now, $e_j = \sum_i X_{ij}$, so $E(e_j) = \sum_{i \,:\, j \in P_i} r_i$. Also, since X_{ij}s are independent for different is, we get

$$V(e_j) = \sum \{r_i(1 - r_i) : j \in P_i\}. \tag{3.36}$$

Although the distribution of s is difficult to compute, Rao and Bandyopadhyay (1987) showed that $E(s) = \sum_{j=1}^{n} r_j T_j / 2$ and

$$V(s) = \frac{1}{2} \sum_{j=1}^{n} r_j T_j - \frac{1}{2} \sum_{j=1}^{n} r_j^2 W_j - \sum_{j=1}^{n} \frac{r_j(1-r_j)}{n_j - 1}(T_j^2 - W_j), \qquad (3.37)$$

where

$$T_j = \sum \{r_i : i \in P_j \text{ and } j \in P_i\} \text{ and } W_j = \sum \{r_i^2 : i \in P_j \text{ and } j \in P_i\}.$$
$$(3.38)$$

If we make the assumptions (i) $i \in P_j$ if $j \in P_i$ and (ii) $r_j = r$ for all j, then

$$E(s) = \frac{mr}{2} \text{ and } V(s) = \frac{mr}{2}(1-r)^2.$$

3.5 MODELS FIXING ALL OUT-DEGREES AND IN-DEGREES OF INDIVIDUAL VERTICES

Model IV.1

This model takes the vertex set $V = \{v_1, v_2, \ldots, v_n\}$ and the out-degree d_i as well as the in-degree e_i of v_i as fixed for $i = 1, 2, \ldots, n$ and assumes that all the digraphs on V with $d^+(v_i) = d_i$ and $d^-(v_i) = e_i$ for $i = 1, 2, \ldots, n$ are actually possible. Note that the d_is and e_is have to satisfy the following conditions: $0 \leq d_i \leq n - 1$ and $0 \leq e_i \leq n - 1$ for all i and $\sum d_i = \sum e_i$. But these conditions are not sufficient. Ryser (1963) and Fulkerson (1966) proved that these together with the following condition are necessary and sufficient for the existence of a digraph with $d^+(v_i) = d_i$ and $d^-(v_i) = e_i$ for $i = 1, 2, \ldots, n$:

$$\sum_{i=1}^{k} d_i \leq \sum_{j=1}^{k} \min(k-1, e_j) + \sum_{j=k+1}^{n} \min(k, e_j), \quad k = 1, 2, \ldots, n, \quad (3.39)$$

where we assume without loss of generality that $d_1 \geq d_2 \geq \cdots \geq d_n$. We will make this assumption for convenience in what follows. Moreover, G will denote a digraph with vertex set $\{v_1, v_2, \ldots, v_n\}$ and with $d^+(v_i) = d_i$ and $d^-(v_i) = e_i$ for all i.

We will prove only the necessity of the above condition. Clearly, there are $\sum_{i=1}^{k} d_i$ arcs $v_i v_j$ with $1 \leq i \leq k$. The number of arcs among these with $1 \leq j \leq k$ is at most $\sum_{j=1}^{k} \min(k-1, e_j)$, and the number with $k+1 \leq j \leq n$ is at most $\sum_{j=k+1}^{n} \min(k, e_j)$, and hence the inequality follows. This proves the necessity. A proof of sufficiency can be found in Berge (1973). One can easily give an example where the inequality is not satisfied: Take both the out-degree and in-degree sequences to be $(3, 3, 1, 1)$. Then the inequality is violated for $k = 2$.

Under the present model, the total number of arcs, out-degrees, in-degrees, and sources, sinks, and isolates is all fixed. The range of the other parameters considered earlier seem to be difficult to find. Rao (1984; unpublished manuscript) gave some lower and upper bounds for $\min s(G)$. These are quite involved, and we only mention a special case. Let $a_i = d_i + e_i$ for all i. If the product of the two largest a_is does not exceed $N + 1$, where N is the number of nonzero a_is, then $\min s(G) = 0$. We next note that $\max s(G) \le \lfloor \sum_{i=1}^{n} \min(d_i, e_i)/2 \rfloor$. To prove this, it is enough to note that there can be at most $\min(d_i, e_i)$ symmetric pairs containing v_i. We do not know any sufficient conditions under which the bound is attained, and we do not have any lower bound for $\max s(G)$. We give an example to show that the above upper bound is not always attained. Suppose there is a digraph G with out-degree and in-degree sequences $(3, 2, 2, 2, 1, 1, 0)$ and $(0, 0, 0, 2, 2, 3, 4)$ and with two symmetric pairs. Then $v_4 v_5$, $v_4 v_6$, $v_5 v_4$, and $v_6 v_4$ should be arcs, and v_7 cannot have in-degree 4, a contradiction. Note, however, that there exists a digraph with the given out-degree and in-degree sequences and with one symmetric pair.

Even though we do not know the minimum and maximum values of $s(G)$ in general, we may be able to find them sometimes by using the technique described below. Suppose we are given one digraph G. By an *alternating rectangle* in G, we mean four distinct vertices u, v, w, x such that uv and wx are arcs and ux and wv are not arcs. (Note that the entries in the cells of the adjacency matrix corresponding to the pairs (u, v), (u, x), (w, x), and (w, v) are $1, 0, 1, 0$—hence the name *alternating rectangle*.) By *switching along this alternating rectangle*, we mean dropping the arcs uv and wx and introducing the arcs ux and wv (this amounts to interchanging 1s and 0s in the four cells of the adjacency matrix referred to above). Note that this does not alter the out-degree or the in-degree of any vertex. Similarly, by a *compact alternating hexagon* in G, we mean three distinct vertices u, v and w such that uv, vw, and wu are arcs and vu, wv, and uw are not arcs. (Note that the entries in the cells of the adjacency matrix corresponding to the pairs (u, v), (w, v), (w, u), (v, u), (v, w), and (u, w) are $1, 0, 1, 0, 1, 0$—hence the name *compact alternating hexagon*.) By *switching along this compact alternating hexagon*, we mean dropping the arcs uv, vw, and wu and introducing the arcs vu, wv, and uw. Again, this does not alter the out-degree or the in-degree of any vertex. Rao, Jana, and Bandyopadhyay (1996) proved that any digraph H with $d^+(v_i) = d_i$ and $d^-(v_i) = e_i$ for all i can be obtained from any other such digraph G by a finite sequence of switches along alternating rectangles and compact alternating hexagons. (In most cases, this can be achieved by using only alternating rectangles.) Using this technique, we may be able to prove in some cases by actual construction that a known lower bound or upper bound for $s(G)$ is actually attained.

We do not know the range of the diameter, the radius, and the number of strong and weak components when both d_is and e_is are fixed. However, we can give the minimum number of weak components. For this, let $m = \sum d_i = \sum e_i$, and let p denote the number of weak components. Let ℓ be the number of is such that $d_i = e_i = 0$. Then min $p = \ell + \max(1, n - \ell - m)$ (when $m < n - \ell - 1$, every weak component of a digraph attaining min p is a "tree" on one or more vertices; when $m \geq n - \ell - 1$, a digraph attaining min p has only one weak component other than the ℓ isolated vertices), but the value of max p is not known. Finally, the range of the clique number is also not known.

Model IV.2

This model takes the vertex set $V = \{v_1, v_2, \ldots, v_n\}$ and the out-degree d_i as well as the in-degree e_i of v_i as fixed for $i = 1, 2, \ldots, n$ and assumes all the digraphs on V with $d^+(v_i) = d_i$ and $d^-(v_i) = e_i$ for $i = 1, 2, \ldots, n$ to be equally likely.

Note that the d_is and e_is have to satisfy the conditions stated in Model IV.1 for the existence of at least one digraph with the given out-degrees and in-degrees. (If the out-degrees and in-degrees are read from an observed network, these conditions will automatically be satisfied.) The number of possible networks is a very complicated function of d_is and e_is and is not known, although some recursive methods have been given by Sukhatme (1938) and Katz and Powell (1954) for computing it. The number can be astronomical even for moderate n like $n = 40$. There is also no easy way of generating (listing) all the networks.

Under the present model, practically nothing is known about the distribution of any of the statistics except those that are trivially fixed by the model. So one has to take recourse to simulation. But even generating a random network (where all possible networks are chosen with equal probabilities) is a difficult problem now.

Pramanik (1994) gave a heuristic procedure to get an approximately random network by generating its incidence matrix. His method basically consists of the following: choose a cell, the (i, j)th with probability proportional to $d_i e_j$; put a 1 in that cell; update the d_is and e_is; and repeat. At each stage including the beginning, the entries in all the cells that are determined by the current d_is and e_is are filled in before applying the above procedure. Although this procedure seems to give an approximately random network, there is no theoretical basis for it or an estimate of how good the approximation is.

Snijders (1991) bypassed the problem of generating a random matrix and gave a way of generating a nearly random network so that its probability could be computed. One can then estimate the distribution of any statistic (under the model where all possible networks are equally likely) using a ratio estimator.

One possible way of generating a random network is the following: Generate a random network with out-degree sequence $(d_1, d_2, \ldots, d_n)$. Accept it if its in-degree sequence is $(e_1, e_2, \ldots, e_n)$; otherwise, reject it, generate another with out-degree sequence $(d_1, d_2, \ldots, d_n)$, and repeat this until a network is accepted. It is easy to see that this gives a random network under the present model, but the rate of rejection will generally be so high that not even one may be accepted in a million even for moderate values of n.

Rao et al. (1996) gave a Markov chain simulation method for generating a random network. We will briefly describe the method without detailed proofs. In the following text, we use the term *alternating cycles* to mean alternating rectangles and compact alternating hexagons as defined in the discussion of Model IV.1.

Let $\mathcal{E}$ denote the set of all networks with vertex set $V = \{v_1, v_2, \ldots, v_n\}$ and with $d^+(v_i) = d_i$ and $d^-(v_i) = e_i$ for $i = 1, 2, \ldots, n$. The basic step of the Markov chain Monte Carlo (MCMC) method is as follows. We start with an initial network belonging to $\mathcal{E}$. At any stage, we enumerate the alternating cycles in the current network, choose one of them at random, and switch along it to get a new network in $\mathcal{E}$. We perform this process a large number of times. Then one believes that the network obtained should be a random network (we shall see presently that this is not quite correct). To try to prove this, let us formulate it as a Markov chain. The states of the Markov chain are the networks belonging to $\mathcal{E}$. We shall say that two states are adjacent if the networks represented by them can be obtained from each other by switching along one alternating cycle. Let $c(i)$ denote the number of states adjacent to the state i. Then the procedure mentioned above obviously gives a Markov chain with transition probability $p_{ij} = 1/c(i)$ if j is adjacent to i and 0 otherwise. Note that the Markov chain is irreducible since every state can be reached from every other state in a finite number of steps. So, there exists a unique stationary distribution (see Feller, 1968), and if the Markov chain is aperiodic, the distribution of the state after q steps approaches this stationary distribution as $q \rightarrow \infty$, whatever the initial state. To find the stationary distribution, note that it is a probability vector $\pi' = (\pi_1, \pi_2, \ldots, \pi_N)$ such that $\pi'\mathbf{P} = \pi'$, where $\mathbf{P}$ is the transition probability matrix $((p_{ij}))$. Taking $\theta_i = c(i)/\sum_k c(k)$, it is easy to see that $\sum_i \theta_i p_{ij} = \theta_j$, and thus $\pi_i = \theta_i$. Thus, according to the stationary distribution, the probability of the ith state is not $1/N$ but is proportional to the number $c(i)$ of alternating cycles in the network corresponding to the ith state.

As observed in the preceding paragraph, the basic Markov chain simulation method given above does not choose the networks in $\mathcal{B}$ with equal probabilities and needs modification. Suppose we know an upper bound K for the $c(i)$s. Then we can modify the basic method as follows: At any stage, if we are currently in state i, we go to any one of the states adjacent to i, each with probability $1/K$, and remain at the state i itself with probability $1 - c(i)/K$. Then the transition probability p_{ij} is $1/K$ if $i \neq j$ and i, j are adjacent, 0 if $i \neq j$ and i, j are not adjacent, and $1 - c(i)/K$ if $i = j$. Clearly, now $\mathbf{P}$ is (symmetric and) doubly stochastic, and so the stationary distribution gives probability $1/N$ to each state provided the Markov chain is aperiodic. If $c(i) < K$ and so $p_{ii} > 0$ for at least one state i, that state and thus (noting that the Markov chain is irreducible) the entire Markov chain are aperiodic, and the distribution of the state after q steps tends toward the discrete uniform distribution as $q \rightarrow \infty$, whatever the initial state.

The difficulty in using the modification mentioned in the preceding paragraph is that one cannot get a good upper bound for the $c(i)$s. If K is too large compared to the $c(i)$s, then the p_{ii}s become close to 1, and the convergence to the uniform distribution will be too slow. The best K would, of course, be the maximum of $c(i)$s over all the states, increased by a small number to take care of periodicity. Since this exact maximum cannot be determined, we do the following: We estimate the maximum $c(i)$ using a pilot study and use the estimate increased by a small amount as the initial value of K. At any stage, if the current state is i, then we go from i to one of the states adjacent to i, each with probability $1/K$, and remain at i with probability $1 - c(i)/K$. If we move to state i', we update K by replacing it with $\max(K, c(i'))$. It can be shown that, in the limit, all states are equally probable.

One decision to make while using the Markov chain simulation method is the following: How long should the Markov chain be run to get a nearly random matrix? We do not have a definite answer, but it is known that any network can be obtained from any other network in t or fewer steps, where $t = \min(m, n(n-1) - m)$. Perhaps running the Markov chain for $2t$ to $3t$ steps will be enough to achieve a reasonably good level of mixing. Note that the network obtained in the $3t$th step is a nearly random network. To get another, we have to run the Markov chain again for $3t$ steps starting from the initial network.

3.6 OTHER MODELS

Model V

Recall that Model III.2 implicitly makes two assumptions: (i) For any fixed i, the probability that v_j is chosen by v_i is the same for all j, and (ii) the choices of different v_is are statistically independent. Assumption (i) was removed in Model III.3. In the present model, which is essentially that proposed by Katz and Powell (1956), we remove assumption (ii). This model is an incomplete model and stipulates that there is a common correlation τ between X_{ij} and X_{ji} for all i and j with $i \neq j$. $P(X_{ij} = 1)$ is still assumed to be $d_i/(n-1)$ for all $j \neq i$.

Now, from the definition of τ, we have

$$P(X_{ij} = X_{ji} = 1) = \frac{1}{(n-1)^2}\left(d_i d_j + \tau\sqrt{d_i d_j(n-1-d_i)(n-1-d_j)}\right)$$

and $E(s(G)|\tau)$ is the sum of the above probability over all i and j such that $i < j$. Equating $s(G)$ to its expected value, we get an estimate $\hat{\tau}$ of τ that can be taken as a measure of reciprocity. A positive value of $\hat{\tau}$ will be interpreted as indicating a tendency toward reciprocation and a negative value toward anti-reciprocation (j not going to i when i goes to j), while a value of 0 indicates neutrality with respect to reciprocation.

Note that when $d_i = d$ for all i, the above expression reduces to

$$P(X_{ij} = X_{ji} = 1) = \frac{d}{n-1}\left(\frac{d}{n-1} + \tau\frac{n-1-d}{n-1}\right).$$

Thus,

$$P(X_{ji} = 1 | X_{ij} = 1) = P(X_{ji} = 1) + \tau P(X_{ji} \neq 1).$$

Summing the above joint probability over i and j such that $i < j$, we get

$$E(s|\tau) = \frac{nd^2}{2(n-1)}(1-\tau) + \frac{nd}{2}\tau,$$

so

$$\hat{\tau} = \frac{2(n-1)s - nd^2}{nd(n-1-d)}.$$

This expression can be used as an approximation when d_is are nearly equal to d. Generalizing the above expression for $E(s|\tau)$ to

$$\frac{\sum\sum_{i<j} d_i d_j}{(n-1)^2}(1-\tau) + \frac{\sum_i d_i}{2}\tau,$$

(τ will not be the correlation coefficient and equation (6) will not hold now), Katz and Powell (1956) obtained the expression

$$\hat{\tau} = \frac{2(n-1)^2 s - S_1^2 + S_2}{(n-1)^2 S_1 - S_1^2 + S_2} \tag{3.40}$$

for $\hat{\tau}$ in the general case, where S_1 and S_2 are as defined in Model III.2. Notice that this reduces to the preceding expression when $d_i = d$ for all i.

For given d_is, the set of values $\hat{\tau}$ takes is contained in $[-1, 1]$. But $\hat{\tau}$ attains the value 1 only when s attains the value $\sum d_i/2$, and $\hat{\tau}$ attains the value -1 only when $d_i = (n-1)/2$ for all i and $s = 0$. When the d_is are all equal, τ is like an intraclass correlation coefficient.

The present model is incomplete since it does not even specify $P(X_{ij} = X_{ji} = X_{k\ell} = X_{\ell k} = 1)$. Thus, even the variance of s under the model cannot be computed.

Model VI

Wasserman and Faust (1999) discuss some useful models for understanding single relational data involving a given number of individuals in a social network of choice relation. We propose providing a description of these models, which are also termed *dyadic interaction models*. Some generalizations of these dyadic models have been recently studied in Em-ot, Tiensuwan, and Sinha (2008), and applications have also been made to real network data. We will provide a detailed description of the model and related data analysis results in Chapter 4 and also in Chapter 6 on graph-theoretic case studies.

As usual, we start with n individuals forming a network based on some form of choice relation between any pair of individuals. The possibilities of choice involving the pair of individuals i and j are

$$(0,0), \quad (1,0), \quad (0,1) \quad \text{and} \quad (1,1),$$

where the first component is 1 or 0 according to whether i chooses j or not, and the second component is 1 or 0 according to whether j chooses i or not.

The body of data arising from a network in the form of the adjacency matrix (or sociomatrix) of order $n \times n$ is referred to as X data. Note that $X_{ij} = 1$ or 0 according to whether there is an arc from i to j or not.

Y **Array**

In general, X data are not symmetric. For modeling purposes, we convert X data into what is called the "Y array." It is a symmetric matrix of order $2n \times 2n$ made up of a 2×2 submatrix $Y_{(i,j)}$ for each pair of vertices i and j.

The rows as well as the columns of $Y_{(i,j)}$ are designated 0 and 1 (instead of the usual 1 and 2). If $X_{ij} = r$ and $X_{ji} = s$, we put 1 in the (r, s)-cell of $Y_{(i,j)}$ and 0s in the other three cells. Clearly, $Y_{(j,i)}$ is the transpose of $Y_{(i,j)}$. The matrices $Y_{(i,j)}$ corresponding to the four possibilities for the pair (i, j) are shown below.

$$X_{ij} = 0, X_{ji} = 0: \qquad Y_{(i,j)} = \begin{bmatrix} 1 & 0 \\ 0 & 0 \end{bmatrix}$$

$$X_{ij} = 0, X_{ji} = 1: \qquad Y_{(i,j)} = \begin{bmatrix} 0 & 1 \\ 0 & 0 \end{bmatrix}$$

$$X_{ij} = 1, X_{ji} = 0: \qquad Y_{(i,j)} = \begin{bmatrix} 0 & 0 \\ 1 & 0 \end{bmatrix}$$

$$X_{ij} = 1, X_{ji} = 1: \qquad Y_{(i,j)} = \begin{bmatrix} 0 & 0 \\ 0 & 1 \end{bmatrix}$$

The contemplated model for the Y array dwells on specific expressions for the multinomial cell probabilities corresponding to the four cells designated by $(r, s), r = 0, 1; \ j = 0, 1$, for every pair of individuals (i, j). Let $P[(r, s); (i, j)]$ denote the probability that the cell (r, s) receives the value 1 in $Y_{(i,j)}$ (i.e., that $X_{ij} = r$ and $X_{ji} = s$). Then the model stipulates the following:

$$\log P[(0, 0); (i, j)] = \lambda_{ij},$$
$$\log P[(1, 0); (i, j)] = \lambda_{ij} + \theta + \alpha_i + \beta_j,$$
$$\log P[(0, 1); (i, j)] = \lambda_{ij} + \theta + \alpha_j + \beta_i, \tag{3.41}$$
$$\log P[(1, 1); (i, j)] = \lambda_{ij} + 2\theta + \alpha_i + \beta_j + \alpha_j + \beta_i + (\alpha\beta),$$

where the logarithm is the natural logarithm (w.r.t. the base e).

In the above, for every pair (i, j), λ_{ij} is a normalizing constant since the four probability expressions have to add up to unity. This yields

$$\lambda_{ij} = -\log\left(1 + e^{\theta + \alpha_i + \beta_j} + e^{\theta + \alpha_j + \beta_i} + e^{2\theta + (\alpha_i + \beta_j) + (\alpha_j + \beta_i) + (\alpha\beta)}\right). \tag{3.42}$$

The other parameters are interpreted as follows:

1. θ represents what may be termed the overall "choice" parameter (like the grand mean in analysis of variance [ANOVA]), and for each choice (by either i or j or by both), its presence in the model expression for probability is thus incorporated.

2. α represents the "expansiveness" or "out-degree" aspect and β the "popularity" or in-degree aspect of an individual, and these are individual specific in general terms.

3. $(\alpha\beta)$ represents the "reciprocity" aspect of the pair of individuals concerned, and it is regarded as a global phenomenon (so that its dependence on specific individuals' features is ruled out).

More general models are discussed in Wasserman and Faust (1999).

Note that while the in-degree and/or out-degree aspects are assumed to be individual specific, the reciprocity aspect is taken to be a "global" phenomenon and not pairwise individual specific. The same is true of θ as a parameter indicating the "global" aspect of choices of individuals in the network. It receives weight 2 for the last case when both the individuals choose each other. We must also note that there are altogether $n(n-1)$ ordered pairs of individuals indexed like (i, j) in terms of X data, but in terms of Y array, we have to consider only $n(n-1)/2$ *dyads*—that is, unordered pairs or, equivalently, ordered pairs (i, j) with $i < j$—since $Y_{(i,j)}$ determines $Y_{(j,i)}$. Furthermore, in the model described above, there are altogether $1 + n + n + 1 = 2(n+1)$ parameters. As a matter of convention, it is assumed that

$$\sum \alpha_i = \sum \beta_i = 0$$

so that, in effect, there are $2n$ parameters to be estimated. For a given pair of individuals, the likelihood function is readily expressible in terms of the multinomial (4-cell) probabilities, using the indicator functions. Hence, the joint log-likelihood function for all such *unordered pairs* of individuals can be written down in a routine manner. The main problem in finding maximum likelihood estimates of the parameters lies in the dependence of the λ_{ij}s on the others—namely, $\theta, \alpha_i, \alpha_j, \beta_i, \beta_j$, and $(\alpha\beta)$. Therefore, the likelihood equations are not analytically tractable, and one has to take recourse to statistical computing.

W **Array**

Having described a general model as above, we can now focus the discussion on some simplified models that are motivated by considerations of possible "grouping" among the individuals. In a sociological context, these groupings may be prompted by family size, occupation, caste, kinship, and the like. If we consider one such "external factor," then the individuals may be classified into several disjoint categories, and the category-specific out-degree and in-degree parameters may be more appropriate to use. That means we can dispense with individual-specific α_i and β_j parameters and replace them by those associated with their groups. Thus, for two groups or categories I and II (like small/large family size), we may use α_I and α_{II} along with the constraint $n_I\alpha_I + n_{II}\alpha_{II} = 0$, where n_I and n_{II} are the group sizes. The same is true of the βs, the in-degree parameters. Of course, m and $(\alpha\beta)$ remain unaltered. This leads to what has been referred to as a W array. It may be noted that under the W array, the number of parameters reduces to $1 + (C - 1) + (C - 1) + 1 = 2C$, where C is the number of categories induced by the external factor.

For the W array with two categories, the model description is given by

$$
\begin{aligned}
\log P[(0, 0); (i, j)] &= \lambda_{I,I}, \\
\log P[(1, 0); (i, j)] &= \lambda_{I,I} + \theta + \alpha_I + \beta_I, \\
\log P[(0, 1); (i, j)] &= \lambda_{I,I} + \theta + \alpha_I + \beta_I, \\
\log P[(1, 1); (i, j)] &= \lambda_{I,I} + 2\theta + 2\alpha_I + 2\beta_I + (\alpha\beta)
\end{aligned}
\tag{3.43}
$$

when the two individuals are *both* in Category I. Similar descriptions apply for the cases: Both are in Category II or one is in Category I, while the other is in Category II. For example, if i and j belong to different categories, we may assume without loss of generality that i belongs to Category I and j to Category II (since we have to consider only unordered pairs of individuals), and then

$$\log P[(0, 0); (i, j)] = \lambda_{I,II},$$
$$\log P[(1, 0); (i, j)] = \lambda_{I,II} + \theta + \alpha_I + \beta_{II},$$
$$\log P[(0, 1); (i, j)] = \lambda_{I,II} + \theta + \alpha_{II} + \beta_I,$$ (3.44)
$$\log P[(1, 1); (i, j)] = \lambda_{I,II} + 2\theta + \alpha_I + \beta_{II} + \alpha_{II} + \beta_I + (\alpha\beta).$$

Moreover, for this model involving two groups, there are altogether six parameters—namely, θ, α_I, α_{II}, β_I, β_{II}, and $(\alpha\beta)$.

V Array

There is yet another simplified version of the Y array. For example, in situations where individual αs and βs are insignificant or sufficiently small compared to the other parameters, we can ignore them in the model description. This is referred to as a V array, and the model with only two parameters reduces to

$$\log P[(0, 0); (i, j)] = \lambda,$$
$$\log P[(1, 0); (i, j)] = \lambda + \theta,$$
$$\log P[(0, 1); (i, j)] = \lambda + \theta,$$ (3.45)
$$\log P[(1, 1); (i, j)] = \lambda + 2\theta + (\alpha\beta).$$

Explicit expression for the maximum likelihood estimate of $(\alpha\beta)$ can be obtained under the present model (see Rao & Bandyopadhyay, 1987). Rao and Bandyopadhyay (1987) also discuss the special case of this model obtained by dropping the parameter θ and keeping only the parameter $(\alpha\beta)$.

Each of the parameters θ, α_is, β_is, and $(\alpha\beta)$ can be estimated, for example, by the method of maximum likelihood. However, there are no closed formulae for the estimates, and they have to be computed by iterative procedures (for details, see Wasserman & Faust, 1999). We will discuss some aspects of model fitting and model validation in Chapter 4, wherein the problem of estimating these parameters will also be briefly addressed. Illustrative examples will be discussed in Chapter 6 on case studies.

Model VII

Model VII, due to Holland and Leinhardt (1981), assumes that the probability of obtaining any particular network is

$$\text{const. exp} \left\{ \theta m + \sum_{i=1}^{n} \alpha_i d_i + \sum_{i=1}^{n} \beta_i e_i + \rho s \right\},$$

where θ, ρ, α_is, and β_is are real valued parameters such that $\sum \alpha_i = 0$ and $\sum \beta_i = 0$. Note that only n is fixed, and m, d_is, and e_is are variables.

Under the present model, the distributions of (X_{ij}, X_{ji}), and $(X_{k\ell}, X_{\ell k})$ are independent if i, j, k, and ℓ are distinct. Thus, it allows for correlation between X_{ij} and X_{ji}, but disjoint pairs are independent. Here, θ represents density (or overall choice), α_is represent the differential expansiveness of the vertices, β_is represent the differential popularity of the vertices, and ρ represents overall reciprocity. It can be verified that

$$\frac{P(X_{ji} = 1 | X_{ij} = 1)}{P(X_{ji} = 0 | X_{ij} = 1)} \bigg/ \frac{P(X_{ji} = 1 | X_{ij} = 0)}{P(X_{ji} = 0 | X_{ij} = 0)} = e^{\rho}$$

is independent of i and j. Thus, ρ is a log-odds ratio. One can get special cases of the present model corresponding to Models II.2 and III.2 as follows: For II.2, drop the terms containing d_is, e_is, and s. For III.2, drop the terms containing e_is and s. On the other hand, it turns out that the dyadic model (described in the preceding section and expanded by Wasserman & Faust, 1999) encompasses this model as the "joint likelihood of the parameters" based on the entire body of dyadic interaction data on all pairs of vertices with the identification of ρ as $\alpha\beta$.

As mentioned before, each of the parameters θ, ρ, α_is, and β_is can be estimated, for example, by the method of maximum likelihood. However, there are no closed formulae for the estimates, and they have to be computed by iterative procedures. For details, see Holland and Leinhardt (1981) and Wasserman and Faust (1999).

REFERENCES

Achuthan, N., Rao, S. B., & Rao, A. R. (1984). The number of symmetric edges in a digraph with prescribed out-degrees. In *Combinatorics and applications: Proceedings of the Seminar in Honour of Professor S. S. Shrikhande* (pp. 8–20). Calcutta: Indian Statistical Institute.

Berge, C. (1973). *Graphs and hypergraphs.* Amsterdam: North-Holland.

Em-ot, P., Tiensuwan, M., & Sinha, B. K. (2008). Some aspects of stochastic modeling of dyadic relations in social networks: Theory and applications. *Journal of Statistical Theory and Applications, 7,* 303–322.

Feller, W. (1968). *An Introduction to probability theory and its applications* (Vol. 1, 3rd ed.). New York: John Wiley.

Fulkerson, D. R. (1966). A network flow computation for project cot curves. *Management Science, 7,* 167–178.

Harary, F. (1988). *Graph theory*. New Delhi, India: Narosa.

Holland, P. W., & Leinhardt, S. (1981). An exponential family of probability distributions for directed graphs. *Journal of the American Statistical Association, 76,* 33–50.

Katz, L., & Powell, J. H. (1954). The number of locally restricted directed graphs. *Proceedings of the American Mathematics Society, 5,* 621–626.

Katz, L., & Powell, J. H. (1956). Measurement of tendency towards reciprocation of choice. In J. L. Moreno (Ed.), *Sociometry and the science of man* (pp. 403–409). Beacon, NY: Beacon House.

Katz, L., & Wilson, T. R. (1956). The variance of the number of mutual choices in sociometry. *Psychometrika, 21,* 299–304.

Pramanik, P. (1994, January). *Generating random (0, 1)-matrices with given marginals.* Paper presented at the Third International Conference on Lattice Path Combinatorics, New Delhi, India.

Rao, A. R. (1984). *Bounds for the number of symmetric edges in a digraph with specified out-degrees and in-degrees.* Unpublished manuscript, Indian Statistical Institute.

Rao, A. R. (2002, December). *The number of reachable pairs in a digraph.* Paper presented at the R. C. Bose Centenary Symposium on Discrete Mathematics and Applications, Indian Statistical Institute, Kolkata, India.

Rao, A. R., & Bandyopadhyay, S. (1987). Measures of reciprocity in a social network. *Sankhyā,* Series A, 49, 141–188.

Rao, A. R., Jana, R., & Bandyopadhyay, S. (1996). A Markov chain Monte Carlo method for generating random (0, 1)-matrices with given marginals. *Sankhyā, Series A, 58,* 225–242.

Ryser, H. J. (1963). *Combinatorial mathematics.* New York: John Wiley.

Snijders, T. A. B. (1991). Enumeration and simulation methods for 0–1 matrices with given marginals. *Psychometrika, 56,* 397–417.

Sukhatme, P. V. (1938). On bipartitional functions. *Philosophical Transactions of the Royal Society of London, 237,* 375–409.

Wasserman, S., & Faust, K. (1999). *Social network analysis: Methods and applications.* Cambridge, UK: Cambridge University Press.

⊰ FOUR ⊱

VALIDATION OF STATISTICAL MODELS

———•◦◆◦•———

4.1 INTRODUCTION

In this chapter, we discuss at length the methodological issues in model validation in the context of social networks. In Chapter 3, we introduced various deterministic (graph-theoretic) and probabilistic (statistical) models. As far as the deterministic models are concerned, the question of model validation cannot be answered based on a given network. One has to seek possible explanations from the contextual scenario. However, for probabilistic models, we will make an attempt to provide validation techniques. By model validation, we mean acceptance or rejection of a given model based on the given network, say G_0. In other words, we will examine whether the given network can be regarded as a possible realization of a random network underlying a given model. In the process, we will employ standard statistical techniques after carefully formulating the model validation problem as one of testing statistical hypotheses. In this context, we refer to Rao (1973) for the basic concepts.

We will discuss the models one by one, and wherever necessary, we will also project meaningful submodels in our endeavor toward model validation.

The general approach toward model validation is as follows: We look for a "statistic" (e.g., T) whose distribution is completely known whenever the assumed model is true. Next we compute the value T_0 of the statistic for the given network G_0. We also examine the nature of T for all conceivable random digraphs (i.e., random networks) under the stipulated model (or submodel). This is done by exploring "sampling distribution" of T. Next we argue that for the model to be valid, the observed value of T (i.e., T) should behave in a "normal fashion" with respect to the above-mentioned sampling distribution of T. Any extreme behavior of T_0 should indicate that the stipulated model is not likely to be tenable.

Hunter, Goodreau, and Handcock (2008) have explained that any attempt to validate a model for social networks mostly results in failure. When the distribution of a statistic T is either derived from analytical considerations or empirically determined based on a large number of simulated networks, these networks frequently bear little resemblance to the observed network, and as a result, the observed value T_0 seldom behaves in a normal fashion. Our attempt in this chapter, therefore, is to acquaint the reader with various methodologies that can be developed in this endeavor. As we will see, mostly we are not in a position to validate the models. As we proceed, we will provide necessary explanations for model failure.

4.2 MODEL VALIDATION

Model I.2

We start with Model I.2 of Section 3.2. This model stipulates that all the $2^{n(n-1)}$ possible digraphs are equally likely to be realized. For any moderate to large n, this seems to be an impossible proposition, and therefore, the model is not likely to be tenable. However, the methodologies are described below for general awareness.

We are given an observed network G_0 with n vertices, and we have to examine if G_0 can be regarded as a random realization among all networks arising out of the above model. We will propose a number of "statistics" for this purpose. Note that in Model I.2, we have already worked out the distributions (exact and simulated) of some of the statistics such as the number of arcs, the out-degrees and maximum out-degree, number of sources, number of isolates, diameter, radius, and so on.

(i) $T = m$, *the number of arcs or one-way ties.* It has been argued that m is distributed as a binomial variable with parameters $[n(n-1), 1/2]$ whenever the model is valid. Therefore, the observed value of m, such as m_0, should not show any sign of *extremeness* with reference to this binomial distribution. The procedure to test this feature is well known in the statistical literature. There are *exact* and *approximate* tests available. For large n, we may use an approximate test, which rests on computation of the Z score:

$$Z = \frac{m - n(n-1)/2}{\sqrt{n(n-1)/4}}. \tag{4.1}$$

Then we check if it is larger in absolute value than 1.96 at a 5% level of significance. We now discuss the following illustrative example.

Illustrative Example. Consider the network for the village Baghra (reference: block—Bengabad, dist.—Giridih, state—Jharkhand) constructed in 2002. In particular, we will restrict our attention to the Koiri community comprising 40 households. It turns out that these households include 7 "isolates." The entire village network is given at the end of the book in Diagram 7. (Four major networks are used for validation of Model VI.) So effectively, we will deal with $n = 33$ households. From the observed digraph, we count the value of m as 37. Then the Z score is computed as $Z = (37 - 33.32/2)/\sqrt{33.32/4} = -30.22$, which is very large in absolute value. Therefore, we conclude that the hypothesis is not tenable at all, or in other words, we do not have any justification to accept the model as a true model.

Remark 1. It has been stated and proved earlier (Model I.2) that the model description in terms of a random digraph is equivalent to the one in terms of the random variables X_{ij}s having independent and identically distributed (*iid*) Bernoulli distribution with success probability $1/2$. This suggests a

Submodel: All X_{ij}s are *iid* with success probability p, (4.2)

and we may assume that this submodel is a priori *true*. In that case, validation of the original model means examining the validity of $p = 0.5$ from the given digraph. It turns out that for the assumed submodel, m carries *all* information about p, and hence once a test for $p = 0.5$ is constructed as above using m, there is no need to carry out any further tests. If we do *not* assume the submodel described above or assume different submodels, we can focus on the use of other statistics as well. Keeping this in mind, we now describe the use of other statistics.

(ii) *What if we want to use the out-degree values?* A little reflection shows that in case the maximum out-degree is too high or the minimum out-degree is too low, we will have reason to suspect the validity of the model. Therefore, a reasonable approach would be to compute d_{max} and d_{min} from the given graph G_0 and examine these values in terms of their extremeness. Now we can follow a standard approach in testing statistical hypotheses. It uses two-sided *cutoff* points, one for d_{max} and the other for d_{min}, each one with a 2.5% cutoff so that on the whole, it is a test with a 5% level of significance. We call these points critical values and denote them by d_0 and d_{00}, respectively. Once these are determined, we accept the model whenever d_{min} is above d_{00} and d_{max} is below d_0.

We now describe the procedure by using the above illustrative example once more.

Illustrative Example (continued). From the observed digraph, we find $d_{max} = 2$ and $d_{min} = 0$. Now we compute d_0 and d_{00} using normal approximation to binomial distribution of d with parameters $n = 33$ and $p = 0.5$. These are standard computations, and we obtain $d_0 = 24$ and $d_{00} = 8$. Thus, for $8 < d_{min} < d_{max} < 24$, we accept the model; otherwise, we reject the model. Since in this example, $d_{min} = 0$, we reject the model. In other words, the model is not tenable, given the observed digraph.

Here we used normal approximation to the binomial for large n. For moderate or small values of n (i.e., for small-sized digraphs), we can use exact binomial probabilities to compute the critical values.

Remark 2. To validate the model above, we could also compare the in-degree values with the out-degree values. We simply indicate the details of the calculations below. Based on the given digraph with effectively $n = 33$ vertices, we have $e_{max} = 6$ and $e_{min} = 0$. The cutoff points are the same as those in the case of using the out-degrees. Hence, based on a study of the in-degrees as well, we reject the model.

Remark 3. The use of both sets of out-degree and in-degree values is another possibility. However, because of dependence of the pairs of random variables of the type d_i and e_j on $X_{i,j}$, joint probability distribution of the $2n$ out-degree and in-degree variables is quite complicated. Therefore, simultaneous use of them is a nontrivial exercise. We do not pursue this here. Use of the Bonferroni inequality provides a workable solution.

(iii) *Uses of source and sink data.* Once more, it is not difficult to argue that whenever the hypothesis involving the parameter p of the submodel breaks down, the number of sources (or sinks) will be too high or too low. Thus, extreme values of these statistics will lead to the model being questionable. We can now count the actual values of these statistics from the given digraph G_0 and examine if these are extreme values. Here again, we can use the 2.5% cutoff value on each side—high and low. Thus, use of either source count or sink count is quite straightforward. Of course, one should take care of both scenarios: small and large values of n. Again, what if we want to use both counts? It is possible to develop a working formula to take care of both (using the Bonferroni inequality). The main point of concern is that these two counts (source and sink) are *not* statistically independent, so an exact test is difficult to formulate.

(iv) Conceptually, *use of the number of symmetric pairs* is quite straightforward since whenever model violation occurs, this number tends to be too high or too low. Also, the exact distribution of this statistic under the stipulated model is binomial. Therefore, use of exact and approximate (Z score) tests is fairly routine. In the above data set, we have $s_0 = 5$. On the other hand, under the assumed model, $E(s_0) = n(n-1)/8 = 132$ and $\text{Var}(s_0) = 3n(n-1)/32 = 99$. Hence, the z statistic $= (5 - 132)/\sqrt{99} = -12.76$, which is very large in absolute value. Therefore, the model is rejected outright.

Remark 4. What about using the count of isolates in the observed graph? It will also lead to the same conclusion since under the assumed model and for $n = 40$, the distribution is supposed to be degenerate at 0, which means we should not expect any isolate at all. However, we have as many as 7 isolates in the graph. Hence, the model is not tenable.

Remark 5. Diameter, radius, number of strong and weak components, and clique number can also be used to check the validity of the models.

Model I.3

We now examine the validity of Model I.3 (Section 3.2) based on the realization G_0. Note that the model does *not* specify the value of the parameter p. Therefore, large or small values such as the statistics mentioned above are *not* indicators of the possible violation of the model (since p value itself could be large or small to justify the extreme nature, if any, of the values assumed by various statistics). On the other hand, it seems justified to use $m/n(n-1)$ as an estimate of p, although its value computed from the given digraph cannot be *tested* against a standard stipulated or expected from the model, assuming that the model is true. In such situations, we use what is known as *conditional* argument. We condition on m and examine the performance of other statistics under the hypothesis that the assumed model is true. In other words, we work with the conditional distributions of various statistics, given m, and try to develop techniques for examining the validity of the original model. It is interesting to note that such conditional distributions are the same as those arising out of Model II.2 described in Section 3.2. We will study Model II.2 and discuss tests for model validation later. Below we will describe several submodels and develop techniques for the validity of the original model based on the submodels.

Use of Submodels. Consider the following submodels:

$$\text{For each } i, \ P[X_{ij}=1]=p_i. \tag{4.3}$$

In the above submodel, p_i depends only on i and is independent of all js different from i, and all random variables are independent.

Assuming that this class of submodels is true, we can test for the validity of the original model by testing if the p_is are all equal. Note that under these submodels, all the ds are independently distributed and that there is *no* restriction on them. To test for equality of the p_is, we now apply a standard test, known as the contingency chi-square test. We form a $2 \times n$ table with the first row having the numbers d_is and the second row having the numbers $n-1-d_i$s in the corresponding positions. This forms what is known as a $2 \times n$ contingency table. Now we apply the standard formula for contingency chi-square and compute its value. For small n, we compare this value with a "tabulated" value from the chi-square distribution with $(n-1)$ degrees of freedom (df), and if it exceeds the tabulated value, we reject the validity of the original model. Otherwise, we transform the observed chi-square value into the corresponding Z score as

$$Z = \frac{\chi^2 - (n-1)}{\sqrt{2(n-1)}} \tag{4.4}$$

and, as before, compare it (in absolute value) with 1.96 at the 5% level and decide accordingly.

One can show that the formula for the above chi-square is given by

$$\chi^2 = \sum (d_i - \bar{d})^2 / \bar{d}, \tag{4.5}$$

where $\bar{d} = m/n$. It is known that chi-square simplifies to $\chi^2 = (\sum d_i^2)/\bar{d} - n\bar{d}$.

Illustrative Example (continued). The d values give rise to the following frequency distribution: $[(0 - 5); (1 - 19); (2 - 9)]$. Routine calculations yield the value of chi-square as 12.054, which is less than $n - 1 = 32$. Therefore, the hypothesis of the validity of the submodels is accepted.

On the other hand, we may use the following submodels:

$$\text{For each } j, \ P[X_{ij} = 1] = q_j. \tag{4.6}$$

In the above submodel, q_j depends only on j and is independent of all is different from j, and all random variables are independent. Then we will use the in-degree values e_is instead of the out-degree values in the above formulae.

Illustrative Example (continued). In-degree values give rise to the following frequency distribution: $[(0 - 10); (1 - 14); (2 - 7); (3 - 1); (6 - 1)]$; $\bar{e} = 37/33 = 11{,}212$. Next we compute chi-square $= \sum e^2/\bar{e} - n\bar{e} = 40.595$, whence the Z score $= (40.595 - 32)/\sqrt{64} = 1.0744$, which also indicates a good fit. Therefore, we may conclude that the submodels indicating the in-degree-based networks are also homogeneous (i.e., they do not differ significantly among the households).

Remark 6. In the above example, it is interesting to note that all the out-degree and in-degree values are remarkably small, given the value of n. That explains why the submodels (governed by the respective p_i or q_j values) do not differ significantly among themselves. Note also that we have assumed the submodels to be true and examined whether the submodels are identical in nature.

At this stage, we may also be interested in using a model for which $P[X_{ij} = 1]$ depends on *both* i and j. Below we will present one such model:

$$P[X_{ij} = 1] = \frac{e^{\alpha + \beta c_i + \gamma d_j}}{[1 + e^{\alpha + \beta c_i + \gamma d_j}]}, \tag{4.7}$$

where c and d are meaningful "covariates" (i.e., auxiliary quantitative factors) that possibly govern the choices of individuals i and j for such a tie to emerge.

If we assume the validity of such a model for all pairs (i, j) with $i < j$, then the original model will be valid whenever $\beta = 0$ and also $\gamma = 0$. Thus, we will have to develop testing procedures for these two parameters in the submodels.

In the literature, such models are known as logistic regression models, and these have been studied extensively from various perspectives. We have already introduced a variation of this model in Section 3.6 in the spirit of "dyadic models" since in the context of a network, it seems natural to develop a model explaining the flow of out-degree for pairs of individuals. See more under Model VI below.

Model II.2

This model stipulates that the number of arcs (m) is given; otherwise, the digraph is random. It is also far from being a true scenario in reality. Not all arcs are generated purely on a random basis. However, as before, we can derive and use the conditional distributions of meaningful statistics, given m.

(i) *Use of* ds. It is well known that under the stipulated model, the joint distribution of ds, given m, is called the *multivariate hypergeometric distribution* with parameters $[n; n-1, n-1, ..., n-1; m]$. Also note that ds are subject to the following constraint: sum of ds is equal to m. In such a case, we say that ds form a singular distribution. To develop a test statistic based on the ds, we first compute the means, variances, and covariances of the ds. It follows that they possess the same mean, same variance, and same pairwise covariance. Writing $M = n(n-1)$, these are given by

$$\text{mean} = \frac{m}{n},$$

$$\text{variance} = \frac{m(n-1)(M-m)}{n^2(M-1)}, \tag{4.8}$$

$$\text{covariance} = -\frac{m(M-m)}{n^2(M-1)}.$$

Now we can use $(n-1)$ of the ds (leaving aside one of them, such as the last one) and form a test statistic based on the vector $\mathbf{d}$ of the selected d_is and the vector of their means, $E(\mathbf{d})$, and the associated variance-covariance matrix Σ. The test statistic is basically a chi-square statistic and is defined as

$$\chi^2 = (\mathbf{d} - E(\mathbf{d}))' \Sigma^{-1} (\mathbf{d} - E(\mathbf{d})), \tag{4.9}$$

which is approximately the chi-square with $(n - 1)$ *df*, and for reasonably large n, we may use the transformed Z score as in (4.4).

This Z score may be compared in absolute value against 1.96 to decide on the validity or otherwise of the hypothesis of validity of the model.

For small values of n, we can consult the chi-square table for the critical value and decide accordingly.

Remark 7. No matter how different the argument leading to the test construction above looks as compared with the test based on chi-square outlined in the previous subsection, it turns out that the two tests are the same. They simply have been framed using two different arguments.

Remark 8. Use of es instead of ds is analogous.

Remark 9. Use of both the ds and es is another possibility. However, as mentioned before, there is intrinsic interdependence between these two sets of variables. We will skip this procedure.

Remark 10. Use of maximum and minimum out-degree is another possibility.

(ii) *Use of the number of reciprocal pairs of vertices.* If the original model is true, then conditionally on m, the distribution of the number of symmetric pairs (s_0) has been derived earlier in Section 3.1 in Chapter 3. Also, the distribution of s_0 has been tabulated for some combinations of values of n and m. Now we argue that whenever the original model is *not* valid, s_0 will behave in abnormal fashion so that it will tend to assume significantly high or low values. Hence, a high or a low value of observed s_0 will cast doubt on the validity of the original model. To find "tabulated" values of s_0, we use a 2.5% cutoff at both ends.

(iii) *Use of other statistics.* In Section 3.3 in Chapter 3, we discussed and tabulated probability distributions (exact/simulated) of various other statistics. Thus, for example, we can use the number of "sources" as a test statistic. When the model is valid, its conditional distribution, given m, is known to be approximately binomial with parameters n and $p = \exp[-m(n - 1)/(M - 2n/3)]$. Therefore, based on this statistic, we can develop a routine test for validity of the model. Likewise, we can use "sinks" only or both sources and sinks, number of "isolates," and so on.

Model III.2

This time, d_is are given (to be those in the observed digraph); otherwise, it is stipulated that all underlying models with the stated values of the d_is are equally likely. This also mostly fails to depict a real situation. Given d_i, it is not at all likely that the ith household (HH) will make a random choice from among the remaining HHs, and this act of random choice will prevail among all HHs.

However, to validate the underlying model, we can use suitable statistics. Naturally, the idea of using the in-degrees (es) comes first. Note that under the model, the means and variances of the es already have been worked out. It can be shown that the pairwise covariances among the e_is are given by

$$\text{cov}(e_i, e_j) = -[(n-1)(S_1 - d_i - d_j) - (S_2 - d_i^2 - d_j^2)]/(n-1)^2. \quad (4.10)$$

Since the sum of the es is the same as the sum of the ds, which is fixed (since ds are given as in the observed digraph), es jointly define a singular distribution. Therefore, we will discard one of them and use the rest to form a chi-square as follows (recall similar use of the ds toward validation of Model II.2(i) above).

$$\chi^2 = [\mathbf{e} - E(\mathbf{e})]' \Sigma^{-1} [\mathbf{e} - E(\mathbf{e})]. \quad (4.11)$$

Next we can use the number of symmetric pairs and standardize it by using its mean and variance, which already have been calculated. Furthermore, its exact distribution is also available and has been described earlier (Model III.2). We can use both-sided cutoff values for this statistic to carry out a test of validity of the model.

Model III.3

Here again we can use (a) the in-degrees and also (b) the number of symmetric pairs to develop tests for validity of the model. In the case of in-degrees, we will base our test on chi-square, while for the other, we can use its mean and variance and carry out an approximate Z score test. For use of the in-degrees, we already have available their means and variances. We display below only the expression for pairwise covariance terms. Define $r_i = d_i/N_i$, where N_i is the size of the potential set P_i for unit i in the population. For details, we refer to Section 3.4 in Chapter 3.

$$\text{cov}(e_i, e_j) = \sum_{k \,:\, P_k \text{ contains } i \text{ and } j} \tau_k (1 - \tau_k)/(N_k - 1). \quad (4.12)$$

On the other hand, for use of the number of symmetric pairs (i.e., number of reciprocal pairs), we already have available expressions for its mean and variance under the present model. There we can use normal approximation and the z statistic to check for the validity of the model.

Model VI

This model already has been discussed in Section 3.6 in Chapter 3. For a reader with the necessary statistical background, we can provide further analytical results as follows. These are needed for the purpose of estimating the model parameters. Normally, we use the maximum likelihood method of estimation of the parameters, and hence we need to explicitly write down the joint likelihood function under different models. In this context, it is important to know how the likelihood depends on the data or, rather, which *summary statistics* are involved in the likelihood function. These summary statistics are referred to as *sufficient statistics*. For the Y array, the summary statistics are the individual out-degrees and in-degrees (i.e., d_i, e_i values apart from s, the total number of reciprocal pairs). The likelihood involves $\sum d_i$ as well, which is the same as $\sum e_i$. For the W array, the sufficient statistics are $\sum_I d_i, \sum_{II} d_i, \sum_I e_i, \sum_{II} e_i$, and s. Finally, for the V array, we only need $\sum d_i$ (which is the same as $\sum e_i$) and s.

We will now elaborate on the nature of the solutions under the V and W arrays. These are relatively much easier to determine, unlike the Y array, which is computation intensive.

For the V array, the log-likelihood is given by

$$\log L = \lambda \binom{n}{2} + \theta \left(\sum d_i\right) + (\alpha\beta)s, \qquad (4.13)$$

where λ is given by

$$\lambda = -\log[1 + 2e^\theta + e^{2\theta + (\alpha\beta)}]. \qquad (4.14)$$

First note that

$$\frac{d\lambda}{d\theta} = -2e^\theta \frac{1 + e^{\theta + (\alpha\beta)}}{1 + 2e^\theta + e^{2\theta + (\alpha\beta)}} \qquad (4.15)$$

and that

$$\frac{d\lambda}{d(\alpha\beta)} = -\frac{e^{2\theta + (\alpha\beta)}}{1 + 2e^\theta + e^{2\theta + (\alpha\beta)}}. \qquad (4.16)$$

Next note that

$$\frac{d\log L}{d\theta} = \binom{n}{2}\frac{d\lambda}{d\theta} + D; \quad \frac{d\log L}{d(\alpha\beta)} = \binom{n}{2}\frac{d\lambda}{d(\alpha\beta)} + s. \qquad (4.17)$$

Here, $D = \sum d_i$. From the above, we can easily write down the two equations. Set $D^* = [\frac{D}{2s} - 1]^{-1}$. It follows that

$$e^{\theta + (\alpha\beta)} = D^*. \qquad (4.18)$$

We now use this defining relation involving m and $\alpha\beta$ in the first equation and derive, upon simplification,

$$\frac{D}{2} = e^{\theta}\left(\binom{n}{2}(1 + D^*) - \frac{D}{2}(1 + D^*) - \frac{D}{2}\right), \qquad (4.19)$$

whence we can solve for $\hat{m}$. Subsequently, we solve for $(\alpha\beta)$ from the defining relation given above.

For the W array involving two categories I and II with sizes n_I and n_{II}, respectively, the dyadic model is given above when both individuals belong to the first category. Note that in this case, the $\lambda_{I,I}$ parameter is given by the relation

$$\lambda_{I,I} = -\log[1 + 2e^{\theta + \alpha_I + \beta_I} + e^{2\theta + 2(\alpha_I + \beta_I) + (\alpha\beta)}]. \qquad (4.20)$$

Similar expressions are available for $\lambda_{I,II}$ and $\lambda_{II,II}$. To write down the log-likelihood for the W array, let us use the following notations:

$$D_I = \sum_I d_i, \quad D_{II} = \sum_{II} d_i, \quad E_I = \sum_I e_i \text{ and } E_{II} = \sum_{II} e_i.$$

Then we can write

$$\begin{aligned}
\log L = {} & \lambda_{I,I}n_I(n_I - 1)/2 + n_I n_{II}\lambda_{I,II} + \lambda_{II,II}n_{II}(n_{II} - 1)/2 \\
& + \theta[(b + 2c) + (e + f + 2g) + (q + 2r)] \\
& + \alpha[(b + 2c + f + g) - n_I/n_{II}(e + g + q + 2r)], \\
& + \beta[(b + 2c + e + g) - n_I/n_{II}(f + g + q + 2r)] \\
& + (\alpha\beta)[c + g + r]
\end{aligned} \qquad (4.21)$$

where we have used the symbols $a, b, c; d, e, f, g$; and p, q, r to denote the frequencies corresponding to the cells:

$$[(0, 0), (0, 1), (1, 1); (0, 0), (0, 1), (1, 0), (1, 1); (0, 0), (0, 1), (1, 1)],$$

with the first set of three corresponding to Category I, the second set of four corresponding to the crossed Categories $I \times II$, and the last set of three corresponding to the Category II. Moreover, α denotes α_I, and β stands for β_I. We have naturally expressed α_{II} and β_{II} in terms of α and β, respectively. The following table shows the frequency counts in different cells.

Frequencies of the W Array

		G1		G2	
		0	1	0	1
G1	0	a	b	d	c
	1	b	c	f	g
G2	0	d	f	p	q
	1	e	g	q	r

Note that

$$(i) \quad a+b+c = \binom{N_I}{2},$$

$$(ii) \quad d+e+f+g = N_I N_{II}, \tag{4.22}$$

$$(iii) \quad p+q+r = \binom{N_{II}}{2}.$$

As we have mentioned before, the difficulty in obtaining explicit solutions to the likelihood equations lies in the complex nature of dependence of the λs on other parameters. These parameters have *exclusive* and *common* roles to play. Thus, for example, θ and $(\alpha\beta)$ are common, whereas the others are exclusive to the cross-categories. Fortunately, we have only four independent parameters to estimate from the data. However, the equations can be written down in a routine manner. It would help to "initiate" the solution by writing down some initial conditions.

We suggest the following:

$$\alpha^{(0)} = (b + f + c + g)/n_I(n-1),$$

$$\beta^{(0)} = (b + e + c + g)/n_I(n-1), \tag{4.23}$$

$$(\alpha\beta)^{(0)} = (c + g + r)/\binom{n}{2},$$

and then we start solving for $\theta^{(1)}$. The cycle goes as follows: θ, $(\alpha\beta)$, α, β.

Remark 11. Computational aspects of various dyadic model-fitting procedures will be discussed in Chapter 6, wherein we will deal with data sets of the

Baghra village, in particular. The network of the entire the Baghra village is given at the end of the book in Diagram 7. All of the important communities are also shown in the network. The theoretical results are discussed in Em-ot, Tiensuwan, and Sinha (2008).

Remark 12. We do not elaborate on validation/fitting of Model VII here. We refer to Holland and Leinhardt (1979) for necessary results.

REFERENCES

Em-ot, P., Tiensuwan, M., & Sinha, B. K. (2008). Some aspects of stochastic modeling of dyadic relations in social networks: Theory and applications. *Journal of Statistical Theory and Applications, 7,* 303–322.

Holland, P. W., & Leinhardt, S. (1979). *Perspectives on social network research.* New York: Academic Press.

Hunter, D., Goodreau, S., & Handcock, M. (2008). Goodness of fit of social network models. *Journal of the American Statistical Association, 103,* 248–258.

Rao, C. R. (1973). *Linear statistical inference and its applications.* New York: John Wiley.

FIVE

GRAPH-THEORETIC
AND STATISTICAL
MEASURES AND METHODS

————————◆◆◆————————

5.1 INTRODUCTION

I n this chapter, we consider a few features or characteristics of a social
network and explain how these features can be measured. The possibility
of using graph theory to derive sociological indices has already been argued in
the previous chapters.

Our main emphasis will be on the parameter or statistic X of the network,
which measures the given characteristic. The final measure is obtained by
standardizing X either by using a graphical (nonprobabilistic) model or a
probabilistic model, as explained in Chapter 3. We will concentrate more on
the first type of measure, which is easier to deal with and yet gives reasonably
good results in most cases. Different uses and statistical inference regarding
some of the measures will be discussed in the next chapter.

*Unless otherwise mentioned, the measures computed in examples will be
those obtained by using graphical models.*

For many of the characteristics, we will consider both global and local
measures. Often, the local measure for a vertex u is simply the global measure
for the network induced by the neighborhood of the vertex u (i.e., u together
with the set of all vertices v such that uv is an arc, vu is an arc, or both).

It is worth mentioning that a measure (global or even local) of a characteristic can also be applied to the subnetwork induced by any subset S of the set V of all vertices. This will definitely be meaningful when there is no arc between S and $V - S$ and possibly even when there are arcs between S and $V - S$.

5.2 THREE LOCAL MEASURES OF EGOCENTRIC CHARACTERISTICS

5.2.1 Expansiveness

The *expansiveness* of an individual refers to how well connected he or she is, how many others he or she goes to, and so on. If the network is of individual choice or preference, the expansiveness of the ith node indicates its capacity for sociability, the extent of its social congeniality, or the level of becoming integrated with others in the network.

Instead, suppose the network is based on going for assistance or help, whether financial, material, or physical, or for counseling and advice when it is urgently needed. Then the expansiveness of a node can be an indicator of buffer against vulnerability of the resource poor in the community. It can also reveal the extent of dependency. The exact interpretation to be given depends on an assessment of the ground situation based on contextual data.

Clearly, the expansiveness of the ith node is indicated by its out-degree d_i. The number of sinks (explained and introduced in Chapter 2) in a digraph indicates the number of vertices each of whose out-degree, is 0. One can standardize d_i using Model I.1 and get $d_i/(n-1)$ as the standardized measure of expansiveness of the ith vertex.

Under Model I.2, d_i has the distribution $B(n-1, 1/2)$. Using this, one can get a probabilistic version of the measure of expansiveness of the ith vertex.

The standardized measure of expansiveness is 0.75 for the top vertex in the first network of Figure 1.1 in Chapter 1 and 1.00 for each of the bottom vertices. It is 0.083 for the top two vertices as well as the bottom two vertices in the last network.

5.2.2 Power, Popularity, and Socioeconomic Status

The power, popularity, potential for leadership, or influence or socioeconomic status of an individual can be gauged by looking at his or her in-degree in the social network of preferences. If the network is based on financial help (i.e., if uv is an arc when u goes to v for financial help), the in-degree can also indicate resource potential. The number of sources (explained and introduced in Chapter 2) in a digraph indicates the number of vertices each without any in-degree (i.e., lacking power, influence, popularity, etc.).

The in-degree e_i of the ith vertex can be standardized using Model I.1 to get the standardized measure $e_i/(n-1)$. The probabilistic version can be obtained by using the fact that e_i has the distribution $B(n-1, 1/2)$ under Model I.2.

The individuals with a high in-degree have the potential for influencing others and will be the ideal persons to start the diffusion of an innovative idea or process (see Coleman, Katz, & Menzel, 1966). One can also think of various extensions of the in-degree that may be better measures of power. For example, we may look at the number of vertices that can reach the particular vertex in at most two or three steps instead of directly in one step. One may also give some weights depending on the number of intermediaries one has to go through and so forth. Some of these will be considered later.

The standardized measure of popularity is 1.00 for the top vertex in the first network of Figure 1.1 in Chapter 1 and 0.75 for each of the bottom vertices. It is 0.333 for the top two vertices and 0 for the bottom two vertices in the last network.

5.2.3. Structural Equivalence

We say that two vertices u and v are structurally equivalent if they play similar roles in the network w.r.t. all other nodes. There are two slightly different interpretations of this. The more stringent one requires that for any vertex $w \neq u$, v, (i) uw is an arc if and only if vw is an arc and (ii) wu is an arc if and only if wv is an arc. When these hold, u and v are substitutable for each other while keeping the other vertices fixed. The less stringent one requires that there is an automorphism of the network taking u to v. What this means is that there is a permutation f of the vertex set such that f preserves adjacency (i.e., for all vertices x and y, xy is an arc if and only if $f(x)f(y)$ is an arc) and $f(u) = v$. Under either of these definitions, if u and v are structurally equivalent, then clearly, they have the same out-degree and the same in-degree, and each of them is involved in the same number of reciprocal pairs. But the converse is not true. In the network of Figure 5.1, v_7 and v_8 are structurally equivalent under either definition. Under the stringent definition, no other pair of distinct vertices is structurally equivalent. Under the less-stringent definition, v_2 and v_5 (but not v_2 and v_6) are structurally equivalent.

Figure 5.1

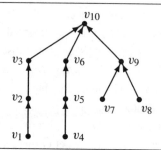

Subgroups of a social network can be identified using either the concept of a clique or the concept of a maximal set of structurally equivalent vertices. These can give entirely different sets of subgroups as one can easily see. Both the definitions, given above, of structural equivalence are too stringent (just like that of a clique) to identify subgroups in practice, so clustering techniques have to be used (Burt, 1978; Lorraine & White, 1971; Scott, 1991).

5.3 THREE LOCAL-CUM-GLOBAL MEASURES OF EGOCENTRIC AND GLOBAL CHARACTERISTICS

5.3.1 Cohesion

The first characteristic of a social network that we are likely to consider is the cohesiveness of the network or how well the nodes are tied up. As noted in Chapter 1, *cohesion* can be measured by the *density of ties D*, defined as $m/n(n-1)$. Clearly, D is obtained by standardizing m using the graphical Model I.1. Note that D is a global measure in the sense that it is for the network as a whole.

By standardizing m using Model I.2, we can get a probabilistic measure of cohesion. Note that m has the binomial distribution $B(n(n-1), 1/2)$ under this model.

One can easily give a local measure of cohesion for a node. Let d_i be the number of arcs leaving the ith node and e_i the number of arcs entering it. Then one can use d_i, e_i, or, better, $d_i + e_i$ to get the measure. The measures based on

d_i and e_i are $d_i/(n-1)$ and $e_i/(n-1)$. The measure based on $D_i := d_i + e_i$ is $(d_i + e_i)/(2n-2)$ since the ith node is involved in $d_i + e_i$ ties out of a maximum possible $2n-2$. Note that since m equals the sum of all d_is as well as the sum of all e_is, the global density D is the average of the local densities $D_1, D_2, \ldots, D_n$.

Under the Model I.2, the distribution of $d_i + e_i$ is $B(2n-2, 1/2)$ since d_i and e_i are independent and have the common distribution $B(n-1, 1/2)$. Using this, one can get a probabilistic version of local density.

The densities of the five networks in Figure 1.1 in Chapter 1 are 0.90, 0.133, 0.40, 0.20, and 0.102, respectively. Under Model I.2, the standardized values of m (i.e., $(m - E(m))/\sigma(m)$) are 3.58, -6.96, -0.89, -3.29, and -9.93, respectively. The corresponding probabilistic measures (i.e., $P(m \leq$ the observed value)) are 1.000, 0.000, 0.252, 0.001, and 0.000, respectively. The local density (using D_i) is 0.208 for each of the top two vertices in the last network of the figure and 0.041 for each of the bottom two vertices. The corresponding probabilistic measures under Model I.2 are all 0.000. The local density (using d_i) is 0.083 for each of the top two and the bottom two vertices in this network. The corresponding probabilistic measures under Model I.2 are all 0.003.

5.3.2 Reciprocity

Reciprocity refers to the ties being reciprocated (i.e., vu being a tie when uv is a tie). It indicates some sort of balance or harmony that can nullify the negative effects of social stratification. Local reciprocity of a vertex in the network of a social choice relation is an indicator of its social congeniality or level of being integrated with others in the network.

Reciprocity can be measured by the number s of symmetric (or reciprocal) pairs. However, this needs to be standardized. One may standardize s under Model I.1 to get the measure of reciprocity $2s/n(n-1)$. However, this model assumes that everybody can really go to everybody else, which is unrealistic when n is even moderately large, say, 50 or more, in many types of social networks. Actually, $2s/n(n-1)$ is a combined measure of reciprocity and cohesion. Rather, one may want a measure of the extent to which the arcs present in the network (whether they are small or large in number) are reciprocated. Then one fixes both n and m and considers Model II.1. If $m \leq n(n-1)/2$, the minimum and maximum values of s are 0 and $\lfloor m/2 \rfloor$, and the standardized measure of reciprocity becomes $2s/(m - \epsilon)$, where ϵ is 0 or 1 according to whether m is even or odd. If $m > n(n - 1)/2$, the minimum value of s becomes $m - n(n - 1)/2$, and the measure of reciprocity becomes

$$\frac{2s - (2m - n(n - 1))}{n(n - 1) - m - \epsilon}.$$

One may go a step further and standardize s under Model III.1, which assumes the out-degrees of the vertices to be fixed. The minimum and maximum values of s under this model were given in Chapter 3. These are rather complicated in general. However, the minimum reduces to 0 if all d_is are less than $n/2$, and the maximum reduces to $(\sum d_i - \epsilon)/2$ when the d_is do not differ too much among themselves. Here ϵ is 0 or 1 according to whether $\sum d_i$ is even or odd. Thus, when d_is are small compared to n, the measure of reciprocity becomes $2s/(\sum d_i - \epsilon)$, which is the same as $2s/(m - \epsilon)$ obtained earlier.

One may go still one step further and standardize s under Model IV.1, which assumes both the out-degrees and the in-degrees of the vertices to be fixed. Now neither the minimum nor the maximum value of s is known. However, if $d_i + e_i \leq \sqrt{N}$ for all i, where N is the number of nonisolated vertices, then the minimum value of s is 0. The maximum value of s is at most $\lfloor \sum \min(d_i, e_i)/2 \rfloor$, and equality holds in many cases. Thus, the measure of reciprocity under Model IV.1 is either exactly or approximately $2s / \sum \min(d_i, e_i)$ in many cases.

One can also standardize s using any of the probabilistic Models I.2, II.2, III.2, and IV.2. Under Model I.2, s has the distribution $B(n(n - 1)/2, 1/4)$. Under Model II.2, the exact distribution of s is not known. But the distribution is unimodal. The mean and variance are given under Model II.2 in Chapter 3. If $m << n(n - 1)$, then $E(s) \sim m^2/2n^2$ and $V(s) \sim E(s)$, and the distribution can be approximated by a Poisson distribution. Under Model III.2, the mean and the variance are given in Chapter 3. If the d_is are small compared to n, $E(s) \sim \bar{d}^2/2$ and $V(s) \sim E(s)$, the same as those under Model II.2. We do not know anything about the mean and variance of s under Model IV.2.

The probabilistic Model III.3 assumes a potential set for each vertex from which the vertex makes its choices. The mean and variance of s under this model are given in Chapter 3. If "v_j is potential for v_i implies that v_i is potential for v_j," and if the potential set of the ith vertex has exactly d_i/ρ elements for each i, then the mean and variance reduce to $m\rho/2$ and $m\rho(1 - \rho)^2/2$, respectively. As already mentioned in Chapter 3, the main difficulty with this model is in determining the potential set for each vertex.

The probabilistic Model III.4 is an incomplete model. It assumes that there is a common coefficient of correlation τ between X_{ij} and X_{ji} for all i and j. This parameter τ may be thought of as a measure of reciprocity. Note that this may be positive or negative. A positive value of τ will be interpreted as indicating a tendency toward reciprocation and a negative value toward anti-reciprocation (j not going to i when i goes to j), while a value of 0 indicates neutrality in respect to reciprocation. With a slightly modified definition (which coincides with the earlier one when the d_is are all equal), τ is estimated by

$$\hat{\tau} = \frac{2(n-1)^2 s - S_1^2 + S_2}{(n-1)^2 S_1 - S_1^2 + S_2},$$

where $S_1 = \sum d_i$ and $S_2 = \sum d_i^2$. It may be noted that although $\hat{\tau}$ takes values in $[-1, 1]$, the values 1 and -1 may not always be attainable. τ is like an intraclass correlation coefficient. But since the model is incomplete, its significance cannot be tested.

The probabilistic Model V assumes an exponential-type probability distribution for the observed network. Here, the parameter r indicates reciprocity. It is a log-odds ratio. Its estimate can be used as a measure of reciprocity. There is no closed formula for the maximum likelihood estimate of r, but it can be computed using an iterative procedure.

We now turn to the local reciprocity of a node. This refers to how reciprocal the ties of that particular node are. Suppose first that only n is fixed. Then $s_i/(n-1)$ may be taken to be the measure of local reciprocity of the ith vertex, where s_i is the number of reciprocal pairs in the network containing the ith vertex. Since the sum of all s_is equals $2s$ (recall that the definition of s involves unordered pairs), the global measure $2s/n(n-1)$ is the average of the local measures for all the vertices. If d_i is fixed, the local measure may be taken to be s_i/d_i. Notice that now the global measure $2s/\sum d_i$ (which is valid under some assumptions on d_is) is a weighted average of the local measures with the weight of s_i/d_i being d_i. If both d_i and e_i are fixed, the local measure may be taken to be $s_i/(\min(d_i, e_i))$, and (under some assumptions) the global measure will be a weighted average of the local measures, with with the ith vertex getting weight $\min(d_i, e_i)$.

Note that while considering the measure s_i/d_i, we are fixing only the out-degree of v_i and not the out-degrees of all the vertices (in the latter case, it may not be possible for s_i to attain the values 0 and d_i). A similar clarification holds for the measure $s_i/(\min(d_i, e_i))$.

The measure $2s/n(n-1)$ of reciprocity (fixing only n) is $0.80, 0.133, 0.40$, 0, and 0.013 for the five networks of Figure 1.1 in Chapter 1. When both n and m are fixed, the measure of reciprocity is $0, 1, 1, 0$, and 0.125 for the five networks. (For the first network, the only possible values for s are 8 and 9; thus, there is very little variation possible, and one might say the measure is not quite applicable here.) Under Model II.1, the corresponding values of $(m - E(m))/\sigma(m)$ are $-0.23, 6.93, 3.26, -0.86$, and 0.28, respectively. The local measure of reciprocity $s_3/(n-1)$ of v_3 in the first network of the figure is 0.75 if n is fixed. The measure s_3/d_3 obtained by fixing d_3 alone is also 0.75, and the measure $s_3/(\min(d_3, e_3))$ obtained by fixing both d_3 and e_3 is 1.00 for the same vertex.

5.3.3 Indirect Reciprocity

Reciprocity refers to vu being an arc when uv is an arc. But even if vu is not an arc, the arc uv may be reciprocated indirectly (through others) in the sense that there may be a path from v to u. We will refer to this as *indirect* or *generalized* reciprocity compared with the usual notion of reciprocity, which may be treated as *direct* reciprocity.

Clearly, the number S of arcs uv such that u is reachable from v is a crude measure of indirect reciprocity. Note that S is the same as the number m_w of arcs within strong components. If n alone is fixed, the range of S is $\{0, 2, 3, \ldots, n(n-1)\}$. When both n and m are fixed, we do not know the range of S, but the minimum and maximum of S have been given under Model II.1 of Chapter 3. S can be standardized using these.

The above definition of indirect reciprocity may be considered too liberal by one who thinks that paths of large length are of no practical use. Suppose we allow only paths of length 1 and 2 to reciprocate an arc. Then we take the number c of arcs uv such that $d(v, u) \leq 2$ is the indicator of indirect reciprocity. When n alone is fixed, the range of c is again $\{0, 2, 3, \ldots, n(n-1)\}$, and c can be standardized using this. When n and m are fixed, the range of c is not known.

For the first network in Figure 1.1 of Chapter 1, fixing n, the range of c is $\{0, 2, 3, \ldots, 20\}$, and the observed value of c is 18, so the measure of indirect reciprocity is $17/19 = 0.894$ or $18/20 = 0.9$ accordingly as the range or only the maximum and minimum are taken into consideration. If m is also fixed, c has to be m, so the corresponding measure is not defined. For the third network, fixing n, the range of c is $\{0, 2, 3, \ldots, 20\}$, and the observed c is 8, so the measure is $8/20 = 0.4$.

5.4 SIX MEASURES OF GLOBAL CHARACTERISTICS

5.4.1 Connectedness and Fragmentation

We say that a social network is connected if everybody in it can reach everybody else either directly (in one step) or indirectly through one or more intermediaries (i.e., by a path of any length). If the network is not connected, it breaks up into several components. The idea of a network being connected is that it at least has the scope for becoming a *social group* in the same sense as we have described earlier the two terms (social network and social group) in Chapter 1. The definition of connectedness depends, of course, on the type of paths allowed. If we insist that the ties in the path all have to be directed forward, we consider strong connectedness. If we ignore directions (i.e., if we allow the ties to be used in both forward and reverse directions), we consider weak connectedness. Ignoring direction of a path between vertices u and v can be sociologically interpreted as if it does not matter whether u goes to v or vice versa. This may happen if u and v are placed in the same class or category. Note that the third network in Figure 1.1 in Chapter 1 is strongly (and so weakly) connected, while the last network is weakly but not strongly connected.

The opposite of connectedness is fragmentation. If the network is not even weakly connected, it breaks up into two or more networks with no tie between any two of these. The number of these (*weak*) *components* is a measure—in a negative sense—of weak connectedness. If the network is not strongly connected, it splits into two or more *strong components*, but now there can be arcs between two strong components, although they will all be in the same direction. The number p of strong components can be used to measure strong connectedness. Since p can take any value from 1 to n, $(n - p)/(n - 1)$ is a standardized measure of strong connectedness. Note that the measure is 0 if each vertex is a strong component by itself and 1 if all the vertices form a single strong component. Similarly, $(n - q)/(n - 1)$ is a standardized measure of weak connectedness, where q is the number of weak components.

Isolates (i.e., vertices with neither any out-degree nor any in-degree) are simply weak components consisting of a single vertex. This is a particularly important phenomenon worth studying (Laumann & Pappi, 1976; Wellman & Berkowitz, 1988). The occurrence of a large number of isolates may have important ramifications in the social context as discussed earlier in Chapter 1. Usually, it is considered as an indicator of a lack of integration or atomization within a community for whatever the reason may be. However, it may also indicate resourcefulness of individuals. The appropriateness of the interpretation will depend on ground data.

It may be noted that each of the first, third, and fourth networks of Figure 1.1 in Chapter 1 has only 1 strong and only 1 weak component. The second network of the figure has 5 strong and 5 weak components. The last network of the figure has 12 strong components and 1 weak component (note that vertices 1 and 2 form 1 strong component). Thus, the measure of strong connectedness is 1 for the first, third, and fourth networks; 0.556 for the second network; and 0.083 for the last network. The measure of weak connectedness is 0.556 for the second network and 1 for the other four networks.

5.4.2 Reachability

A concept closely related to connectedness is reachability. We say that node v is reachable from node u if u can go to v either directly or indirectly through one or more intermediaries (i.e., if there is a directed path from u to v). One can consider the number R of pairs of distinct nodes (u, v) such that v is reachable from u, as an indicator of the extent of reachability in the network as a whole. Since the maximum possible number of reachable pairs is $n(n-1)$, $R/n(n-1)$ may be taken to be a standardized *reachability index* for the network as a whole. The number of vertices reachable from the ith vertex (excluding itself), divided by $n-1$, gives a local measure of its reachability.

One may take the view that the existence of a path from u to v with a large length may not serve any purpose since, to reach v, u has to go through many intermediaries, which may be practically impossible. Thus, we may consider reachability in k or fewer steps for any fixed k. If $R^{(k)}$ is the number of pairs of distinct vertices (u, v) such that $d(u, v) \leq k$, then the range of $R^{(2)}$ is $\{0, 1, \ldots, n(n-1)\}$, so $R^{(2)}/n(n-1)$ may be taken to be a measure of reachability in two steps. One can similarly consider a measure of reachability in k steps. Since the number of vertices reachable from v_i in k steps can vary from 0 to $n-1$, this number divided by $n-1$ gives a local measure of reachability in k steps for the ith vertex.

The measure of reachability is 1.00 for the first, third, and fourth networks in Figure 1.1 in Chapter 1. It is 0.156 for the second network and 0.237 for the last network. The local measure of reachability is 0.083 for v_1, 0.167 for v_3, 0.333 for v_8, and v_{12} and 0.25 for v_{11} in the last network of the figure. The measure of reachability in two steps is 1.00 for the first and third networks, 0.156 for the second network, 0.40 for the fourth network, and 0.205 for the last network. The local measure of reachability in two steps is 0.083 for v_1, 0.167 for v_3, and 0.25 for v_8, v_{11}, and v_{12}.

5.4.3 Connectivity

Our discussion on connectivity will not include directions; therefore, connectedness refers to weak connectedness, paths mean semi-paths, and so on. Even when a network is connected, there can be a vertex u such that when u is removed from the network, the remaining vertices get disconnected. A vertex u with this property is usually called a *cut vertex*. It can be shown that if u is a cut vertex, then there exist at least two vertices v and w such that every path between them passes through u. Thus, u plays a critical role in keeping the network connected. If there is no cut vertex, the connectedness of the network is ensured when any one node leaves the network and the network is robust in a sense. The *connectivity* of a network is the smallest number of vertices to be removed to make it disconnected. This is a measure of the robustness of the network w.r.t. connectedness. It can be shown that if the connectivity is k, then between any two vertices, there will be k disjoint paths. Usually the connectivity of the network is of interest, and there is no need to standardize it.

The connectivity of the networks in Figure 1.1 in Chapter 1 are 4, 0, 1, 2, and 1, respectively. Vertex v_1 is the only cut vertex in the third network, and the fourth network has no cut vertex. The vertices v_1, v_2, v_4, v_5, and v_7 are the cut vertices in the last network.

5.4.4 Cliques

In graph theory, taking a very stringent view, a *clique* is defined as a set of nodes such that (i) each of the nodes in the set is tied up both ways with each other in the set directly, and (ii) no other node can be included in the set without losing the property (i). Thus, a clique is a maximal subset of V that induces a complete symmetric digraph.

The term *clique* usually refers to an exclusive set of people with some common interests that they protect strongly. Although all the nuances of this cannot be captured in a social network, a clique can be conceptualized in a social network as a set of nodes with high interaction among themselves and with lower interaction with those who are not in the clique. What is considered as a high interaction is a matter of judgment.

One is usually interested in the *clique number* ω, defined as the maximum number of vertices in a clique. One may also be interested in the actual subsets that form cliques and the *partition number* θ, defined as the minimum number of cliques whose union contains all the vertices of the network.

The clique number of a digraph G is the same as that of the symmetrization of G obtained by including vu as an arc whenever uv is an arc and vu is not. Even after this, finding the value of ω for a general network is a difficult (what is known as an NP-*hard*) problem. For example, to show that the clique number is k, one has to find k vertices $v_1, v_2, \ldots, v_k$ such that $v_i v_j$ is an arc for all i and j with $i \neq j$ and also show that no set of $k + 1$ vertices has this property. The number of subsets with $k + 1$ vertices is $\binom{n}{k+1}$, which is astronomical even for moderate n and k like $n = 50$ and $k = 20$. However, here another graph-theoretic concept can help reduce the amount of checking. Suppose we have disjoint sets $V_1, V_2, \ldots, V_\ell$ such that their union is the set V of all vertices and the subdigraph induced by each V_i has no arc. (Incidentally, then, each V_i is known as an *independent set*, and the minimum ℓ for which such a partition of V exists is known as the *chromatic number* of the digraph.) Then it is easy to see that any clique can contain at most one vertex from each V_i (and $\omega \leq \ell$). Using this can reduce tremendously the number of subsets of size $k + 1$ to be checked. Finding the partition number is also a difficult (NP-hard) problem.

We note that two different cliques can have one or more vertices in common. Thus, unlike strong or weak components, cliques do not form a partition of the vertex set. One can think of some other parameters related to cliques such as the average size of a clique, but these are all difficult to determine for an arbitrary network.

The idea of components or cliques is that they are, in some sense, the (maximal) sets of vertices that have a potential to become social groups. The weak component is the weakest such concept. Next comes the strong component. The strongest such concept is that of a clique as defined above. Since the above definition of clique is very stringent, various relaxed versions have been considered in the literature (for undirected graphs)—namely, (a) the distances between the vertices in the clique being at most k, (b) the degrees in the network induced by the clique being at least k, or (c) the degrees in the network induced by the clique S being at least $|S| - k$. The corresponding modifications of a clique have been called *k-clique*, *k-core*, and *k-plex*, respectively (see Scott, 1991).

We think that it is better to identify a *near clique* as a maximal set S of vertices such that the subdigraph H induced by S has the following properties: (a) The density of H is at least 0.9, and (b) $d_i \geq 0.75(|S| - 1)$ and $e_i \geq 0.75(|S| - 1)$ in H if $|S| \geq 5$. Note that (a) is equivalent to the average out-degree (which equals the average in-degree) within H, which is at least $0.9(|S| - 1)$. The idea of the definition is that the local density of each vertex, as well as the global density, is high in H. It is easy to see that if S is a near clique, the diameter of H is at most 2 (for any two vertices u and v, the sets $\{w : uw \text{ is an arc}\}$ and $\{x : xv \text{ is an arc}\}$ cannot be disjoint). Note that with the above definition, a near clique on three vertices is completely symmetric, a near clique on four vertices may have one arc missing, and a near clique on five vertices may have two arcs missing, but these two cannot have the same initial vertex or the same terminal vertex. The cutoff values 0.9 and 0.75 are somewhat arbitrary and may be changed if needed. The determination of the maximum number of vertices that form a near clique, not to speak of determining all the near cliques, is a difficult problem for a general network.

The clique number is 3, 3, 2, 1, and 2, respectively, for the five networks in Figure 1.1 in Chapter 1. Incidentally, the chromatic numbers of these networks are 5, 3, 2, 2, and 3, respectively. The first network is a near clique as defined above.

5.4.5 Centrality

Centrality is a multifaceted concept (Bavelas, 1950; Freeman, 1979). It has been discussed by various researchers from various theoretical considerations. We, however, consider it only minimally as is required for our purpose.

We assume that the digraph is strongly connected. We start the study with local centrality rather than with the global centrality. The idea of a vertex being central is that it is highly connected with others and is *at the center of things*. Thus, the *local centrality* of a vertex is measured by its out-degree d_i. A standardized measure of local centrality, which can be used to compare two vertices in possibly different networks, is $d_i/(n-1)$, which happens to be the same as the standardized measure of expansiveness of the ith vertex. Note that even though we assumed that the network is strongly connected, and so the minimum possible value of d_i is 1 and not 0, we are ignoring this fact while standardizing d_i.

There is another centrality of a vertex—namely, its in-degree. Although sometimes this latter type may be more important, we will discuss mostly the former type. The latter type can be studied by applying the former type to the converse digraph (obtained by reversing the direction of each arc).

The centrality of the ith vertex defined as $d_i/(n-1)$ does not take into account the vertices that can be reached from i indirectly. But considering the number of vertices reachable from the ith vertex does not help since it is $n-1$ for every i. Let n_k be the number of vertices reachable from the ith vertex in k steps but not in $k-1$ steps (i.e., the number of vertices at distance k from i). Then we may take a weighted sum $\sum_{k=1}^{n-1} w_k n_k$ of the n_ks as an indicator of the centrality of i. Note that $d_i = n_1$ is obtained by taking w_k to be 1 or 0 according as $k=1$ or $k \geq 2$. Since the effect of the ith vertex on a vertex reachable in k steps decreases with increasing k, w_k should also decrease with increasing k. The choice of the w_ks will be somewhat arbitrary, but perhaps $w_k = 1/k^2$ is a reasonable choice. Thus, the local centrality of the ith vertex may be taken to be $\sum_{k=1}^{n-1} n_k/k^2$. Clearly, the maximum possible value of this is again $n-1$ attained when $n_1 = n-1$, so we may take

$$\frac{1}{n-1} \sum_{k=1}^{n-1} \frac{n_k}{k^2}$$

as a standardized measure of centrality of the ith vertex. We are again ignoring the minimum value under the assumption of strong connectedness, which is attained when $n_k = 1$ for $k = 1, 2, \ldots, n-1$.

In the above approach, we got an initial measure, which is positively related to the centrality of a vertex. Another approach uses an initial measure that is negatively related to the centrality of a vertex. This is the sum σ_i of the distances from the ith vertex to all other vertices. Note that $\sigma_i = \sum_{k=1}^{n-1} k n_k$. It is easy to see that the minimum possible value for σ_i is $n-1$, and the maximum possible value for σ_i is $1 + 2 + \cdots + (n - 1) = \binom{n}{2}$, so a measure of centrality of the ith vertex is

$$\frac{\binom{n}{2} - \sigma_i}{\binom{n}{2} - (n - 1)} \quad \text{or} \quad 1 - \frac{\sigma_i}{\binom{n}{2}},$$

the latter obtained by ignoring the minimum value of σ_i.

In the preceding paragraph, we took the sum of the distances to all the other vertices as an initial measure (in a negative sense). Clearly, taking the average instead of the sum does not alter the final measure of centrality. Thus, the final measure of centrality of the ith vertex is based on the average distance of a vertex from it. There is another possibility: instead of taking the average, taking the maximum and thus guarding against the worst possibility. To do this, we consider the *eccentricity* E_i of the ith vertex, defined as the maximum distance of any vertex from it. $1 - E_i/(n - 1)$ is the corresponding standardized measure of centrality. Sometimes, one may be interested in the value of E_i itself rather than in the standardized measure.

A vertex with the maximum centrality is called a *central vertex*. If we take $1 - E_i/(n - 1)$ as the centrality of v_i, this definition coincides with the usual definition of a central vertex as one at which $\min_i E_i$ is attained. The set of all central vertices is called the *center*. It is worth pointing out that the vertices in the center of a network need not be closely tied up among themselves; in fact, they may even form an independent set. Vertices with the smallest centrality are called *peripheral vertices*.

We now turn to global centrality, which may also be called centralization (like concentration). This refers to the central vertex having very high local centrality and all others having much lower local centrality. This is measured (in a negative sense) by the sum of the differences between the centralities of the center and the other vertices. This sum is then standardized with respect to its range (see Scott, 1991).

For the vertex v_1 in the first network in Figure 1.1 in Chapter 1, $n_1 = 3$ and $n_2 = 1$, so the measure $\frac{1}{n-1} \sum_{k=1}^{n-1} \frac{n_k}{k^2}$ is $13/16 = 0.812$. The eccentricity E_1 of the vertex is 2, so the measure $1 - E_1/(n - 1)$ is 0.5. For the vertex v_3, these two measures are 1 and 0.75. Next consider the *converse H* of the last network in Figure 1.1 in Chapter 1. The n_is for v_1 in H are $n_1 = 4$, $n_2 = 6$, and $n_3 = 2$, so the measure $\frac{1}{n-1} \sum_{k=1}^{n-1} \frac{n_k}{k^2}$ for v_1 is 0.477, and the measure $1 - E_i/(n - 1)$ for v_1 is 0.75. The two measures for v_2 in H are 0.465 and 0.75. For v_5, $n_1 = 2$,

$n_2 = 3$, and $n_\infty = 7$, so the first measure is 0.228, and the second measure is not defined.

5.4.6 Hierarchy

We first discuss the concept of hierarchy and then discuss the measures. Hierarchy generally refers to stratification into levels. In the context of social networks, we will take levels to be the integers $1, 2, \ldots, k$ (for some k) assigned to the vertices in such a way that arcs can go only from one level to a strictly higher level. If such an assignment of levels can be made, clearly the network is acyclic (i.e., it has no circuits). Conversely, suppose the network is acyclic. Then there exists a source u. Assign Level 1 to u. The network obtained by dropping u is also acyclic and so has a source v. Assign Level 2 to v. Proceeding like this, we can assign the Levels $1, 2, \ldots, n$ to the vertices as required.

The above definition of hierarchy seems to work well for the network of an organization where the vertices are the employees and the existence of an arc uv means that u reports to v. But notice that it misses something since we would not like to say that a network without any arc is hierarchical. So we insist that the network is also weakly connected (note that this condition would be satisfied by the network of an organization). Thus, we say that a network is hierarchical if it is weakly connected and there is an assignment of levels as above (i.e., the network is weakly connected and acyclic).

Note that in the above definition of hierarchy, which we shall call *weak hierarchy*, it is possible that two vertices u and v may not be comparable in the sense that there is no path from u to v and there is no path from v to u. (This can very well happen in the network of an organization.) However, sometimes we are interested in what we call *strict hierarchy* or *linear hierarchy*, where we insist that any two vertices are comparable. *We emphasize that we are not insisting that if* uv *and* vw *are arcs,* uw *is not an arc.* That is, we allow the hierarchy to be short-circuited, but arcs have to go upward. It is easy to see that a network is strictly hierarchical if and only if it has a path containing all the n vertices and is acyclic.

How do we find a measure of weak hierarchy of a network G? Let p and q denote the numbers of strong and weak components in G. Now, two vertices belong to a circuit if and only if they belong to the same strong component. Since there is no hierarchy between two vertices on a circuit, there is no hierarchy within a strong component. Thus, we may take that the hierarchy of G equals the hierarchy of the condensation H of G obtained by contracting each strong component of G to a vertex. H has p vertices and q weak components, with each weak component being an acyclic tree. Clearly, there is no hierarchy between different weak components, so the hierarchy is 0 if $q = p$ and increases as q decreases. Thus, we take $p - q$ as a measure of hierarchy of G. Since the minimum and maximum values of $p - q$ are 0 and $n - 1$ when n is fixed, we may take $(p - q)/(n - 1)$ as a standardized measure of weak hierarchy.

The measure of hierarchy obtained above has the same value for the two networks shown in Figure 5.2.

Figure 5.2

First network   Second network

However, one may feel that the second network is more hierarchical since there are arcs from both the vertices of Level 1 to the vertex at Level 2 in it. If we want to measure hierarchy taking this into account, we may consider the number m_b of hierarchical arcs (i.e., arcs between strong components). Since the minimum and maximum values that m_b can take are 0 and $n(n - 1)/2$, we may take $2m_b/n(n - 1)$ as a standardized measure of weak hierarchy. The values of this measure are 0.33 and 0.67 for the two networks in Figure 5.2.

We note that in both the measures, $(p - q)/(n - 1)$ and $2m_b/n(n - 1)$, we are fixing only n and *not* m. Suppose we want to fix n and m. Then the minimum and maximum values of $p - q$ and m_b are given under Model II.1 of Chapter 3. Using these, standardized measures of weak hierarchy can be obtained. We, however, mention that the range of m_b is not continuous.

We next consider the measurement of linear hierarchy. One can think of taking the minimum number of paths that together include all the vertices as a measure (in a negative sense) of linear hierarchy. However, using this criterion, a circuit will be perfectly linearly hierarchical, which is unrealistic. Therefore, we consider the minimum number P of paths in G, formed with arcs joining different strong components of G, which together include all the vertices of G. (We allow single-vertex paths that have length 0.) When n is fixed, the range of P is $\{1, 2, \ldots, n\}$, so $(n - P)/(n - 1)$ may be taken to be a standardized measure of linear hierarchy.

Perhaps one could also consider, instead of P, the minimum number Q of paths in G, formed with arcs joining different strong components of G, whose transitive closure includes all the arcs between strong components of G. We do not know of any nice procedures to find P and Q for a general network.

For all the networks in Figure 1.1 in Chapter 1 except the last, the measure of hierarchy is 0 since the strong and weak components coincide. The last network has 12 strong components and 1 weak component, so the measure of weak hierarchy based on $p - q$ for it is $11/12 = 0.917$. The measure $2m_b/n(n - 2)$ for it is $2 \times 14/(13 \times 12) = 0.179$. For this network, $P = 7$ (note that we have to use different paths for the vertices v_3, v_8, v_9, v_{10}, v_{11}, v_{12}, and v_{13}), so the measure $(n - P)/(n - 1)$ of linear hierarchy is 0.5.

Before we leave the topic of hierarchy, we make a few observations. Although hierarchical arcs are one-way (unreciprocated) ties, the converse is not necessarily true. A one-way arc uv is hierarchical provided there is no *path* from v to u (i.e., u can reach v directly, but v cannot reach u directly or even indirectly). This gives another way of looking at hierarchy. It is in a sense the opposite of what may be called *generalized* or *indirect reciprocity* where an arc uv may be reciprocated by a path of any length from v to u instead of an arc.

REFERENCES

Bavelas, A. (1950). Communication patterns in task oriented groups. *Journal of the Acoustical Society of America, 22,* 271–282.

Burt, R. S. (1978). Cohesion versus structural equivalence as a basis for network subgroups. *Sociological Methods & Research, 7,* 189–212.

Coleman, J. S., Katz, E., & Menzel, H. (1966). *Medical innovation: A diffusion study.* Indianapolis, IN: Bobbs-Merrill.

Freeman, L. C. (1979). Centrality in social networks: I. Conceptual clarification. *Social Networks, 1,* 215–239.

Laumann, E. O., & Pappi, F. U. (1976). *Networks of collective action: A perspective on community influence system.* New York: Academic Press.

Lorraine, F., & White, H. C. (1971). Structural equivalence of individuals in social networks. *Journal of Mathematical Sociology, 1,* 49–80.

Scott, J. (1991). *Social network analysis: A handbook.* Newbury Park, CA: Sage.

Wellman, B., & Berkowitz, S. D. (Eds.). (1988). *Social structures: A network approach* (pp. 19–61). Cambridge, UK: Cambridge University Press.

⊰ SIX ⊱

GRAPH-THEORETIC CASE STUDIES

——————◦●◦——————

6.1 INTRODUCTION

We know that various characteristics of social structure are not amenable to direct measurement due to a gap between the "measure" and the "reality" one intends to measure. "Cohesion" or "solidarity within a community, extent of "fragmentation," prevalence of "reciprocity," "hierarchy" (i.e., "hierarchical layering" of social ties within it), and so on are some such examples. The use of these concepts to describe a society is quite common, but these are used rather metaphorically without any quantitative measure (Adhikari, 1960). In Chapter 5, we discussed how one can derive measures to indicate such characteristics of social structure by social network analysis. In that chapter, we also gave some hypothetical examples for discussion.

In this chapter, we illustrate applications of graph-theoretic and statistical measures using social network data from "ordinary everyday social behavior" in real-life situations. Apparently, social behavior and interactions in everyday life, in their totality, may look chaotic. We endeavor to "reveal . . . some intellectual order" out of this "chaos" of everyday life by social network analysis (SNA; Homans, 1961). Regularity of empirical social behavior and interactions in day-to-day life establish social relationships among human beings, and its articulation among the "actors" produces hidden social networks, linking them. This chapter contains two case studies based on field investigation to explain our point of view.

In addition, there is a section on reciprocity with multiple arcs as an illustration of social network analysis of weighted digraphs. We will conclude this chapter with yet another section on statistical analysis of a specific and small social network data, illustrating the use of Model VI in Section 3.6 and also in Section 4.2.

However, with respect to the case studies, in addition to "observation, recording, and analysis" of social network data, which have been already discussed by Mitchell (1969), we need to resolve some of the other complexities kind that one faces at different stages of study.

Before we proceed further, let us first list the salient complexities. We list below the chain of stages with built-in complexities, as they arise.

1. Choice of social action and interaction in daily life for the study

2. Obtaining an appropriate social network from among one's multiple social networks, which emerge empirically in the course of the chores of social action and interaction in daily life

3. Whether to study one of the social networks—if so, which one or combination of them and, in that case, how do we combine the networks?

4. Compatibility in the meaning of the social action performed as imputed to it by an actor (ego) and the object (alter)

5. Reference time period

6. Actor's (ego's) selection of the object (alter) for social action: appropriateness of random selection model

7. Choice of appropriate methodology for statistical analyses

We shall now briefly discuss the above issues one by one for our case study.

    1. Often vulnerable situations crop up in a household (HH) as a matter of crisis or emergency that the HH cannot withstand by its own resources at hand—whether financial, material, physical, or otherwise (such as advice, consultation, expertise, etc.)—nor is there any institutional source that can provide the facilities for access to such resources on request. While facing these vulnerabilities, a household can survive only by mobilizing the available informal resources (i.e., social capital). We discussed in Chapter 1 that despite the implementation of various measures to promote economic development in rural areas, a household in a village still suffers from a lack of such resources

when it faces a crisis or emergency. As for a buffer, it has to marshal resources from different informal sources by dint of a tie such as being a neighbor, friend, employer, relative, local leader (*Matabbar*), and so on. But why does one person help another? Various sources of motivation to help and support flow along this tie. The motivation can broadly be commitment to traditional values or normative duties, nurturing of sentiments of personal obligation, a matter of social consideration, or a matter of rationale and an instrument of utilitarian strategy of assessing alternative payoffs in the future (unlike in the case of market transactions).

Hence, the present study of a household's buffer against vulnerability at the time of a crisis or emergency differs from a study of spontaneously organized self-help/mutual aid groups that form a category of "informal, voluntary associations" (Katz, 1981).

A household makes a request to another household for urgent help and support when a crisis or emergency suddenly impinges upon the former. The response of the latter provides the key to social action and interaction. Considering the critical importance of circulating informal help and support in maintaining survival in the life and living of the villagers, it has been chosen as the objective of the case study. The data obtained related to the above feature were put to SNA for an in-depth study of social structure by graph-theoretic and statistical measures.

2. Since there are multiple dimensions of social behavior and interaction, an actor can belong to multiple social networks, and the same set of actors can build a number of different social networks. Which one do we decide to work with? This is, no doubt, a matter to be decided according to the objective of the study.

3. The present case study is based on the aggregated flow of different types and purposes of requests for help and support as shown earlier in Chapter 1 (Tables 1.1 and 1.2)—that is, a social network obtained by a combination of the above items. A social network derived from a single component gives a precise but partial, narrowly bound view of the pattern of distribution of social relations. On the other hand, the network based on a combination of such related components will indicate a comprehensive perspective, giving a more relaxed view of social structure. The aggregated social network can be obtained in two ways. One is that multiple social networks of, say, K types, based on the same set of vertices (N) with different out-degree sequences ($d^\alpha, \alpha = 1, ..., K$), can be aggregated by combining K sets of out-degree

sequences (d) by the rule of union (inclusion-exclusion), for the vertices indexed as $i = 1, 2, \ldots \ldots, N$ (Jana, Bandyopadhyay, & Choudhuri, 2007). The other approach is to gather data for a social network from the field by using an integrated concept of help and support (i.e., a household requests another for help and support of any kind, whether financial, material, physical, or an other type). Such a request and the response to it provide ties of social relationship. This situation is depicted by the social network with a vertex denoting a household and a directed arc in it showing the direction of any request sent at all to anyone.

4. The social action and interaction under consideration should carry the same meaning to both the actor (ego) and the object (alter) to ensure standardization of data for the construction of a social network. Help and support seem to be quite unambiguous and apparently are very easily understood by the alter. But in reality, field enquiries expound different meanings imputed by different alters of the term *help*, denoting the same social action. A household may not have enough groceries sufficient to treat some guests who have suddenly come for a visit. The head of the household rushes to the local grocery shop, but he does not have enough money on hand to buy the foodstuffs. He faces an extremely embarrassing situation. However, based on his good acquaintance with the local grocery shop owner, he decides to rush to him to request the required foodstuffs. Of course he will pay later, whether at one time or in installments. But the shop owner may or may not comply with his request. He has to decide only on the basis of the strength of belief of the verbal assertions and the latter's goodwill. Enquiries were made in the villages in two different parts of the same region (in the villages where shop owners were found to have provided the foodstuffs under such circumstances). In one part of the region, the households that made the request considered it a matter of tremendous help by the shop owners, while in the other part of the region, it was not at all considered a matter of help. It was taken to be a matter of subtle investment to bargain in the future to demand for higher prices. Hence, the ties with shop owners should be excluded from the ties of help in an emergency in the latter part of the region but not in the former.

5. We note that a temporal (e.g., 1, 2, or 5 years) boundary sets a limit to what extent the articulation of social action and interaction among the actors of a social network will be recorded for SNA. An extended boundary is likely to include more ties than a relatively less extended one, and thus the boundary

may alter the estimated values of the graph-theoretic measures. For the purpose of our study, the former may be too relaxed and hence runs the risk of being largely contaminated by problems of recall, while the latter may be too rigid to be meaningful at all. Hence, we need to use a balanced time period to compare different social networks. We do this by qualitatively specifying the period of time within which social actions are recorded.

The mode of qualitative reference to time that we use is what happens "normally," "usually," or "generally." This is based on the self-perception of ego. For example, to record the out-degree of a vertex, one may ask, "To which the HHs does ego send requests for help?" The reference the period may be "past year," "past 5 years," or "normally goes to whom." On one hand, when the point of origin and the endpoint are fixed, the data obtained from actors can be compared directly. On the other hand, qualitatively identified time needs standardization prior to SNA. For our case studies, we have followed a qualitative definition and cross-checked by matching one's out-degrees with the in-degrees of the others in the network.

6. We previously discussed that the nature of an urgent need for help or assistance required by a household to face a crisis may be of different types. Help and cooperation may flow along different kinds of relationships in the community, varying from traditional primordial obligations and normative duties of kinship, friendship, and sharing a common neighborhood to a contractual one of economic ties or some sort of expectation of return in the future. Regardless of the type of help required or the individual who is being asked, it is important also to note how the ego (i.e., the actor [head of HH]) who needs help chooses the alter (i.e., the HH whom the actor approaches with the request for help). We find that this is not a matter of random choice or an outcome of a random process. On the contrary, this is a semi-deterministic decision-making process where the action is perceived as a purposeful, sequentially organized deliberate process with unambiguous goals and objectives that are known in advance. This is similar to the rational-comprehensive-analytic model of Janis-Mann (Michie, 2001). For this reason, we have considered deterministic graph-theoretic models of social networks along with a probabilistic version in Chapter 3.

Again, the fact that our finding has not yet become redundant is evident from the basic assumption of the methodology of modeling social network data based on the concept of a random graph or a exponential random graph model (ERGM). A random graph is generated by a random process. Also, the nodes and edges of a social network are random variables. In an earlier study, we compared the properties of deterministic and probabilistic measures of the same characteristic—namely, reciprocity in a social network. We have discussed and compared the effectiveness of various (graph-theoretic and probabilistic) measures using empirical data on 21 village communities (see Chapter 1). The comparison has demonstrated relative effectiveness of deterministic measures (Rao & Bandyopadhyay, 1987).

The collection and processing of data for SNA has received attention for many decades (see Mitchell, 1969). But our fieldwork experience with respect to empirical social networks has prompted us to realize the relevance of this side of the coin, which differentiates the underlying logistics of the methodology of SNA from that of survey research in general. In the latter case, randomness plays a basic role. Again, it is also to be noted that unlike in the field of macro decision making in economics, political science, business policy, or the policy of running an organization, decision-making processes of an ego for urgent support at the time of a crisis or emergency are characterized by different types of parameters. The most striking ones are as follows: type and quantum of help required; availability of the "alter," "donor," or "patron"; time, nature, and context of urgency; past experience with the alter; and social status, personality, credibility, and social connectedness of the ego or the recipient. Broadly speaking, on the basis of these parameters, egos decision-making process runs along the following sequence: The first step is that the ego has a mental construct of a list of those HHs (either within or outside the local community) who may provide help to him or her at a time of a need. This is the ego's universe or set of potential helpers. The next step is for the ego to classify the potential set into subsets of HHs, according to the parameters of decision making given above. These subsets are not necessarily mutually exclusive or exhaustive in the analytical sense of these terms. The subsets may rather be also a sort of "fuzzy" set—not explicitly defined. As and when required, the ego, facing a crisis, decides, as if spontaneously, which of the potential HHs to approach for help.

Construction of a social network based on empirical social behavior thus requires not only an understanding of the interaction of the subsystems of the social system (as is usually perceived and described in social science parlance identifying) but also going deep below the surface of social action along with of underlying parameters and relevant actors.

7. Assumption of the normality of the distribution of statistics related to the parameters may not be valid in all cases. Quite commonly, the ones such as in-degrees and weak and strong components are "scale free." Power curves fit them well (cf. Barabasi & Bonabeau, 2003). Hence, nonparametric distribution-free statistical methods demand attention in such cases.

6.2 RATIONALE OF SOCIAL NETWORK ANALYSIS BY CASE STUDIES

Before we venture into the details of the case studies, we make the following brief submission regarding the appropriateness of SNA to examine the pattern of social structure in terms of sociological theory.

There are various streams of thought in the parlance of sociological thinking regarding the concept of social structure. One thought is, as we have tangentially touched upon earlier in Chapter 1, a behavioral or interactional version. It identifies social structure from the actual pattern of regular social interaction among actors, rather than defining it as a construct out of a set of a priori criteria. Most notable among the criteria are "value orientation" or normatively ascribed components of a social system construed as its "structural-functional" requisites.

Following this view, a social network obtained for a community from interactions among its actors produces an image of its social structure. Its different characteristics can then be measured, as described earlier, by graph-theoretic measures derived from a social network. Given this premise, one can compare communities whether cross-sectionally or longitudinally and study differences in their structures. In a way, our endeavor may be referred to as a comparison by a "whole-network study" (Wellman & Berkowitz, 1988).

The queries of SNA, however, require various types of ground data on characteristics of each actor in the network as well as on the structure and pattern of mutual help and support gathered from multiple sources for interpretation of SNA findings. As such, it needs an analysis by many more variables than data points. Again, the overall logistic of our study is not to drive toward a generalization from a random sample to a universe, as is aimed in usual survey research. Our approach is to draw inference from a comparative study of cases. (Robinson, 1951). A village is treated as a "case," and hence the design of a village-based case study, as well as the SNA of its social network of help and support at the time of emergencies, has been considered the most appropriate methodology for the purpose (Yin, 1994). Accordingly, the global social network of a community, whether a "village community" or its segment identified by a social or economic attribute, is treated as the unit of SNA. Moreover, one can also estimate the statistical properties of the characteristics of a single "case" by simulation under an appropriate model, be it a village community or its segment (Dawson, 1962). Hence, a statistical analysis of the findings of SNA of a case study is no longer an unsolvable proposition. Thus, global comparison of social structures becomes a feasible quantitative proposition by SNA. In fact, this is how SNA has become the meeting ground of computer science, statistical science, mathematical science, and social science. For example, we have given values of some parameters of a social network of a community estimated by computer simulation in Table 6.1 and we have compared a few of them with their mathematically derived values. We now turn to the case studies. We have undertaken two case studies to delineate two types of changes in social structure: longitudinal change and cross-sectional variation. We discuss their details as follows.

6.3 OBJECTIVES

6.3.1 Case Study Type I

In this part of the study, we intend to compare longitudinal changes in social structure. We do this by SNA, obtaining the values of graph-theoretic measures of some global characteristics of social networks at two time periods: One, the baseline, refers to the pattern of ties as those that had circulated about three decades ago, during 1971–1972, and the other, during 1997–1998. The social network of a village community depicts the sum total of interactions of various processes in a spatially and temporally bounded sociocultural entity (i.e., a village). Moreover, as a matter of revealing out some in-depth stories to explore internal dynamics hidden behind a global scenario, we have subsequently desegregated the global findings by a few selected categories of "caste" and "class" (as occupationally identified). A caste provides,

All tables in Chapter 6 are presented at the end of the chapter.

among different things, a ritualistically ascribed mode of status division prevalent in India, while an occupation indicates the mode of participation of an actor in a local system of production. That way, it also explicates one's class position. These two categories of caste and class are commonly used structural and cultural dimensions of social stratification in India (Beteille, 1971). These comparative findings at two levels, global and stratificational, enable us to gather an idea regarding whether any connection exists between the change in a social network and the change in its social and economic settings, whether the measures of development implemented in the region have influenced the characteristics of local rural society only at the surface or have percolated deep below to create an impact at the level of the pattern of social relational structure as well. In the present case study, we examine whether the measures of development have retarded integratedness within a community. Contextually, the following graph-theoretic measures as described in Chapter 5 have been selected to compare the social networks. The measures are cohesion, reciprocity, connectedness, fragmentation, and hierarchy.

6.3.2 Case Study Type II

The second case study examines cross-sectional variation in the pattern of circulating social ties of a community across villages. We have chosen the case of a minority religious group (the Muslim community) for this purpose. Because this community is regarded as culturally homogeneous, robust in religiosity, and a structurally well-integrated community, we decided to analyze and compare the pattern of articulation of ties within the Muslim community in a few villages situated in the same region. These villages have been inhabited by Muslims for generations. Numerically, they form a minority community in the villages we plan to study. Socially, they constitute a marginalized group rooted in the villages where non-Muslims, particularly the Hindu community, predominate. Whatever the sociocultural environment, it is commonly held that the Muslim community remains noteworthy for its religious devoutness, which generates a sort of rigid internal cohesion that extends help and support as and when needed to meet the emergencies in daily life. Under the influence of triangulation of these factors, it may be reasonably hypothesized that the graph-theoretic measures for this community will be more or less robust, tending to show inappreciable variation across the villages. The characteristics of the social structure of the Muslim community are treated as variables. Accordingly, we ask the following: Does the flow of ties in the interface with societal forces impinging on the villages produce different types of patterns in social networks of the Muslim community in different villages? In other words, we ask whether the social networks of the Muslim community of the study villages are similar to one another and cluster together.

6.4 SELECTION OF VILLAGES FOR CASE STUDIES

6.4.1 Type I Case Study

Earlier in Chapter 1, we described how the highlights of implementing official measures of rural development led to an alteration in the pattern of articulating ties of social help and support within the village community in Kabilpur during the period of 1971–1972 and 1997–1998. In fact, we have extensively researched social network data related to the HHs of Kabilpur. This background has prompted us to treat this particular village as the nodal village for our longitudinal study.

Furthermore, empirical evidence has also pointed out the need to take note of another attribute: the proximity of a village to an all-weather road, an indicator of the quality of its connectedness with urban market centers. This is observed to be an important attribute contributing to catalyze the implementation of measures of development and its impact on a village (see the section on uneven development in Bandyopadhayay & von Eschen, 1995). Proximity to all-weather roads is a global attribute of a village, and for the purpose of analysis, it can be treated as a dichotomous variable with two values: "near" the road and "far" from the road. The proximity quite likely promotes the influence of an urban way of life and market orientation. Again, urban market cultural influence, it is often lamented, will tend to make individualistic orientation in social behavior more pronounced in the "near" villages, dampening the flow of groupwise circulation of ties of help and the support connecting a number of households within a village.

Since Kabilpur belongs to "near" stratum by proximity to all-weather roads and facilities of communication, we decided to select another similarly located village, Maladanga, which was matched with Kabilpur so that at least a minimum idea about the consistency of the findings could be examined. In the next step, to contrast with two "near" villages, we selected two other villages that were situated "far" from the roads. These two villages are Raspur and Baidyanathpur. Altogether, these four villages constitute our sample cases for a whole-network study at two time periods, 1971–1972 and 1997–1998.

6.4.2 Type II Case Study

For the Type II case study, we used SNA to compare the structural pattern of a Muslim community inhabiting a few multicommunity villages. Namely, we studied six villages altogether. The Hindus form the numerically dominant group in each of these villages and the Muslims are a minority community. The selected villages are located at the tail-end region of the east Indian plateau. The sociocultural milieu of this region is not characterized by Hindu religious orthodoxy. It has rather flourished historically as a frontier land exposed to the interface of two cultural streams, one emanating from the miscegenation of indigenous nonorthodox local cultural traits, softening the other, flowing from Brahminical Hinduism of the East. The case study refers to the findings from SNA of the social networks of the Muslims of these six villages, treated as six "cases," selected against this cultural background.

Two villages (Maladanga and Raspur) among the four selected for the first case study are also inhabited by the Muslims. We have included these two villages for the present case study and supplemented them by adding four other villages from the same region (Harsingraidih, Chitmadih, Baghra, and Mahacho). Administratively, however, these four villages belong to a different district of Giridih in the neighboring state of Jharkhand. The first two villages, like Maladanga, are situated within walking distance of less than 3 km from roads as well as market centers, while the location of Mahacho, like Raspur, is far away (around 15 km). The distance of the remaining village, Baghra, lies in between (5–7 km). We will use the following abbreviations for the six villages: Harsingraidih (Hd), Chitmadih (Cd), Baghra (Bg), Mahacho (Mh), Maladanga (Md), and Raspur (Rp). Hence, on the whole, we get four (including Bg) "near" villages and two "far" ones. Among the four "near" villages, Md is located just beside a major market center at the crossing of two important that link linking the village with many other market and urban centers. One may wonder if we are overdoing it by referring to the differences among the villages so meticulously with respect to their distance from the roads. On the contrary, in the rural areas where we are doing our case studies, categories of location formed by walking distance are important for facilitating interaction with urban markets and, in that way, for diffusion of the urban way of life. The network of the Muslim community of each of these selected six villages is shown for ready reference in Diagrams 8 to 13 at the end of this book.

6.5 FINDINGS FROM CASE STUDY I

6.5.1 Integration

We examine what has happened with time to integration within village communities. The question we have raised is not new, but the way in which it was asked and discussed was different. It was examined meticulously in a historical perspective but according to a somewhat egocentric point of view (cf. Wellman, 1997). In our case study, we have endeavored to answer the question of integration within the community with respect to the social network of a community, whether a village or caste or class as a whole—that is, the global view. Data relevant for measures of characteristics of social structure stated earlier in Section 6.3.1 are presented in Tables 6.2 to 6.8. The highlights of our findings are as follows.

The actual number of ties of help and support at the time of crisis articulating in the network is observed to be quite a small proportion to the maximum number of ties possible in the network, given the number of vertices. This is evident from the measure of density of social networks, whether a village-, caste-, or class-based community. This is true for the base period, 1971–1972, as well as two to three decades later, 1997–1998. Compactness of social structure was thus loose and subsequently has become more so. This is, however, reasonable to expect as a matter of demographic consequence, with the base being related to the size of the community (for a discussion on density, see Albert & Barabasi, 2002; Knoke & Kuklinsky, 1982; Mitchell, 1969, p. 18; it has been discussed as a measure of egocentric clustering in a social network with its global version).

Although density in social interaction was very low in social networks in all the villages, SNA further shows that social structure was also considerably fragmented (F_w) in the "near" villages during the baseline period of 1971–1972. However, it has decreased sharply during the past few decades. In contrast, very low fragmentation characterizes the social structure of the "far" villages from the baseline through the recent period.

6.5.2 Why Fragmentation?

Why were the "near" villages so fragmented as opposed to the "far" villages during the early 1970s? We selected them due to their ready access to roads and transport communication facilities, but this could not be a plausible factor for explaining the characteristic. With the presence of the same factor, the incidence of the same characteristic fell steeply, with the "near" villages remaining "near" rather than becoming "more near," while the fragmentedness of structure got reduced. Alternatively, therefore, we have to look for an explanatory factor from within the social system of the "near" villages. To do this, we begin with the findings of an earlier study of cooperatives in which, we examined why the level of cooperation was low in the villages. The highly polarized system of stratification was revealed as the most contributory factor (Bandyopadhyay & von Eschen, 1988). A small number of upper-class households owned most of all the cultivable land along with the sources of irrigation, which provided sources of livelihood for most of the villagers, but it pushed the vast majority of villagers to the state of becoming wholly dependent on saying that they were "at their mercy" would not be an exaggeration. But that was the type of social stratification prevalent in both the villages of Kabilpur and Baidyanathpur (i.e., one "near" and one "far" village). Hence, one has to go further in depth to explore the cause of variation in the extent of fragmentation between the two villages.

6.5.3 Specificities of Mode of Social Stratification: Kabilpur

Within the same system of social stratification, we find that SNA shows a subtle difference between the social structures of the two villages. The levels of two apparently contradictory characteristics of social structure, fragmentedness (F_w) and reciprocity (s_3), were both high in one of them, Kabilpur, but not in the other, Baidyanathpur. The social structure of Kabilpur thus shows an apparent paradox. The differences in the values of the measures between the two villages led us to answer our query concerning large-scale fragmentation in Kabilpur as well as how it was so despite high reciprocity in the village. Because, one may expect a highly reciprocal village to be endowed with a low level of stratification. To resolve the apparent inconsistency of findings from SNA, we discuss the qualitative anecdotes gathered by genealogical and historical case studies in the villages. It is beyond the scope of this work to reconstruct a detailed history; rather, we will highlight the features that are relevant for the interpretation of findings from SNA.

Our explanation is based on the premise that the system of stratification provides an outline of the topology of the structure, which is a necessary requirement to grasp the background of social actions and interactions. But to have a valid appraisal of the paradox in social structure of Kabilpur— paradox of a high incidence of fragmentation, conjoint with a high reciprocity in the village—one needs to dig below the surface to learn about the forms and purpose of social actions shaped by the specificities of the arena (Wrong, 1988). Accordingly, in the context of Kabilpur, we now discuss why, being embedded in the same system of social stratification, one village has become simultaneously much more fragmented and reciprocal than the other (i.e., Baidyanathpur). The relevant data obtained by SNA are presented in Table 6.5.

A characteristic of the upper class differentiated its system of social stratification in Kabilpur from that of Baidyanathpur in that a clique of seven upper-class households dominated the economy and societal scenario of Kabilpur. The major source of their earning was by appropriation, not by production. The clique was empowered by the support received from other upper-class households, using ties of kinship and caste, and had usurped almost all of the agricultural land in the village as well as access to sources of natural irrigation such as canals, ponds, and so on. They continued to maintain their dominance by force, coercion, and manipulation.

In addition, the households forming the clique at the top were highly integrated because of their small size. They belonged to the same caste of high ritual status (Sadgop caste) and were bound by kinship relations. In addition, ties of mutual help and support added to further strengthen their cohesion.

Moreover, two households of the clique had formed a virtual hub in the social network of the village of Kabilpur. The two (0.84%) together could directly pressurize 35 (15.09%) of the remaining households outside the clique (or 17.86% of households of castes other than the Sadgopes). In addition, they could also exert their influence over at least another 23 (9.91%) of the remaining households. Thus, these two households could exercise control, in some way, of least approximately 25% of the households in the village by a veiled threat of withdrawal or refusal of help during an emergency. As instruments of manipulation of power, the two households used to offer small gratifications and endowments to others for different reasons on various occasions. The instrument of gratification and discrimination had fragmented the villagers, particularly the Bagdi and Santal households, into mutually exclusive segments, which was tangentially touched upon in Chapter 1.

At this point, we add briefly how the clique has risen in the village. In a way, this sketch will help to partly explain the cohesiveness within the clique. All seven households had descended from the same "root ancestor." In collating information from the genealogical histories we have gathered, we learn that there were several waves of migration from an arid region in the district of Burdwan in the west. The migrants mostly belonged to the Goala caste (cowherds/milkmen). The shortage of grazing land pushed them out of their ancestral places of residence to move across the Ajay river to the present neighboring district of Birbhum. Over generations, they had spread out to different villages in this part of Birbhum. Partly due to the availability of plenty of agricultural land and partly because of very low land-to-man ratio, the migrants turned to cultivation as the major source of livelihood. They became "farmers" and began to assert themselves, forming a separate caste of agriculturists, the Sadgope caste, as differentiated from the Goala caste of the milkmen, who were engaged mainly in business of milk and milk products. For an elaborate discussion on social mobility of the Sadgope caste, one may refer to Sanyal (1981).

The "root ancestor" had migrated to this village in the course of one of those waves of migration around five generations back and settled down as a leaseholder of agricultural land from a Brahmin proprietor. Over time, the former pushed out the latter from land ownership and began to acquire land mainly through usury and coercion in which he was joined by his other caste members. Eventually with the acquisition of landed property, the Sadgopes amassed ample wealth and aspired to the same ritually prescribed high social status as that of the Brahmins. It was denied particularly by the potter and barber caste members. These two castes were traditionally ascribed the social status of middle rank along with the Sadgope caste. Since the former two castes were opposed to oblige the Sadgopes, the intercaste rivalry over status had also combined with the drive of the clique at the top to continue to appropriate local resources to deepen fragmentedness in the village. Because they were situated in a fragmented village society, the households forming a segment had to be cohesive and support each other, which led to a high level of global reciprocity (cf. Srinivas's concept of "Sanskritization" and a critical discussion of the same by Bandyopadhyay, 1997).

6.5.4 Baidyanathpur

The upper class in the village of Baidyanathpur consisted of mostly the households of the Rajput community. They claim to have migrated many generations back from a North Indian state (Rajasthan) as part of the infantry of the Moghul emperor in Delhi. In lieu of the services in the army, they received land grants from the emperor in this part of the country. But since the land situation of the village and its surroundings was not very conducive to good farming, nor did it enjoy sufficient facilities of natural irrigation, the Rajputs slowly moved over to business and services going out from the village to various urban areas. Hence, rivalry over land grabbing or status or motivation to exploit maximally village resources by appropriation had not emerged noticeably in the village. The level of reciprocity (s_3) was low, but the villagers remained largely connected by ties through intermediaries (C_w). Fragmentedness was also low (F_w). We have included at the end of the book four networks from Baidyanathpur for ready reference. These correspond to the Santals community (Diagrams 14 and 15) and the Rajput community (Diagrams 16 and 17) for the years 1971–1972 and 1997–1998, respectively.

6.5.5 Impact of Development

In this situation, the official measures of rural development that were implemented—particularly those of land reforms, registration of share-croppers, increased wages for agricultural laborers, local administration by elected village councils (Panchayats and Gram Sabhas), and a total literacy campaign—have led to the empowerment of the rural poor and have curtailed the continuity of the power base of the upper class, dismantling the top clique in particular. The virtual hub and its links became vulnerable to the impact of the official measures and splintered under villagers' mobilization to implement them. Though these features have disappeared, the so-called integration of village community continues to exist. On the contrary, new types of linkages have arisen, and new mini-virtual hubs endowed with new type of societal significance have emerged. Connectedness among the households in the social network has widened much more through indirect links. This is how the dynamicity of the social world distinguishes itself from the natural or biological world (cf. Barabasi & Bonabeau, 2003). We have described these changes in the socio-economic and political scenario in detail in Chapter 1. The observation that the change has penetrated deep beyond the surface of the social structure becomes apparent from the graph-theoretic measures we have obtained from SNA.

As far as our query about the integratedness of the village community is concerned, it has not disappeared but has changed its form. Multilaterality binding a plurality of actor-households has become a prominent mode of the articulation of ties. Incidence of dyadic reciprocity was, in a way, an instrument of fragmentation of the community into narrow segments. Instead, circular reciprocity has surfaced, extending the periphery of connectedness while reducing fragmentedness within the social network.

6.5.6 Generalization

Before we conclude this case study, it may be further added that we have so far explained the joint occurrence of a high incidence of F_w (fragmentation of a village community into a large number of mutually exclusive segments) and s_3 (standardized reciprocity) in terms of typical specificities of a "case" (i.e., Kabilpur). A rank correlation analysis of some parameters of social network also indicates the possibility of drawing a generalized inference concerning the positive relationships between these two characteristics of social structure. We give below the rank correlation matrix of five characteristics of social structure obtained by SNA of social networks of a subsample of 12 villages drawn from the collection of 21 referred to in Chapter 1. In addition to F_w and s_3, the other characteristics considered are the size of a village by number of HHs (n), fragmentation based on direction of ties (F_s), and hierarchy (h).

Rank Correlation Matrix Based on Findings From SNA of 12 Village Communities

-	n	s_3	F_w	h	F_s
n	–	0.03	0.46***	–0.13	0.13
s_3	–	–	**0.74***	**–0.85***	0.45***
F_w	–	–	–	**–0.56****	0.07
h	–	–	–	–	0.74*
F_s	–	–	–	–	–

*Significant at the 1% level. **Significant at the 5% level. ***Significant at the 20% level.

A triangulation of three characteristics of social structure is immediately visible from the bold figures in the above matrix—F_w and s_3 show highly significant positive correlations across the villages, while their correlation with h is negative. Reciprocity thus can be hypothesized to vary directly over social networks as the extent of their splintering into mutually exclusive fragments. For various reasons, a social structure may become fragmented. Usually, a fragment is not likely to be very large in size, and the actors constituting it can directly interact among themselves more frequently. The ties are more likely to be marked by sustained "intensity," to use Mitchell's (1969) criterion of interaction. That way, under the conditions of deprivation, lack of access to common public resources, and an absence of any formal, institutional modality to mitigate the vulnerabilities in life and living, the fragments become conducive to mutual help and support among themselves. The "fragmented" social structure becomes conspicuous by a preponderance of symmetric ties of mutual help. An explanation of their negative correlation with hierarchy is obvious, and so also is a positive correlation of hierarchy with fragmentation by directed ties.

6.6 CLUSTERING AND SEGREGATION OF SOCIAL NETWORKS

Our cross-sectional case study is aimed to examine clustering and segrega-tion of social networks by applying distance based on Mahalanobis's D^2. The concept and methodology of Mahalanobis's D^2 as a measure of "distance" between two societal categories have been already applied in regional science, physical anthropology, social psychology, and sociology. Substantively, it is a multivariate statistical method to differentiate societal groups or categories in terms of their different characteristics taken together. Social networks can certainly be compared in terms of one characteristic at a time, say, reciprocity, connectedness (fragmentation), hierarchy, and so on. But the intriguing ques-tion would be to examine the relative performances of the networks when these features are studied jointly. Since study of a single attribute only gives a partial picture of the social structure, it seems almost imperative to exploit the rele-vance and usefulness of multivariate methods in such studies involving social networks.

6.6.1 Rationale of Applying the Methodology of Mahalanobis's D^2

A comparison of networks, however, is simple to do with respect to any one of the attributes of social structure considered singly. We select a structural characteristic and its appropriate graph-theoretic measure. We then compare the values of the measure across the networks as it happens when we ask whether reciprocity prevails in social behavior to the same extent in different groups or, say, whether the incidence of fragmentation of social structures changes significantly over time or from community to community and so on.

Because social structure is a multidimensional totality, its valid appreciation requires studying it by combining multiple attributes. Here we face a complex situation. We are required to combine graph-theoretic measures of some selected characteristics of social network structure and compare. This is where the concept of a "whole-network study" becomes a pertinent methodological orientation; however, analytical constraints have severely restrained its application (Wellman, 1997, p. 26). In our view, the constraints of whole-network study have been rooted in not taking recourse to an appropriate multidisciplinary methodology. It requires combining the needs of sociological theory "with formal mathematical, statistical and computing methodology," which is explicitly made available by SNA (Wasserman & Faust, 1994). In this context, the concept of "distance" provides a valid quantitative measure to obtain the extent of gap or segregation and clustering among social structures by combining multiple characteristics. Application of the concept of distance in SNA is not new. The literature refers to the methodology of comparing social distances in terms of a single characteristic (Beshers & Laumann, 1967). It was also used to measure structural equivalence (Knoke & Kuklinsky, 1982), but that was an intranetwork, egocentric application.

In the present case study, we intend to examine distances between social networks, each of them being considered as a unit case. We illustrate how the distance-based analysis application can enable us to combine graph-theoretic measures of social networks corresponding to various characteristics of social structures, estimate their statistical properties by computer simulation, and compare them. Mahalanobis's distance (or Mahalanobis's D^2) provides an appropriate methodology to study global differences of social networks. We next show how distances among social networks can be estimated by computer simulation of statistical properties of graph-theoretic measures obtained by social network analysis and use them to indicate global similarities and dissimilarities of social structures.

As stated above, we use social networks as "surrogates" of social structures and values of Mahalanobis's D^2 among pairs of them as measures of distances among them. (Incidentally, for a detailed discussion of mathematical and statistical properties of the statistic D^2, see Mahalanobis, 1930, 1936 [also republished in Bandyopadhyay, 2006].)

For examples of application in various fields of social research, one may refer to Rao and Slater (1949), Stone (1960), and Mukherjee and Bandyopadhyay (1965).

We discuss the cross-sectional study of social networks below.

6.6.2 Objective of the Case Study of the Muslim Community

Our aim is to study differences among social structures of a minority community—namely, the Muslim community—globally in six villages mentioned earlier by application of Mahalanobis's D^2. We use a social network as a substitute of social structure and the value of a graph-theoretic measure obtained by SNA as the value of a respective social structural characteristic.

The reasons for our choice of the Muslim community in these villages are as follows. The six villages are located in the same ecological region at the tail end of the east Indian plateau. The Muslim households of these villages belong to the same Atrap (low-status) subgroup consisting of the Ansaris. They have been inhabiting the same village in the same hamlet (except Cd and Mh, where they are residing in four and two hamlets, respectively) for at least five to seven generations. Thus, in each village, the Muslim community has been endowed with ample scope of developing a stable pattern of regular social interaction among them related to various issues of daily life and living. The social networks we refer to have been empirically derived by linking the heads of households who are the principal actors. Linking has been done according to the direction of flow of a request for help or support made by an actor (a head) to another as and when required at the time of an emergency or crisis in the household. We repeat that in terms of a digraph, a vertex represents a head (or a household), a tie within a pair of vertices indicates that there is flow of help or support between them (otherwise, if there is no tie, it means there is no flow), and the direction of flow is shown by an arrowhead.

Also, as stated earlier, the type of help could be not only financial, but also material or physical. If a household had approached another for advice or guidance, that was also considered a request for help. In fact, it concerned a household's request to provide for any kind of help when it had faced any urgent matter of life and living.

Clearly, in the choice of networks, we have been guided by the fact that the households belong to the same subgroup of the same religious community within a village; therefore, they are expected to share the same structural norms and cultural values being embedded in similar social and cultural moorings. Our logic of selecting networks of the Muslim community for SNA has also been influenced by the parameters that they have been traditionally exposed to the same field of interaction. Hence, there exists a strong reason to expect that the pattern of social structure of the Muslim community in these villages should not diverge significantly; rather, they would tend to become clustered, with distances among them being statistically insignificant. To test this trend as the null hypothesis, we intend to study if distances among the social networks are significantly different and can be interpreted meaningfully.

6.6.3 Characteristics of Social Network Used for D^2 Analysis

In the present case study, we consider five social network-based attributes of social structure. These represent characteristics of two different aspects of social structure. One aspect is the pattern of intranetwork transaction or exchange flowing among the actors or groups of actors directly or through intermediaries. The other aspect is the span and type of linking of the actors, either individually or groupwise, or of various components of a network. The former reproduces the horizontal profile of the network, while the latter reproduces its span.

On the basis of the four primary attributes of a network—the number of actors (vertices or n) constituting a network, the number of reciprocally tied pairs of actors (s), and the number of strong (Cs) and weak (Cw) components of a network—we derive five standardized measures of characteristics of a network which we have used for purposes of comparison. These are standardized measures of reciprocity, strong connectedness, weak connectedness (extent of fragmentation), reachability by directed path, and hierarchy in the pattern of distribution of paths linking actors (individually or component-wise) in a network. These, on the whole, indicate the nature of integration of the actors among themselves within a network. Altogether, we have used these five characteristics jointly to measure the extent of segregation or closeness among the social networks by Mahalanobis's distance. We use these measurements in two stages. First, we estimate distance in terms of the former three attributes. Next, the two remaining attributes are added to complete the picture.

Our study, based on a selection of some attributes of social network, is in tune with the logistic of evaluating the goodness of fit of statistical models by selected structural measures.

6.6.4 Computational Details

Since there exists ample statistical literature on Mahalanobis's D^2 and its application, we mention only one that is relevant for the present analysis (Majumdar & Rao, 1960). The substantive part of the guideline to estimate the value of the D^2 statistic (or Mahalanobis's distance) is to obtain the transformed set of an uncorrelated set of the given number of variables in the standardized form (i.e., with unit variance) corresponding to the original set of the variables. The original set of variables need not be in the standardized form. The sum of squares of the differences between the mean values of the transformed variables, such as the p characters, of any two groups under consideration, gives the value of D^2 between them.

The moot question in estimating distances among the social networks is how to obtain the pooled variance-covariance matrix since each network is a case by itself minimally with two given parameters: n, the number of vertices (actors), and m, the given number of edges (ties) connecting them. With n and m being given for each social network, we generate by simulation a variance-covariance matrix for each of them. Since the social networks are given, they do not overlap. We take them as statistically independent and obtain the pooled variance-covariance matrix by adding the six simulated variance-covariance matrices of six villages and dividing by 36 (Tables 6.9 – 6.21). Incidentally, we could do the same by taking n and d (out-degree sequence) as being given.

Using the pooled variance-covariance matrix, we compute the required coefficients for transformation of the original set of variables (Table 6.16). The original set of variables (Table 6.17) is next transformed into an uncorrelated standardized set using the coefficients as and where required (Tables 6.18 – 6.20).

Finally, we obtain the values of D^2. As stipulated, we have worked out two sets of Mahalanobis's distance: one with respect to three characteristics— reciprocity in exchange, strong connectedness, and weak connectedness (fragmentation)—depicting an intranetwork flow of exchange (Table 6.21a), and the other considering the five characteristics jointly (Table 6.21b).

6.6.5 What Do the Findings Indicate?

All the pairwise D^2 values, except the one between Cd and Hd, are large, whether estimated with respect to the three or five attributes considered jointly. Statistically, each of the pairwise values is highly significant. According to Mahalanobis's distance, social networks of the six villages can be arranged by three and five attributes, as shown at the end of the book in Diagrams 18 and 19, respectively.

One immediate implication of the findings is that the social network of the Muslim community in each village, generated by articulation of social relations of help and cooperation, is an entity as such segregated from each other. Thus, the global pattern of articulation of social ties of providing help and support is distinctly different from village to village, even though the actors belong to the same Muslim cultural niche. Hence, there is no valid reason group them together as Muslim basket because of the common religious or traditional cultural denomination of the actors. Sociologically, we note that the empirical finding from a quantitative analysis of social network data deviates from the prevalent notion eulogizing the solidarity orientation of the Muslim community. However, if we take a step back and put this against what has been learned from a qualitative historical analysis, it fits in appropriately. In the course of a historical analysis, it has been explicated that ritually, the Muslim community stands "vaguely unified by a common allegiance to the essentials of its members," but with respect to social behavior, it has remained "in every sense a fragmented society even at the turn of the century" (Ahmed, 1988).

Furthermore, despite large values of D^2, the following features are also noteworthy. One is that the value of D^2 between Hd and Cd indicates the path with the shortest distance among all the pairs irrespective of whether three or five attributes are considered.

On the contrary, values of Mahalanobis's D^2 of social networks of Mh and Md compared with those of Hd and Cd are extremely large, with the distances with Bg and Rp coming in between. In fact, the social networks of Mh and Md stand out as "outliers." The social network of Bg is located as an intermediary between Mh, on one hand, and Hd and Cd, on the other, while Rp is between Md, on one hand, and Hd and Cd, on the other.

Sociological derivatives of the values of Mahalanobis's D^2 obtained from the measures of social networks appear to be embedded neither in the sphere of morphological characteristics of size, composition, infrastructural facilities of life, and livelihood nor in access or contact with market or urban centers (Table 6.12). It is rather confounded with expansion of the economic activities generating mobility—upward mobility, to be more specific—as indicated by a changing pattern of livelihoods of the Muslim households (Table 6.13). This is explicated at the end of the book in Diagrams 1 and 2 by a sort of stable "togetherness" of Hd and Cd, marked by indications of upward economic mobility, on one hand, and "scatteredness" of Bg, Rp, Mh, and Md, on the other.

Economic activities of Hd have been mostly tied up with the market in Giridih. Cd was a subsistence village even a few decades back. Due to demographic growth and partitioning of families, many villagers were pushed out to migrate for livelihood to distant places such as Surat (in Gujrat), Jaipur (in Rajasthan), and Jullunder (in Punjab). They saved part of their cash earnings and sent them back to their families left behind in the village. This extra off-farm income was partly invested for the development of agriculture, partly irrigation and growing vegetables, which found a readily expanding market in nearby weekly markets (*Hat-s*) as well as in distant areas. Improved access to paved roads and transportation facilities contributed tremendously in this regard. At the beginning of marketization, the farmers themselves sold the surplus agricultural produce in the neighboring markets at Nayatanr, Bengabad, and also in the *Hat-s* to the retailers as well as to the agents of wholesalers (*Pharia-s*). Nowadays, since the volume of produce has increased so much and has also become a regular feature of the village, the agents themselves come to the village "to make deals" and offer "advances for next year's purchases." Thus, Cd became immersed in the external economy of expanding agriculture.

On the contrary, Bg, also a subsistence village, was interested in the mica industry in Giridih town. Most of the women in this village were engaged at home in part-time jobs as "mica sorters," which had made the villagers quite affluent. But with the crash in the international mica market, its prosperity dwindled. Only very recently have a few villagers turned their attention to improved farming.

The remaining "near" village, Md, is marked by migration from outside. The villagers have settled in the area to earn lucratively from business in stone chip and chalk quarries in neighboring areas. In fact, they are engaged either as "middlemen" or as laborers.

Thus, only two of the four "near" villages, Hd and Cd, have become substantially part of the wider market economy and have flourished that way. The new input for economic development induced by interaction with the external economy has opened up a vista of opportunity for upward occupational mobility among the Muslims. In fact, the percentage of Muslim households whose principal source of income has increased is 41.76% (in Hd) and 37.74% (in Cd), while in Bg, Md, Rp, and Mh, the rates are 14.29%, 13.63%, 11.11%, and 10.00%, respectively.

We argue that the drive toward upward economic mobility lies behind the stable "closeness" of characteristics of the social structure of Hd and Cd and the scatteredness of the other villages. We further argue that the proximity to road links is a necessary factor, no doubt, but that is not sufficient by itself. The nature of market economy with which it is becoming integrated provides the clue to that condition. This is reflected in Diagrams 18 and 19 at the end of the book, which portray notional graphs plotting the six villages by estimated values of Mahalanobis's distance.

6.7 RECIPROCITY WITH MULTIPLE ARCS

This section was written a few decades back, based on secondary data and the then country classification. We are aware that the data and country classification are now outdated in the contemporary context. We have included it only to illustrate the SNA of a weighted digraph.

The United Nations compiles and publishes figures of international trade among all the countries and regions of the world (United Nations, 1984). These publications contain the year-wise figures of total values of export and import from one country to another as well as their breakdowns by each of the commodities or groups of commodities (in millions of U.S. dollars free on board [FOB]). The value of export from one country (i) to another (j) and the value of import by (i) from (j) indicate the quantum of exchange, or flow of trade, in two opposite directions within that pair of countries (i) and (j). The values of export and import between a pair of countries can be used to compare and indicate the extent of the lack of equality in trade between them. The measures of reciprocity, circularity, and balance, as derived above, if obtained by using the values of exports and imports among the countries of the world, can be substituted as measures of overall balance (or lack of it) in world trade. Furthermore, these measures, obtained as time-series data over a period of years, show the trend in the equilibrium of the world's system of trade.

The statistics of export and import of each commodity for which data are found to be numerically noteworthy can be collated from the publications mentioned above. However, instead of dealing with the voluminous data available for each commodity, we illustrate how to apply the above measures in the case of total world trade and the six categories formed out of so many different commodities. We have arrived at these six groups on the basis of an internationally recognized standard classification of commodities (SITC; United Nations, 1986), which are described as follows:

I Crude materials (hides, skins, oilseeds, textile fibers, crude fertilizers, metal scraps, etc.), edible oils (except fuels), animal and vegetable oils, and fats and waxes (SITC codes 2 and 4)

II Mineral fuels, lubricants, and related materials (coal, coke, petroleum, gas, electric current, etc.) (SITC code 3)

III Chemicals and related products (organic and inorganic fertilizers, excluding crude) (SITC code 5)

IV Machinery and transport equipment (metal-working and power-generating machinery, telecommunications equipment, road vehicles, electrical appliances, etc.) (SITC code 7)

V Manufactured goods, classified chiefly by materials (textile yarn and fabrics, iron and steel, etc.) and other miscellaneous manufactured articles (clothing, furniture, heating and lighting fixtures, etc.) (SITC codes 6 and 8)

VI Food (including cereals), live animals, beverages, and tobacco (SITC codes 0 and 1)

VII Total trade in all the commodities (SITC codes 0–9)

We may briefly mention that the first three of the above six groups contain chiefly different types of industrial raw materials. The fourth group includes infrastructural materials, which are important for industrial production and also for general consumers. The last two groups consist of commodities that are produced mainly for general consumption. In addition, for further elaboration, our analysis also includes one or two specific items such as cereals, textile yarns and fabrics, and clothing. One may be tempted to know what the findings would be when these items have a special interest of their own. Last, the seventh group shows the overall trend combining all the groups.

The values of exports and imports for the commodities as specified above have been obtained for all countries of the world pooled together. In addition, the same data were also collated in a desegregated way, but in a manner that the data add depth to our analysis and interpretation. The large number of countries was pooled and reduced to a moderate yet suitable number for the present purpose. To do this, however, we have followed the same logic of standard country classification by type of market economy as developed by the United Nations for international trade.

For the present purpose, however, we first divided the countries into three broad categories by respective type of market economy and then further classified each such category as and where found to be meaningful and feasible (United Nations, n.d.).

1. First, the countries governed by a centrally planned economy (CPE)—for example, the socialist countries of Europe and Asia (e.g., USSR, Vietnam, Mongolia, People's Republic of China, Poland, Albania, East Germany). They are pooled and retained as such.

Second, the countries with a developed market economy were classified as follows:

2. The United States (by itself, being the major developed country);

3. The rest of the developed market economy countries (PDM)—for example, European countries other than those of CPE-EEC and EFTA members, such as England, West Germany, France, Sweden, Italy, Canada, Japan, Australia, and South Africa.

Third, the countries with developing market economies were classified as follows:

4. Latin America (DLA), which includes all the countries, mainland and island, of Central and South America except Cuba;

5. Middle East (DME), including countries such as Saudi Arabia, Syria, Iraq, Tunisia, Algeria, Egypt, and Libya;

6. Asia and Oceania (DAO)—for example, India, Bangladesh, Pakistan, Sri Lanka, Burma, Malaysia, Indonesia, Hong Kong, Fiji, Papua New Guinea, and Polynesia;

7. Africa (DAF), consisting of all the countries of Africa except South Africa.

We next arranged and pooled the data on exports and imports for each group of commodities from one country to another and obtained the corresponding values of exports and imports of the same group of commodities from one type of market economy or its subdivision to another. We thus obtained the data in a condensed form of a 7×7 matrix of flow from one type of economy to another and obtained the values of reciprocity, circularity, and balance.

Furthermore, we also obtained the values of these measures at different periods of time. Beginning with 1970, we considered at a 5-year gap the years 1975 and 1980. We have also added the year 1983, which was the latest year for which we could obtain the published data. We could thus look at a trend over at least a short period of time as well.

We shall now briefly indicate how to compute the values of the proposed measures. Since this is just for illustration, we shall use somewhat in detail the data on international trade in one group of commodities, those of manufactured goods (group V of commodities) in the year 1970. Table 6.22 contains the relevant data of international trade in manufactured goods in the form of a 7×7 matrix. We give this as an illustration. Values of graph-theoretic measures of reciprocity in international trade in manufactured goods among countries grouped by respective political structure were, on the whole, in a symmetrically balanced state in 1970. That is, the state of the system was not that some groups of countries exported much more. In other words, the direction of flow was more bilateral than unilateral.

In 1970, the total value of international trade in manufactured goods was U.S.\$42.797 million. In Table 6.22, the figure within parentheses is the minimum of the two figures for the pair of countries (i) and (j)—export from (i) to (j) and import to (i) from (j). This minimum is, therefore, the reciprocated amount between (i) and (j). Thus, the bracketed grand total of U.S.\$14.519 million is the total of all the "minimums," which is consequently the empirically observed total amount of reciprocation in the worldwide trade of manufactured goods in 1970. In other words, for the Table 6.22,

$$m = 42,797$$

and

$$s_0 = 14,519.$$

Now, under the assumption that the total value of world trade remains fixed, allowing each category of market to alter its export or import value to another, to attain a perfect balance, the empirically attainable maximum amount of reciprocation is $s_{max} = m/2$. Hence, the measure of reciprocity becomes

$$s_2 = 100 \times 14{,}519/(42{,}797/2) = 67.9.$$

Under the assumption that each category of market keeps fixed the total value of its exports (or imports)—that is, its row (or column) total in the above-mentioned table—then the empirically attainable maximum amount of reciprocation shall depend on the nature of the fixed total values of exports (or imports), that is, the row (or column) totals.

If a row total exists that is greater than half of the grand total value of world trade, then this row total (q) is to be subtracted from the grand total value and $(m - q) = s_{max}$ because the row total, which is greater than half of the grand total, cannot be reciprocated.

If each row total is equal to or less than half of the grand total of world trade, then $s_{max} = (m/2)$.

For the above table,

$$
\begin{aligned}
s_3 &= 14{,}519/(42{,}797 - 22{,}852) \\
&= 72.8.
\end{aligned}
$$

In case both the total value of exports (row total) and the total value of imports (column total) of each type of market are considered as given data or as fixed, then to obtain s_4, it is to be checked whether the minimum amount of reciprocation is 0. Because, unlike in the case of the assumptions held for the measures s_2 and s_3, some minimum amount of reciprocation can become "forced"—the lower floor, so to say—by the very nature of the given two totals of exports and imports for each category of market. To standardize for this forced amount of reciprocation, if any, this amount needs to be deducted as for differences in origin. Since this minimum can be different for different cases, it is very important to check before comparing reciprocities. However, the difficulty involved in finding the exact value of this minimum is also to be noted. This "forced" minimum reciprocation is U.S.\$4.984 million for the above-mentioned table.

Second, one must note for each category of market the minimum of its two totals, of row and column, and then obtain the grand total of the set of these minima (b_0), which is U.S.\$32.202 million for the above table. Again, it is to be noted whether any one of these minima is greater than half their grand total.

If yes, then deduct this minimum and also the "forced" minimum calculated earlier from the latter grand total and use the remainder as a denominator to obtain s_4; otherwise, consider half of the grand total of the set of minima, less the "forced" minimum as the denominator, to obtain s_4.

Since none of the row totals is greater than half of 32,202 for the data given above, we shall consider $\frac{1}{2}(32,202) - 4,984 = 11,117$ as the denominator.

Third, the "forced" amount of reciprocation, if any, is also to be deducted from, so the remainder shall be the numerator to get s_4. In our case, we shall therefore deduct 4,984 from 14,519 and get

$$s_4 = 9,535/11,117 = 85.8.$$

It may have been noticed that so far, in the case of obtaining various measures of reciprocity, s_2, s_3, and s_4, our primary focus was the amount of flow from one category to another and back from the latter. Instead, in our proposed measures of balance, b_2 and b_3, we deal with only the closeness or gap between the marginal total of exports (rows) for each category and their corresponding marginal totals of imports (columns) irrespective of what happens between pairs of countries. Then, b_2 is b_0 divided by the grand total of world trade in manufactured goods. In the present case,

$$b_2 = 32,202/42,797 = 75.2.$$

For b_3, we consider (as for s_4) the column of the set of values of the minima and find out which of this set of values is the lowest (say, $\min x_i$). In the present case, $\min x_i = 163$. We shall now recall the maximum amount of reciprocation possible as in the case of obtaining s_3 (say, $s_{max}^{(3)}$), which is 19,945. Then,

$$b_3 = (32,202 - 2.153)/(2.19,945 - 2.153)$$
$$= 80.6.$$

As the procedure to obtain the value of the measure of circularity (c_2) is very complex and quite difficult to determine exactly, we can only show the minimum and the maximum limits by using the relationship $s_2 < c_2 < b_2$. In the present case, therefore, $0.68 < c_2 < 0.81$.

6.8 ILLUSTRATION OF DYADIC MODEL FITTING: BAGHRA VILLAGE

We have chosen a small village network for illustration of the computations involved in fitting dyadic models of the type described in Sections 3.6 and 4.2 in Chapters 3 and 4, respectively.

An extensive survey was conducted in the village of Baghra near Giridih, Jharkhand, India, in 2002. The survey had multiple purposes and covered, among other items of enquiry, information on "financial help" received from HHs in the village during the 12-month reference period from 2001–2002 until the date of the survey. It resulted in a social network covering a total of 104 HHs. A substantial number of these HHs were "isolates" scattered over four main communities—Muslim, Koiri, Gowala, and Turi—and these communities collectively covered more than 90% of the HHs. The network is exhibited in Figure 6.1. We addressed up the study of modeling the dyadic relations among the HHs in the communities separately. For this, again we deleted the isolates in each community. Thus, effectively, we are left with 14 Muslim HHs, 36 Koiri HHs, 12 Gowala HHs, and 20 Turi HHs.

For each of the communities listed above, we examined the dyadic relational models based on W arrays. For this, we needed to adhere to a "grouping" mechanism, and we used two criteria: HHs (small family/large family) and occupation (primarily agriculture/nonagriculture). Thus, for each community, we have fitted dyadic interaction models for data in the form of W arrays resulting from both the grouping criteria. The results are given in Table 6.23 for all communities.

In the same spirit, we also examined the dyadic relational models based on V arrays. For this, there is no need for grouping. The results are given in Table 6.24.

For the V array, we have also tested the hypotheses about common θ and $(a\beta)$.

First, we test the common θ parameter

$$H_0 : \theta_M = \theta_K = \theta_G = \theta_r.$$

The chi-square statistic has a value of 31.018 with 3 degrees of freedom. We reject H_{04} since $31.018 > \chi^2_{0.05}(3) = 7.815$. Thus, there is no significant common θ parameter.

Next, we test the common $(a\beta)$ parameter

$$H_0 : (a\beta)_M = (a\beta)_K = (a\beta)_G = (a\beta)_r.$$

The chi-square statistic has a value of 5.9569 with 3 degrees of freedom. We accept H_{05} since $5.9569 < \chi^2_{0.05}(3) = 7.815$, and the estimated common $(a\beta)$ parameter is 1.9689.

Although the movement parameters of all four communities have a difference, there is a common reciprocal parameter of all four communities.

For the W array, we have also tested the hypotheses of significance of the a and β parameters—those whose estimates are approximately 0.10 or smaller in absolute value. The tests were based on the computation of the maximum likelihood under the original model and then under the restricted mode, assuming the insignificance of the parameter(s) being tested. Then the difference of the two log-likelihoods is asymptotically chi-square with 1 degree of freedom for each parameter being tested.

The results indicate the following:

(a) For the Muslim community, $a = 0$ for both HHs and occupation, and furthermore, $\beta = 0$ for occupation only; chi-square values are 0.135, 0.019, and 0.019, respectively.

(b) For the Koiri community, $a = 0$ for HHs; chi-square value is 0.1751.

(c) For the Gowala community, $\beta = 0$ for both HHs and occupation; chi-square values are 0.1178 and 0.2183, respectively.

(d) For the Turi community, $a = 0$ for HHs; chi-square value is 0.001.

After deleting the insignificant model parameters, all others have been estimated using the method of maximum likelihood once more. The results are given in Table 6.25.

Remark 1. It is evident from the computations in Tables 6.24 and 6.25 that we can also address the problem of simultaneous testing of significance of a and β with respect to each of the communities. It is a routine task to compute the log-likelihood values under the usual (full) model and under the submodel when the null hypothesis (of insignificance of the parameters) is assumed to be true.

In a recent paper (Em-ot, Tiensuwan, & Sinha, 2008), we addressed the problem of modeling the dyadic relational network when the two classifications are crossed with each other, thus resulting in four crossed categories with respect to HH size and occupation (with two options for each). The reader is referred to the article for further details.

We conclude this section with the tables (Tables 6.1–6.25) presented serially with reference to the text in various sections and subsections.

Table 6.1   Values of Parameters s, p, and q of Social Networks of the Muslim Community of the Villages: Observed and Simulated Values Under Model II.2, Given n and m

Panel I: s = number of reciprocally tied pairs of vertices

Village	N[a]	Observed Values (0)	Simulated Values $E(s)$	$\sigma(s)$	Standard Values $(0 - E(s))/\sigma_s$	Theoretical Values[b] $E(s)$	σ_s
Baghra	14	4	1.94	1.20	1.7240	1.94	1.20
Harsingraidih	34	8	0.94	0.92	7.7133	0.92	0.92
Chitmadih	53	14	0.79	0.86	15.2940	0.80	0.86
Mahacho	10	4	1.55	1.02	2.4011	1.53	1.02
Maladanga	22	2	0.08	0.27	7.0878	0.08	0.27
Raspur	9	0	0.15	0.36	−0.4008	0.12	0.34

Panel II: p = number of strong components

Village	N[a]	Observed Values(0)	Simulated Value $E(p)$	$\sigma(p)$	Standard Values $(0 - E(p))/\sigma_p$
Baghra	14	2	5.73	2.46	−1.5208
Harsingraidih	34	26	26.35	4.87	−0.0719
Chitmadih	53	38	44.51	6.07	−1.0733
Mahacho	10	4	5.05	2.03	−0.5185
Maladanga	22	20	21.88	0.42	−4.4770
Raspur	9	9	8.80	0.49	0.4092

Panel III: q = number of weak components

Village	N[a]	Observed Values (0)	Simulated Values $E(q)$	$\sigma(q)$	Standard Values $(0 - E(q))/\sigma_q$
Baghra	14	1	1.16	0.38	−0.4139
Harsingraidih	34	8	3.19	1.25	3.8377
Chitmadih	53	12	5.38	1.70	3.8845
Mahacho	10	1	1.15	0.37	−0.4124
Maladanga	22	15	13.17	0.39	4.6898
Raspur	9	4	4.28	0.47	−0.5845

a. Number of Muslim HHs in a village.

b. Not shown for p and q due to complexities in derivation and computation.

Table 6.2   Graph-Theoretic Measures

Graph-Theoretic Measures	Two "Near" Villages Combined		Two "Far" Villages Combined	
	1971–1972	1997–1998	1971–1972	1997–1998
$D_0(\%)$	1.40	0.35	1.89	0.72
s_0(numbers)	461	56	87	25
$s_3(\%)$	82.76	10.67	24.23	6.56
Isolates	176	116	8	8
C_s	33.51	13.10	58.43	13.43
C_w	48.71	82.24	96.25	95.32
F_w	51.29	17.76	3.73	4.48
h	15.21	69.13	37.83	82.09

Note: D_0 = density of within-village ties (i.e., $m/n(n-1)$, with m = the number of ties and n = the number of HHs); s_0 = number of reciprocal (symmetric) ties; s_3 = standardized measure of reciprocity; C_s = strong connectedness (i.e., $(n-p)/(n-1)$); C_w = weak connectedness (i.e., $(n-q)/(n-1)$); F_w = weak fragmentation (i.e., $(q-1)/(n-1)$); h = hierarchy (i.e., $(p-q)/(n-1)$).

Table 6.3   Graph-Theoretic Measures of "Near" Villages

Graph-Theoretic Measures	Kabilpur		Maladanga	
	1971–1972	1997–1998	1971–1972	1997–1998
$D_0(\%)$	1.53	0.39	1.07	0.28
s_0(numbers)	386	45	75	11
$s_3(\%)$	88.74	12.30	61.98	6.88
Isolates	93	41	83	76
C_s	37.82	20.88	26.67	3.24
C_w	52.94	89.79	42.00	72.65
F_w	47.06	10.21	58.00	27.35
h	15.13	68.68	15.33	6.41

Table 6.4   Graph-Theoretic Measures of "Far" Villages

Graph-Theoretic Measures	Raspur		Baidyanathpur	
	1971–1972	1997–1998	1971–1972	1997–1998
$D_0(\%)$	3.54	1.00	1.32	0.63
s_0(numbers)	57	10	30	18
$s_3(\%)$	32.20	6.67	16.43	6.50

Table 6.4 (Continued)

Graph-Theoretic Measures	Raspur		Baidyanathpur	
	1971–1972	*1997–1998*	*1971–1972*	*1997–1998*
Isolates	2	7	6	1
C_s	74.26	8.67	48.80	16.22
C_w	97.03	95.95	95.78	95.27
F_w	2.97	4.05	4.22	4.73
h	22.77	87.28	46.99	79.05

Table 6.5 Graph-Theoretic Measures: Bagdi Community of a "Near" and a "Far" Village

Graph-Theoretic Measures	Kabilpur		Baidyanathpur	
	1971–1972	*1997–1998*	*1971–1972*	*1997–1998*
$D_0(\%)$	0.40	0.30	9.94	4.95
s_0(numbers)	20	5	0	0
$s_3(\%)$	82.61	5.56	0.00	0.00
Isolates	73	83	2	0
C_s	14.02	2.29	0.00	4.55
C_w	20.56	55.50	38.89	40.91
F_w	79.44	44.50	61.11	59.09
h	6.54	53.21	38.89	36.36

Table 6.6 Graph-Theoretic Measures: Santal Community of a "Near" and a "Far" Village

Graph-Theoretic Measures	Kabilpur		Baidyanathpur	
	1971–1972	*1997–1998*	*1971–1972*	*1997–1998*
$D_0(\%)$	2.52	0.71	4.73	3.57
s_0(numbers)	30	3	2	4
$s_3(\%)$	86.11	11.54	10.53	16.67
Isolates	27	34	1	0
C_s	32.08	5.88	13.33	8.89
C_w	39.62	49.41	86.67	80.00
F_w	60.38	50.59	13.33	20.00
h	7.55	43.53	73.33	71.11

Table 6.7   Graph-Theoretic Measures: Rural Poor Category of a "Near" and a "Far" Village

Graph-Theoretic Measures	Kabilpur		Baidyanathpur	
	1971–1972	1997–1998	1971–1972	1997–1998
$D_0(\%)$	1.03	0.30	0.95	0.42
s_0(numbers)	171	34	3	10
$s_3(\%)$	90.48	16.35	12.00	10.42
Isolates	96	87	20	57
C_s	30.89	13.14	4.17	5.16
C_w	37.70	72.92	56.94	69.01
F_w	62.30	27.08	43.06	30.99
h	6.81	59.79	52.78	63.85

Note: The *rural poor* category of occupations includes agricultural laborers, nonagricultural and other laborers, factory laborers, sharecroppers, and marginal and small farmers.

Table 6.8   Graph-Theoretic Measures: 1971–1972 vs. 1997–1998

Graph-Theoretic Measures	1971–1972		1997–1998	
	Sadgopes of Kabilpur	Rajputs of Baidyanathpur	Sadgopes of Kabilpur	Rajputs of Baidyanathpur
$D_0(\%)$	26.19	4.34	2.15	1.74
s_0(numbers)	227	5	24	7
$s_3(\%)$	96.19	11.63	24.49	10.00
Isolates	5	3	5	1
C_s	80.99	27.27	44.21	14.29
C_w	85.71	90.91	92.63	93.41
F_w	14.29	9.09	7.37	6.59
h	4.76	63.64	48.42	79.12

Table 6.9   Computations Based on the Network for the Muslim Community of Harsingraidih (Hd) Village Involving 34 HHs

Summary Statistics	s_3	cns	cnw	reachs	hierarchy
Mean	4.0449	0.2339	0.9365	30.2035	0.7019
Standard error	0.1280	0.0048	0.0012	0.3161	0.0051
Median	4.35	0.21	0.94	28.46	0.73
Mode	4.35	0.24	0.94	33.48	0.76

Table 6.9 (Continued)

Summary Statistics	s_3	cns	cnw	reachs	hierarchy
Standard deviation	4.0464	0.1506	0.0374	9.9971	0.1621
Kurtosis	1.0028	−0.3979	0.0278	0.2001	−0.2866
Skewness	1.0043	0.4173	−0.4288	0.7630	−0.4395
Range	21.74	0.73	0.21	54.41	0.85
Minimum	0	0	0.79	11.94	0.15
Maximum	21.74	0.73	1	66.35	1
Sum	4,044.88	233.91	936.49	30,203.47	701.92
Count	1,000	1,000	1,000	1,000	1,000

Variance-Covariance Terms	s_3	cns	cnw	reachs	hier
s_3	16.3737	–	–	–	–
cns	0.0854	0.0227	–	–	–
cnw	−0.0190	−0.0009	0.0014	–	–
reachs	0.1897	1.3570	−0.0403	99.9422	–
hier	−0.1049	−0.0238	0.0024	−1.4058	0.0263

Table 6.10   Computations Based on the Network for the Muslim Community of Baghra (Bg) Village Involving 14 HHs

Summary Statistics	s_3	cns	cnw	reachs	hierarchy
Mean	15.5369	0.6452	0.9874	70.1659	0.3427
Standard error	0.2906	0.0060	0.0010	0.4346	0.0061
Median	15.38	0.69	1	70.41	0.31
Mode	15.38	0.77	1	87.24	0.23
Standard deviation	9.1901	0.1888	0.0300	13.7429	0.1924
Kurtosis	−0.0741	0.2620	3.0050	−0.5891	0.2914
Skewness	0.4242	−0.6694	−2.0959	−0.1443	0.7002
Range	46.15	1	0.15	67.35	1
Minimum	0	0	0.85	32.65	0
Maximum	46.15	1	1	100	1
Sum	15,536.92	645.17	987.41	70,165.9	342.67
Count	1,000	1,000	1,000	1,000	1,000

Variance-Covariance Terms	s_3	cns	cnw	reachs	hier
s_3	84.4582	–	–	–	–
cns	0.1534	0.0356	–	–	–
cnw	−0.0192	−0.0003	0.0009	–	–
reachs	1.8197	2.4584	0.0383	188.8668	–
hier	−0.1715	−0.0359	0.0017	−2.4197	0.0370

Table 6.11   Computations Based on the Network for the Muslim Community of Chitamandi (Cd) Village Involving 53 HHs

Summary Statistics	s_3	cns	cnw	reachs	hierarchy
Mean	2.4088	0.1611	0.9131	21.1987	0.7547
Standard error	0.0869	0.0037	0.0010	0.2362	0.0041
Median	3.03	0.13	0.92	19.88	0.77
Mode	0	0	0.92	16.02	0.85
Standard deviation	2.7468	0.1181	0.0322	7.4698	0.1297
Kurtosis	1.6182	−0.4222	−0.1651	0.5002	−0.5072
Skewness	1.2232	0.5636	−0.0037	0.8180	−0.5105
Range	15.15	0.56	0.19	44.78	0.63
Minimum	0	0	0.81	7.8	0.37
Maximum	15.15	0.56	1	52.58	1
Sum	2,408.85	161.08	913.09	21,198.71	754.73
Count	1,000	1,000	1,000	1,000	1,000

Variance-Covariance Terms	s_3	cns	cnw	reachs	hier
s_3	7.5448	–	–	–	–
cns	0.0408	0.0139	–	–	–
cnw	−0.0085	−0.0009	0.0010	–	–
reachs	0.3979	0.7692	−0.0468	55.7977	–
hier	−0.0487	−0.0148	0.0019	−0.8175	0.0168

Table 6.12   Computations Based on the Network for the Muslim Community of Mahacho (Mh) Village Involving 10 HHs

Summary Statistics	s_3	cns	cnw	reachs	hierarchy
Mean	19.1875	0.5583	0.9853	66.3480	0.4268
Standard error	0.4019	0.0071	0.0012	0.4478	0.0073
Median	12.5	0.56	1	67	0.44
Mode	12.5	0.67	1	91	0.33
Standard deviation	12.7095	0.2248	0.0384	14.1621	0.2311
Kurtosis	−0.2740	−0.3986	4.3217	−0.6455	−0.4319
Skewness	0.3285	−0.4316	−2.3615	0.1289	0.4243
Range	62.5	1	0.22	64	1
Minimum	0	0	0.78	36	0
Maximum	62.5	1	1	100	1
Sum	19,187.5	558.32	985.26	66,348	426.77
Count	1,000	1,000	1,000	1,000	1,000

Table 6.12 (Continued)

Variance-Covariance Terms	s_3	cns	cnw	reachs	hier
s_3	161.5326	–	–	–	–
cns	0.3597	0.0505	–	–	–
cnw	–0.0692	–0.0007	0.0015	–	–
reachs	–0.9532	2.9356	0.0599	200.5655	–
hier	–0.4296	–0.0512	0.0022	–2.8733	0.0534

Table 6.13   Computations Based on the Network for the Muslim Community of Raspur (Rp) Village Involving 9 HHs

Summary Statistics	s_3	cns	cnw	reachs	hierarchy
Mean	6.85	0.0240	0.5858	20.2414	0.5617
Standard error	0.5531	0.0019	0.0018	0.0789	0.0034
Median	0	0	0.62	19.75	0.62
Mode	0	0	0.62	18.52	0.62
Standard deviation	17.4895	0.0593	0.0576	2.4942	0.1076
Kurtosis	3.5947	7.8278	0.5117	1.7010	2.5768
Skewness	2.2543	2.7174	–1.3038	1.2840	–1.8164
Range	100	0.38	0.24	13.58	0.5
Minimum	0	0	0.38	17.28	0.12
Maximum	100	0.38	0.62	30.86	0.62
Sum	6,850	23.98	585.8	20,241.45	561.69
Count	1,000	1,000	1,000	1,000	1,000

Variance-Covariance Terms	s_3	cns	cnw	reachs	hier
s_3	305.8834	–	–	–	–
cns	0.6909	0.0035	–	–	–
cnw	–0.6664	–0.0023	0.0033	–	–
reachs	–4.4624	0.0245	0.0111	6.2210	–
hier	–1.3629	–0.0059	0.0057	–0.0133	0.0116

Table 6.14   Computations Based on the Network for the Muslim Community of Maladanga (Md) Village Involving 22 HHs

Summary Statistics	s_3	cns	cnw	reachs	hierarchy
Mean	1.975	0.0057	0.4219	7.2785	0.4164
Standard error	0.2133	0.0006	0.0006	0.0226	0.0011

(Continued)

Table 6.14 (Continued)

Summary Statistics	s_3	cns	cnw	reachs	hierarchy
Median	0	0	0.43	7.02	0.43
Mode	0	0	0.43	6.82	0.43
Standard deviation	6.7468	0.019	0.0190	0.7153	0.0343
Kurtosis	7.7889	18.0072	3.3213	6.9921	5.9658
Skewness	3.1262	3.8507	−2.1160	2.1259	−2.5436
Range	25	0.190.1	5.17	0.24	
Minimum	0	0	0.33	6.4	0.19
Maximum	25	0.19	0.43	11.57	0.43
Sum	1,975	5.74	421.95	7,278.5	416.38
Count	1,000	1,000	1,000	1,000	1,000

Variance-Covariance Terms	s_3	cns	cnw	reachs	hier
s_3	45.5199	–	–	–	–
cns	0.0875	0.0004	–	–	–
cnw	−0.0842	−0.0002	0.0004	–	–
reachs	−0.0846	0.0023	−0.0012	0.5117	–
hier	−0.1748	−0.0006	0.0006	−0.0033	0.0012

Table 6.15 Computations Based on the Network for the Muslim Community of Maladanga (Md) Village Involving 22 HHs

Summary Statistics	s_3	cns	cnw	reachs	hierarchy
Mean	1.975	0.0057	0.4219	7.2785	0.4164
Standard error	0.2133	0.0006	0.0006	0.0226	0.0011
Median	0	0	0.43	7.02	0.43
Mode	0	0	0.43	6.82	0.43

Table 6.16 Computation of D^2: Estimated Coefficients (b_{ij}s)

Variables	x_1	x_2	x_3	x_4	x_5
x_1	2.0382	–	–	–	–
x_2	0.0193	0.0561	–	–	–
x_3	−0.0118	0.0014	0.0097	–	–
x_4	0.0422	3.7514	−0.5285	0.9882	–
x_5	−0.0312	−0.0547	0.0096	−0.0003	0.0023

Table 6.17   Computation of D^2: Relevant Data and Graph-Theoretic Measures

Villages	n	m	s_0	p	q	s_3	$cn(s)$	$cn(w)$	$reach(s)$	$hier$
Hd	34	46	8	26	8	34.78	24.24	78.79	9.52	54.55
Bg	14	27	4	2	1	30.77	92.31	100.00	93.37	7.69
Cd	53	67	14	38	12	42.42	28.85	78.85	7.58	50.00
Mh	10	17	4	4	1	50.00	66.67	100.00	62.00	33.33
Rp	9	5	0	9	4	0.00	0.00	62.50	17.28	62.50
Md	22	9	2	20	15	50.00	9.52	33.33	7.44	23.81

Table 6.18   Computation of D^2: Computation of an Uncorrelated Standardized Set of Variable Values

Villages	$x_1(s_3)$	$x_2(cn(s))$	$x_3(cn(w))$	$x_4(reach(s))$	$x_5(hier)$
Hd	0.3478	0.2424	0.7879	0.0952	0.5455
Bg	0.3077	0.9231	1.0000	0.9337	0.0769
Cd	0.4242	0.2885	0.7885	0.0758	0.5000
Mh	0.5000	0.6667	1.0000	0.6200	0.3333
Rp	0.0000	0.0000	0.6250	0.1728	0.6250
Md	0.5000	0.0952	0.3333	0.0744	0.2381

Table 6.19   Computation of D^2: Equations for Transformation of Observed Variables (xs) to Uncorrelated Standardized Variables (ys)

ys	Expressions in Terms of xs
y_1	x_1/b_{11}
y_2	$x_2/b_{22} - (b_{21}/b_{22})y_1$
y_3	$x_3/b_{33} - (b_{32}/b_{33})y_2 - (b_{31}/b_{33})y_1$
y_4	$x_4/b_{44} - (b_{43}/b_{44})y_3 - (b_{42}/b_{44})y_2 - (b_{41}/b_{44})y_1$
y_5	$x_5/b_{55} - (b_{54}/b_{55})y_4 - (b_{53}/b_{55})y_3 - (b_{52}/b_{55})y_2 - (b_{51}/b_{55})y_1$

Table 6.20   Computation of D^2: Values of Transformed Variables (ys)

Villages	y_1	y_2	y_3	y_4	y_5
Hd	17.0641	−1.5558	101.9285	70.7763	5.3631
Bg	15.0967	11.4481	118.8023	115.1798	1.6641
Cd	20.5034	−1.9185	106.2168	72.6375	5.6790
Mh	23.0890	−4.3226	131.4408	150.4297	−192.2185
Rp	0.0000	0.0000	64.2475	51.8509	9.4424
Md	21.8036	1.6970	60.4845	34.3631	179.1241

Table 6.21a   Values of D^2 Based on the First Three Variables

Villages	Hd	Bg	Cd	Mh	Rp	Md
Hd	–	–	–	–	–	–
Bg	457.70	–	–	–	–	–
Cd	30.35	337.06	–	–	–	–
Mh	914.93	472.32	648.72	–	–	–
Rp	1,713.46	3,335.20	2,185.49	5,066.73	–	–
Md	1,750.65	3,541.01	2,106.21	5,072.68	492.44	–

Table 6.21b   Values of D^2 Based on Five Variables

Villages	Hd	Bg	Cd	Mh	Rp	Md
Hd	–	–	–	–	–	–
Bg	2,443.05	–	–	–	–	–
Cd	33.91	2,192.26	–	–	–	–
Mh	46,298.08	39,305.34	45,857.12	–	–	–
Rp	2,088.27	7,406.25	2,631.74	55,451.62	–	–
Md	33,269.45	41,564.42	33,641.32	156,439.47	29,590.10	–

Table 6.22   International Trade in Manufactured Goods, in Millions of U.S. Dollars (FOB), in 1970

From	CPE	USA	RDM	DLA	DME	DAO	DAF	Row Total	Min. of Row Total and Col. Total
(1)	(2)	(3)	(4)	(5)	(6)	(7)	(8)	(9)	(10)
CPE	–	103 (103)	2,135 (2,135)	219 (16)	246 (31)	414 (309)	295 (185)	3,412 (2,779)	3,412
USA	106	–	5,300 (5,300)	1,357 (659)	115 (12)	584 (584)	148 (22)	7,610 (6,577)	7,610
RDM	2,929	10,539	–	2,166 (1,225)	1,260 (87)	3,513 (2,029)	2,445 (1,732)	22,852 (5,073)	12,508

Table 6.22 (Continued)

From	CPE	USA	RDM	DLA	DME	DAO	DAF	Row Total	Min. of Row Total and Col. Total
(1)	(2)	(3)	(4)	(5)	(6)	(7)	(8)	(9)	(10)
DLA	16	659	1,225	–	1 (1)	12 (12)	17 (13)	1,930 (26)	1,930
DME	31	12	87	2	–	4 (4)	27 (20)	163 (24)	163
DAO	309	1,949	2,029	95	171	–	265 (40)	4,818 (40)	4,567
DAF	185	22	1,732	13	20	40	–	2,012 (–)	2,012
Column total	3,576	13,284	12,508	3,852	1,813	4,567	3,197	42,797 (14,519)	32,202

Note: Figures in parentheses state the pairwise minimum of the two values, of export from one to another and of import to the former from the latter.

Table 6.23   Parameter Estimates and Their Standard Error (SE) of a Fitted Model for W Array Data

	$\hat{\theta}$ (SE)	$(\hat{a\beta})$ (SE)	$\hat{a}$ (SE)	$\hat{\beta}$ (SE)
Muslim: HH size[a]	−1.9623 (0.26)	1.0907 (0.69)	0.0561 (0.21)	−0.1376 (0.21)
Muslim: occupation[b]	−1.9501	1.0687	−0.0221	−0.0221
Koiri: size[c]	−3.6596 (0.20)	2.8806 (0.57)	−0.0065 (0.19)	−0.1733 (0.19)
Koiri: occupation[d]	−3.7442 (0.22)	2.8782 (0.59)	−0.1740 (0.27) −0.1050 (0.23)	0.6205 (0.25) −0.5187 (0.25)

(Continued)

Table 6.23 (Continued)

	$\hat{\theta}$ (SE)	$(\hat{a\beta})$ (SE)	$\hat{a}$ (SE)	$\hat{\beta}$ (SE)
Gowala: HH size[e]	−2.2654 (0.38)	0.4889 (1.23)	−0.5634 (0.38)	−0.1199 (0.35)
Gowala: occupation[f]	−2.2256 (0.37)	0.6472 (1.21)	0.1878 (0.22)	−0.0854 (0.18)
Turi: HH size[g]	−2.5866 (0.28)	1.6199 (0.79)	0.0169 (0.23)	−0.2242 (0.23)
Turi: occupation[h]	−2.6977 (0.29)	1.8608 (0.80)	−0.1531 (0.21)	0.2014 (0.22)

a. Small family size ≤ 5 vs. large family size ≥ 6.
b. Carrying coal vs. miscellaneous others.
c. Small family size ≤ 6 vs. large family size ≥ 7.
d. Three categories of occupation: agricultural laborer/daily laborer vs. factory laborer/cloth mill worker–cum–laborer/water carrier/coal carrier/mason/helper vs. all others combined.
e. Small family size ≤ 6 vs. large family size ≥ 7.
f. Agricultural laborer vs. rest.
g. Small family size ≤ 4 vs. large family size ≥ 5.
h. Rickshaw puller vs. rest.

Table 6.24   Parameter Estimates and Their Standard Error (SE) of Fitted Model for V Array Data

	$\hat{\theta}$ (SE)	$(\hat{a\beta})$ (SE)
Muslim	−2.0369 (0.26)	1.2261 (0.69)
Koiri	−3.6829 (0.21)	2.949 (0.57)
Gowala	−2.1751 (0.35)	0.5656 (1.19)
Turi	−2.689 (0.28)	1.843 (0.79)

Table 6.25   Parameter Estimates and Their Standard Error (SE) of Fitted Model for W Array Data After Deletion of Insignificant Parameters

	$\hat{\theta}$ (SE)	$\widehat{(a\beta)}$ (SE)	$\hat{a}$ (SE)	$\hat{\beta}$ (SE)
Muslim: HH size	−1.9568 (0.26)	1.0733 (0.69)	–	−0.1316
Muslim: occupation	−1.9683 (0.20)	1.1034 (0.69)	–	–
Koiri: HH size	−3.6606 (0.20)	2.8844 (0.57)	–	−0.1733 (0.19)
Koiri: occupation	−3.7442 (0.22)	2.8782 (0.59)	−0.1740 (0.27)	0.6205 (0.25)
	–	–	−0.1050 (0.23)	−0.5187 (0.25)
Gowala: HH size	−2.2713 (0.38)	0.5833 (1.19)	−0.55567 (0.38)	–
Gowala: occupation	−2.2087 (0.36)	0.5694 (1.19)	0.1898 (0.22)	–
Turi: HH size	−2.6857 (0.29)	1.8016 (0.79)	–	−0.2213 (0.24)
Turi: occupation	−2.6977 (0.29)	1.8608 (0.80)	−0.1531 (0.21)	0.2014 (0.22)

REFERENCES

Adhikari, B. P. (1960). Construction of socio-economic models for planning. *Eastern Anthropologist*, pp. 84–94.

Ahmed, R. (1988). *The Bengali Muslims 1871–1906: A quest for identity* (2nd ed.). Delhi, India: Oxford University Press.

Albert, A., & Barabasi, A. L. (2002). Statistical mechanics of complex networks. *Review of Modern Physics, 17*, 47–97.

Bandyopadhyay, S. (1997). Caste 'lost' and caste 'regained': Some aspects of sociology of empirical research on village India. In M. N. Srinivas, S. Seshaiya, & Parthasarathy (Eds.), *Dimensions of social change in India* (pp. 115–134). Bombay, India: Allied Publishers.

Bandyopadhyay, S. (2006). A note on Mahalanobis distance (or D^2 statistic). *Journal of the Asiatic Society, 48*, 78–132.

Bandyopadhyay, S., & von Eschen, D. (1988). Villager failure to cooperate: Some evidence. In D. W. Attwood & B. S. Baviskar (Eds.), *Who shares cooperatives and rural development?* (pp. 112–145). Oxford, UK: Oxford University Press.

Bandyopadhyay, S., & von Eschen, D. (1995). Electoral communism and destruction of cooperation in West Bengal. In B. S. Baviskar & D. W. Attwood (Eds.), *Finding the middle path* (pp. 293–322). Boulder, CO: Westview.

Barabasi, A. L., & Bonabeau, E. (2003). Scale-free networks. *Scientific American, 288*(5), 60–69.

Beshers, J. M., & Laumann, E. O. (1967). Social distances: A network approach. *American Sociological Review, 32,* 225–238.

Beteille, A. (1971). *Caste, class, and power changing patterns of stratification in a Tanjore village.* Berkeley: University of California Press.

Dawson, R. E. (1962). Simulation in the social sciences. In H. Guetzkow (Ed.), *Simulation in social sciences readings* (pp. 1–15). Englewood Cliffs, NJ: Prentice Hall.

Em-ot, P., Tiensuwan, M., & Sinha, B. K. (2008). Some aspects of stochastic modeling of dyadic relations in social networks: Theory and applications. *Journal of Statistical Theory and Applications, 7,* 303–322.

Homans, G. C. (1961). *Social behaviour: Its elementary forms.* London: Routledge & Kegan Paul.

Jana, R. N., Bandyopadhyay, S., & Choudhuri, A. (2007, February). *Application of SNA in reciprocity among farmers.* Paper presented at the International Conference on Social Network Analysis: Theory, Methods and Applications, ISI, Kolkata, India.

Katz, A. H. (1981). Self-help and mutual aid: An emerging social movement? *Annual Review of Sociology, 7,* 129–155.

Knoke, D., & Kuklinsky, J. H. (1982). *Network analysis.* Beverly Hills, CA: Sage.

Mahalanobis, P. C. (1930). On tests and measures of group divergence. *Journal of the Asiatic Society of Bengal, 26,* 541–588.

Mahalanobis, P. C. (1936). On the generalized distance in statistics. *Proceedings of the National Institute of Sciences of India, 2,* 49–55.

Majumdar, D. N., & Rao, C. R. (1960). *Race elements in Bengal: A quantitative study.* Calcutta, India: Asia Publishing House, Statistical Publishing Society.

Michie, J. (Ed.). (2001). *Encyclopedia of social sciences: A readers guide.* London: Dearborn.

Mitchell, J. (1969). The concept and use of social networks. In J. Mitchell (Ed.), *Social networks in urban situations.* Manchester, UK: Manchester University Press.

Mukherjee, R., & Bandyopadhyay, S. (1965). Social research and Mahalanobis's D^2. In C. R. Rao (Ed.), *Contributions to statistics (presented to Professor P C Mahalanobis on the occasion of his 70th birthday)* (pp. 259–282). Oxford, UK: Pergamon.

Rao, A R., & Bandyopadhyay, S. (1987). Measures of reciprocity in a social network. *Sankhyā Series A, 49,* 141–188.

Rao, C. R., & Slater, P. (1949). Multivariate analysis applied to differences between neurotic groups. *British Journal of Psychology, 2,* 17–29.

Robinson, W. S. (1951). The logical structure of analytic induction. *American Sociological Review, 16*(6), 112–118.

Sanyal, H. (1981). *Social mobility in Bengal.* Calcutta, India: Papyrus.

Stone, R. (1960). Comparison of the economic structure of the regions on the concept of distance. *Journal of Regional Science, 2*(2), 1–20.

United Nations. (1984). *International trade: Statistics year book: Vol. I. Trade by country.* New York: Author.

United Nations. (n.d.). *The UN standard country code annex II country classification for international trade statistics, statistical papers* (Series M. No. 49). New York: Author.

United Nations, Department of Economic and Social Affairs, Statistical Office. (1986). *Standard international trade classification: Revision 3* (Series M, No. 34/Rev. 3). New York: Author.

Wasserman, S., & Faust, K. (1994). *Social network analysis: Methods and applications.* Cambridge, UK: Cambridge University Press.

Wellman, B. (Ed.). (1997). *Networks in the global village.* Boulder, CO: Westview.

Wellman, B., & Berkowitz, S. D. (Eds.). (1988). *Social structures: A network approach.* Cambridge, UK: Cambridge University Press.

Wrong, D. H. (1988). *Power, its forms, bases and uses.* Chicago: University of Chicago Press.

Yin, R. K. (1994). *Case study research design and methods.* Thousand Oaks, CA: Sage.

SEVEN

SAMPLING AND INFERENCE
IN A SOCIAL NETWORK

————◆•◆•◆————

7.1 INTRODUCTION

In a social network, the subject matter of study primarily centers on under-standing the dyadic relations among pairs of units—namely, the households (HHs) with respect to some specific features of the population that are char-acterized by dyads. Thus, HH-wise, "isolated singleton features" such as HH size, HH income, and HH expenditure and the like are not directly relevant under the purview of social network study.

For large villages (i.e., villages involving a large number of HHs), col-lection of relevant and reliable dyadic data from all pairs of the HHs toward formation of a village network is costly and time-consuming, apart from the common problem of ending up with "missing" data involving dyads. There-fore, this kind of ambitious project may often lend itself to "incomplete" find-ings. An understanding of the global aspect of the network as a whole may thus be prohibitive. Instead, if we are interested in some specific descriptive features of the network (such as the average out-degree or average in-degree, the average reciprocity), sample survey techniques, adequately applied, may provide relevant information based on a sample of HHs suitably chosen and surveyed.

Sampling of population units and estimation of dyadic parameters in social networks is an extremely fascinating topic. This area of survey sampling research, although very much different from standard survey topics, has been thoroughly studied and documented in the literature. It is impressive indeed to note that several researchers have formulated general estimation problems involving dyads (and also triads) and applied random sampling techniques for proposing solutions to the problems. We will review some such results and present them in the right framework, after discussing the basic notions and results in considerable details.

Following works by Cochran (1977), Frank (1977a, 1977b, 1978), and Thompson (2006), we now intend to discuss some aspects of sampling and inference in a large network. In the language of sampling, we may refer to the HHs (or vertices in a digraph) as sampling units or simply as units. To illustrate this concept, let us think of a network having a total of N population units with an incidence matrix A (see Chapter 2, Section 2.2). We refer to this network as a *population network* and imagine a situation where it is *not* possible to enumerate the whole of it in terms of the out-degrees and in-degrees of all the units in the population. In such a situation, we may take recourse to a *sample*, comprising, say, n sample units, where $n < < N$. We assume that all the N units in the population network are *identifiable* and may be labeled as $1, 2, \ldots, N$. Therefore, the selection of a sample of n units should be a routine task. We may use *simple random sampling without replacement* procedure (abbreviated henceforth as the *srswor* procedure) and come up with a random sample of n units out of the total of N population units. According to this procedure, the units can be selected one by one at random and without replacement each time from the rest of the population units, or the units can be selected all at one time (e.g., see Cochran, 1977). Our presentation is at a basic level and involves specific parameters of the network. Complicated sampling methodologies are to be found in works by Goswami, Sengupta, and Sinha (1990) and Sinha (1997), among others.

In the case of "complete enumeration" of the population—that is, a 100% selection of the units (like HHs, in the context of a village)—we collect complete and accurate information regarding the flow of out-degrees and in-degrees associated with each unit. This, in turn, leads to the conceptualization, visualization, and construction of the incidence matrix A, mentioned above, in its totality. From this, in principle, the entire network can be drawn, and all graph-theoretic, sociological, and statistical measures can be ascertained. However, as mentioned above, more often than not, we may end up with rather discouraging scenarios involving missing or unreliable dyadic components, unless we are handling small-sized networks.

Furthermore, in the case of a large network, a 100% study may be extremely prohibitive, and one may wonder if any adequate sampling procedure can be recommended, at least for extracting information on some key features of the population network. In other words, more interestingly, we may ask if selection of a sample of units according to the above *srswor* method (or, for that matter, any other suitable method of sampling) would lead to any meaningful analysis of the "resulting sample network" so obtained. Naturally, we are referring to our exposure only to the selected units (such as the sampled HHs in a village network) and the "incomplete" nature of the network based on the selected units.

Once more, we reiterate that study of the global features of any large network is virtually impossible, as any attempt to conduct a comprehensive survey of such a population-based complete network may result in such inconveniences as handling a large amount of "missing" data. There are standard techniques for handling missing data in sample survey literature. However, we are in a specialized setup involving dyadic relations as our primary data for understanding the network.

While illustrating the notions and basic results of sampling and inference for network data, we have used the networks of the Mahacho village Muslim community (1971–1972) and Kabilpur village (1971–1972 and 1997–1998). We have also provided six small-sized Muslim community networks (including that of Mahacho village) for ready reference (see Diagrams 8–13 at the end of this book). Interested readers may use these networks while studying the concepts and computations.

We conclude this section with the following remark. General theory for sampling and inference is available for network sampling in the works of Frank (1978) and others. We have essentially used these results, but the computations have been carried out in different forms, following an alternative approach. The cases of $n = 2$ and $n = 3$ have been dealt with initially to introduce various notions and computations, and then the general case has been undertaken. It may be mentioned that the Horvitz-Thompson estimator (HTE), together with the general notion of unbiased estimators for linear and quadratic functions, is the basis for the results presented in this chapter. We have not made explicit use of the HTE as such. Further information can be found in the works of Frank (see Frank, 1977a, 1977b, for a description of the HTE and its use toward unbiased estimation; see also Hedayat & Sinha, 1991).

7.2 DATA STRUCTURE IN A RANDOM SAMPLE OF UNITS

What kind of data do we extract from the sample of selected units? At this stage, let us introduce some notations.

Let $s(n)$ denote a typical selected sample with n units. Before we proceed further, let us discuss the nature of *data* that can be "collected" from the selected units contained in the sample $s(n)$.

The following possibilities may be enumerated:

- **Data Type 1:** Data are in the form of a matrix of size $n \times N$, being a submatrix of the incidence matrix A, comprising the rows labeled $i_1, i_2, \ldots, i_n$, corresponding to the units $i_1, i_2, \ldots, i_n$ included in the selected sample $s(n)$.

- **Data Type 2:** Data are just the collection $d_{i_1}, d_{i_2}, \ldots, d_{i_n}$ of the out-degrees of the selected units. Note that the out-degrees correspond to the row totals in the submatrix of the incidence matrix referred to above.

- **Data Type 3:** Data are in the form of a matrix of size $n \times n$, being a submatrix of the incidence matrix A, comprising the rows *and* columns labeled $i_1, i_2, \ldots, i_n$. Note that this data set exclusively refers to the selected units only.

We now interpret the data sets given above one by one. Essentially, we collect data from the selected units only. In Data Type 1, we specifically ask for the out-degree set (i.e., flow of out-degree of each selected unit to all the remaining $N - 1$ population units). In Data Type 2, we only ask for the out-degree (i.e., the head count of the respective out-degree sets), without the details as to their identification (i.e., who they are). In Data Type 3, again we ask for the flow of out-degree (i.e., the out-degree set), *confining* only to the selected units. That means, we seek from each selected unit information on its flow of out-degree among the selected units *only*. This time, it is not enough to spell out the number; we also collect information on its identification.

Clearly, Data Type 1 will capture Data Type 2 (and, possibly, will provide more useful information), while Data Type 3 will provide the least information. It would be interesting to examine if there is any additional gain by Data Type 1 over what is achieved from Data Type 2. It seems quite plausible that detailed information in Data Type 1 would capture some information on the nature of the "interaction network" among the selected units, on one hand, and the complementary set of units (i.e., the rest of the units), on the other. Also, it is interesting to see what information, if any, can be achieved from Data Type 3.

It must be noted that based on a sample of selected units, it is not our aim to "reproduce" the entire network. That is virtually impossible. Instead, our objective is to focus on some specific parameters of the population network and seek information on such parameters, based on the sample network. In earlier chapters, we have discussed at length many such social network parameters, their graph-theoretic and statistical measures, their standardization, and so on. Two such population parameters (relating to the entire population network) will be considered here, and the central problem would be to draw a valid and reasonable inference on such parameters, based on the sample units and data from which they are derived. Technically, this is referred to as statistical inference problem, and there is a sound theory for such inference in the standard survey sampling methodology literature (see Cochran, 1977).

At this point, let us clarify that there is a fundamental difference between survey sampling problems addressed in the literature and the one we are discussing here. In sample surveys, we extract information (on study variables and also on auxiliary variables) from the individual sampling units themselves (without any regard to other sampling units). In the case of studying a network, since our primary focus is on the dyadic relationships, extracting a sample of units will shatter the pattern of dyadic relations among those sampled and those not sampled. This calls for different techniques while dealing with such sample networks. Frank (1977a, 1977b, 1978) and others in a series of articles have systematically studied these sampling and inference problems involved in network sampling.

Our discussion here is based on the studies available in the literature, and to start with, we keep it at a basic level for introducing the notions of estimate/estimator, unbiasedness, mean squared error (MSE), standard error (SE), and so on. General theory for estimation of dyadic-relational parameters is well documented, and we present only specific formulae based on the concept of random sampling, as discussed earlier.

7.3 INFERENCE PROCEDURE

The population parameters to be considered are the (a) average out-degree (which is the same as the average in-degree) and (b) average reciprocity. We will now focus on the technicalities and explain concepts such as unbiasedness of an estimator and its standard error as we proceed.

7.3.1 Estimation of Average Out-Degree Based on Data Type 1/2

We now focus on the problem of unbiased estimation of $\bar{D}$, the average out-degree in the entire population network, and discuss some results at length. We begin by discussing the case of random selection of $n = 2$ units from a small network and explain the concepts and computations. Denote the sample units so selected by the *srswor* approach by the pair (i, j). Depending on the type of information extracted from this pair of units, we will develop related methodology for data analysis, keeping the problem of estimating population average out-degree in mind. First, we address the problem based on Data Type 1 or Type 2. This means that we have been provided with the numbers d_i and d_j relating to the out-degrees of the selected units i and j, respectively. The only other information provided to us is the size of the population network (i.e., the value of N). We will now develop the estimation procedure.

Procedure I. Upon selection of the units i and j according to the *srswor* procedure, for estimating the population average out-degree, we propose the estimator

$$t_I(i, j) = [d_i + d_j]/2, \tag{7.1}$$

based on the available data.

Procedure I uses the realized d values from the two selected sample units, and the estimate of the overall $\bar{D}$ is its sample analog given above. For a general sample size n, the estimate is the sample average (or the sample mean, as is popularly termed) of the realized d values from the selected units. The sample mean is usually denoted by $\bar{d}$, without explicitly showing the units in the sample composition. As a numerically computed quantity, this is known as an estimate, while the form suggested above refers to an estimator. We will not distinguish between the two terms hereinafter. The estimator enjoys the property of unbiasedness. We illustrate this concept with an example of a small network and with a sample of size 2.

Example 1. Consider the network of a Muslim community in the village of Mahacho involving only 10 HHs. Individual d values are respectively given by $1, 1, 1, 1, 1, 4, 1, 2, 2, 3$, with a total of 17. Therefore, the average out-degree in the population as a whole is $\bar{D} = 17/10 = 1.7$. Also, the population variance of the d values is given by

$$S^2 = \frac{\sum (d_i - \bar{D})^2}{N-1} = \frac{\sum d_i^2 - N\bar{D}^2}{N-1}, \qquad (7.2)$$

which simplifies to 1.1222. Note that the divisor for the computation of variance is taken as $N - 1$, instead of N. This definition of variance is common to random sampling contexts (see Cochran, 1977).

We have been discussing the case of sampling of only 2 HHs from the above network for estimation of the average out-degree in the population network. Below we list *all possible* (i.e., 45) samples of 2 HHs (i.e., pairs of HHs), and for each sample, we compute and show the sample average of d values.

A listing of 45 samples and sample average out-degrees is as follows:

[(1, 2); 1]; [(1, 3); 1]; [(1, 4); 1]; [(1, 5); 1]; [(1, 6); 2.5]; [(1, 7); 1];
  [(1, 8); 1.5];
[(1, 9); 1.5]; [(1, 10); 2]; [(2, 3); 1]; [(2, 4); 1]; [(2, 5); 1]; [(2, 6); 2.5];
  [(2, 7); 1];
[(2, 8); 1.5]; [(2, 9); 1.5]; [(2, 10); 2]; [(3, 4); 1]; [(3, 5); 1];
  [(3, 6); 2.5]; [(3, 7); 1];
[(3, 8); 1.5]; [(3, 9); 1.5]; [(3, 10); 2]; [(4, 5); 1]; [(4, 6); 2.5];
  [(4, 7); 1]; [(4, 8); 1.5];
[(4, 9); 1.5]; [(4, 10); 2]; [(5, 6); 2.5]; [(5, 7); 1]; [(5, 8); 1.5];
  [(5, 9); 1.5]; [(5, 10); 2];
[(6, 7); 2.5]; [(6, 8); 3]; [(6, 9); 3]; [(6, 10); 3.5]; [(7, 8); 1.5];
  [(7, 9); 1.5]; [(7, 10); 2];
  [(8, 9); 2]; [(8, 10); 2.5]; [(9, 10); 2.5] $\qquad (7.3)$

It must be noted that under simple random sampling, we select only 2 HHs out of 10 using a random number table or otherwise. For this, the HHs are serially numbered 1 to 10, as we have done while displaying both the network and all possible sample average out-degrees. Suppose the selected HHs are 5 and 8. Then we are "exposed" only to the data arising out of these two HHs (i.e., we only know d_5 and d_8). This is the essence of Data Type 2 and the Procedure I. Once we obtain these two d values, we compute their average, which is 1.5 in this example, and we take this as an estimate of the population $\bar{D}$. This estimator is denoted by $t_1(5, 8) = [d_5 + d_8]/2$, and its value provides an estimate of 1.5.

We now explain the concept of unbiasedness. Note that although we end up with the HHs numbered 5 and 8 in our example, in principle, any one of the possible 45 pairs of HHs would show up as a result of random selection. Therefore, in principle, any one of the 45 possible sample averages would surface as an estimate of the population average. These sample averages are tabulated and shown above. It is readily seen that these sample averages are *not* the same at all. Naturally, then, the question of usefulness of a specific sample average (based on the out-degree values of an actually selected pair of units in a given context) arises. We need to justify this by exploiting some properties of the sample average out-degree.

Note that each pair of HHs has a 1/45 chance to show up in the sample, and hence each average value has a 1/45 chance for actual realization. The average of such averages works out as

$$\frac{1 + 1 + 1 + \cdots + 2 + 2.5 + 2.5}{45} = 76.5/45 = 1.7, \qquad (7.4)$$

which tallies with the population average of d values. It is in this sense that the sample mean of d values of the selected HHs is said to be an unbiased estimator of the population mean. This property ensures that, on average, the sample average essentially targets the population average.

We already mentioned above that there is a variation in the estimate (sample mean of 2 observed d values) across 45 possible sample pairs of HHs. The variance of these 45 sample estimates (i.e., sample averages) gives rise to the concept of "sampling variance" of an estimate, and its square root is known as the standard error of an estimate. Since we are using an estimate based on data arising out of a sample of selected units, it is highly desirable that the standard error of the resulting estimate is small or at least moderate.

That feature of data will speak about the utility of the sample estimate because otherwise, the estimate may turn out to be unstable and unreliable.

Computations yield: variance of the sample estimate = V_I

$$= \frac{(1^2 + 1^2 + 1^2 + \ldots + 2^2 + 2.5^2 + 2.5^2)}{45} - 1.7^2 = 0.45 \text{ (approx.)} . \quad (7.5)$$

Therefore, the standard error of the sample estimate = $\sqrt{V_I} = 0.67$ (approx.).

There is a simple formula for the computation of the standard error of the sample average based on a simple random sample of size n from a population of size N. The formula for the standard error is given by

$$SD \times \sqrt{[(1 - f)/n]}, \quad (7.6)$$

where $f = n/N$ is referred to as the sampling fraction. Here, SD is the population standard deviation of the out-degree values of the N vertices. This is the square root of the population variance with $N - 1$ as the divisor rather than N. The computational formula is already given above in (7.4), and it is denoted by S^2. In this case, we have $N = 10$ vertices, and the average out-degree in the population is already computed as $\bar{D} = 1.7$. The variance was also already computed as $S^2 = 1.1222$. Therefore, $SD = S = \sqrt{1.1222} = 1.0593$. Consequently, the standard error of the sample average = $1.0593\sqrt{[(1 - 0.2)/2]} = 0.67$, as computed above.

It must be noted that for a simple random sample of three HHs, the sample average of the out-degrees would again be an unbiased estimate of the population average, and it would have the standard error given by the above formula with $n = 3$. This yields $1.0593\sqrt{[(1 - 0.3)/3]} = 0.5117$. For a sample of size $n = 4$, this would further reduce to 0.4103 and so on.

Remark 1. We should point out at this stage that the sample of selected units does not provide any virtual representation of the original network at any rate. For some features of the population network, such as the average out-degree, suitable estimates (such as its sample analogs)— enjoying some properties such as unbiasedness—are constructed based on the sample data. Of course, such an estimate would be useful if it possesses a smaller standard error. We find from the above example that the sample size is a governing factor to control and/or reduce the standard error, which reveals a very important contrasting scenario—namely, cost versus precision. Embarking on more units (i.e., increasing the sample size n) will lead to increased cost, but there is gain in precision in terms of reduced standard error of the resulting estimate. These are some of the issues extensively dealt with in the literature of survey sampling theory and methods (e.g., see Cochran, 1977; Hedayat & Sinha, 1991).

Remark 2. Note that our primary objective is to provide an (unbiased) estimate of the population average out-degree based on out-degree values of two or more selected units. At the same time, we also need to attach a value of the standard error of the estimate to ascertain the extent of variation of the estimate from sample to sample. The expression for the standard error of the sample average is given above and involves the population standard deviation, which may seem a bit puzzling. We are starting with the premise that there is a large network so that complete enumeration of the network is not possible. So we are taking recourse to random sampling of some of the vertices. Therefore, there is no question of our having any idea about the variance of the out-degree values in the population as a whole. This means, along with an estimate of the population average out-degree, we also need an estimate of the population variance of the out-degrees based on the sampled units. Furthermore, we need to use that quantity for computation of the standard error of the sample average. The formula for an estimate of the population variance is quite simple again. It is the sample variance based on sample out-degree values with divisor $(n-1)$, where n is the sample size. In other words, an estimate of population variance based on data collected according to the *srswor* procedure is given by its sample counterpart.

Recall the expression for the population variance given in (7.2). Its sample counterpart is given by

$$s^2 = \frac{\sum_{i \in S}(d_i - \bar{d})^2}{n-1} = \frac{\sum_{i \in S} d_i^2 - n\bar{d}^2}{n-1}. \tag{7.7}$$

Therefore, sample "sd" is computed as s, which is the square root of the sample variance s^2 given by the above formula.

Once this is computed, we can then provide an *estimated* standard error of the sample average.

The formula for the estimated standard error is given by

$$sd \times \sqrt{[(1-f)/n]}, \tag{7.8}$$

where $f = n/N$ is, as before, referred to as the sampling fraction. Here, sd is the sample standard deviation of the out-degree values of the n sampled vertices, and it is computed as s above. We refer to Cochran (1977) for details.

Remark 3. With Data Type 1 or Type 2, general results are available for any sample size. We start with a random sample on n units and arrange to collect data on their out-degrees. Then the sample average of the out-degrees serves as an unbiased estimate of the population average, and its standard error is given by the expression above. For large networks (e.g., comprising 100 or more units), even with a moderate sample size (of 30 or so units), the sample average ± 2 times the estimated standard error serves as reasonable bounds for the population average with a confidence coefficient of 95%.

7.3.2 Illustrative Example of Kabilpur Village: 1971–1972

Before proceeding further, we discuss a real case scenario and describe the sampling aspect. Consider the HH population of the village of Kabilpur in 1971–1972. There are $N = 239$ HHs, with the population average out-degree equal to $\bar{D} = 3.6$. Also, there are a total of 387 reciprocal pairs with population average reciprocity equal to 0.036. We draw a random sample of $n = 30$ HHs. Below we display the serial numbers of the selected HHs in ascending order and, for each selected HH, (a) the detailed listing of all other HHs at the receiving end of the ties originating at the selected HH (i.e., its out-degree set as available under Data Type 1), (b) a listing also indicating in bold the HHs from within the selected HHs (Data Type 3), and (c) its d values derived from Data Type 1/2 and also the "curtailed" d values based on Data Type 3.

Listing of 30 selected HHs and detailed sample-based information thereof:

[4; −; 0; 0]; [14; 12, 15, 20; 3; 0]; [27; 218, 219; 2; 0];
[38; 42, 69; **42, 69**; 2; 2]; [42; 38, 69; **38, 69**; 2; 2]; [59; −; 0; 0];
[64; 122, 145; **122**; 2; 1]; [68; −; 0; 0]; [69; 38, 42; **38, 42**; 2; 2];
[76; 218; 1; 0]; [82; −; 0; 0]; [97; 218; 1; 0]; [98; −; 0; 0];
    [110; 111; 1; 0];
[122; 64, 145; **64**; 2; 1]; [132; 34, 218; 2; 0]; [133; −; 0; 0];
    [142; 143; 1; 0];
    [148; 47, 49 − 52; 5; 0];

[174; 175, 177, 179 − 187, 189, 190, 194 − 197, 200;
   183, 187, 194; 18; 3];
[183; 174, 175, 177, 179 − 182, 184, 185 − 190, 194 − 197, 200;
   174, 187, 194; 19; 3];
[187; 174, 175, 177, 179 − 186, 188 − 190, 194 − 197, 200;
   174, 183, 194; 19; 3];
[194; 174, 175, 179 − 190, 195 − 197, 200;
   174, 183, 187; 18; 3];
[199; 198, 201, 203, 207, 215, 218, 226; **203, 215**; 7; 2];
[203; 198, 199, 201, 207, 215, 226; **199, 215**; 6; 2];
[206; 176, 178, 191, 193, 208, 229 − 237; **232, 235**; 14; 2];
[211; 202, 204, 205, 212; 4; 0];
[215; 198, 199, 201, 203, 207, 214, 218, 226; **199, 203**; 8; 2];
[232; 176, 178, 191, 193, 206, 229 − 231, 233 − 237; **206, 235**; 13; 2];
[235; 176, 178, 191, 193, 206, 229 − 234, 236, 237; **206, 232**; 13; 2]   (7.9)

Thus, for example, the selected HH number 14 provides $d_{14} = 3$ (Data Type 2) and also its curtailed d value as 0 (Data Type 3). This last score is based on the fact that there is no tie originating at HH number 14 and terminating at any of the remaining "selected" HHs.

Again, the selected HH number 38 provides $d_{38} = 2$ along with its curtailed d value also equal to 2. As a matter of fact, all 3 units—namely, 38, 42, and 69—possess this property. These patterns will be used later in our study of reciprocity.

We compute the sample average out-degree based on Data Type 1/2 as 5.4667. Sample variance (with divisor $(n − 1)$) is computed as $s^2 = 39.8438$. Next, the standard error of the sample average is estimated as

$$\text{estimated SD} \times \sqrt{[(1 − f)/n]} = sd \times \sqrt{[(1 − f)/n]} = 1.0776. \quad (7.10)$$

Hence, with 95% confidence, we may state that the population average out-degree will lie within the sample average ±2 times the estimated standard error (i.e., within ±2.1552). This yields the confidence limit as [3.3115, 7.6219], which, of course, includes the true (i.e., population average) value of 3.6.

7.3.3 Estimation of Average Out-Degree Based on Data Type 3

We will now discuss another procedure for data analysis based on Data Type 3. We first discuss the case of $n = 2$. Recall that this time, we have meager information on the network. We only know a_{ij} and a_{ji} when the random sample chosen comprises the two units i and j.

Procedure II. Upon selection of the units i and j by the *srswor* procedure, propose the estimator

$$t_{II}(i,j) = (N-1)[a_{ij}+a_{ji}]/2, \qquad (7.11)$$

based on the available data.

Note once more that the estimator proposed here uses information only on the sample network formed exclusively of the two selected units. Based on the randomly drawn sample of units 5 and 8, we go ahead with the computation of $a_{5,8} = 0$ and $a_{8,5} = 0$, thereby resulting in the estimate of 0. With a small sample of units and with very limited information as to the movement of these HHs exclusively among themselves, this sort of unexpected result is quite possible. The remedy would be to either go for Data Type 1 or Type 2 or to increase the sample size under Data Type 3.

In any case, this estimator is also seen to be unbiased. We now verify this statement below, using, as before, a listing of 45 possible samples and sample estimates of the form of $t_{II}(i,j)$ with reference to the Mahacho village network.

[(1, 2); 4.5]; [(1, 3); 4.5]; [(1, 4); 0]; [(1, 5); 0]; [(1, 6); 0]; [(1, 7); 0];
  [(1, 8); 0]; [(1, 9); 0];
[(1, 10); 0]; [(2, 3); 4.5]; [(2, 4); 0]; [(2, 5); 0]; [(2, 6); 0];
  [(2, 7); 0]; [(2, 8); 0]; [(2, 9); 0];
[(2, 10); 0]; [(3, 4); 4.5]; [(3, 5); 4.5]; [(3, 6); 0]; [(3, 7); 0];
  [(3, 8); 0]; [(3, 9); 0];
[(3, 10); 0]; [(4, 5); 0]; [(4, 6); 0]; [(4, 7); 0]; [(4, 8); 0]; [(4, 9); 0];
  [(4, 10); 0]; [(5, 6); 4.5];
[(5, 7); 0]; [(5, 8); 0]; [(5, 9); 0]; [(5, 10); 0]; [(6, 7); 9]; [(6, 8); 0];
  [(6, 9); 4.5]; [(6, 10); 9];
[(7, 8); 4.5]; [(7, 9); 0]; [(7, 10); 0]; [(8, 9); 9];
  [(8, 10); 4.5]; [(9, 10); 9]   (7.12)

The average of the above 45 estimates turns out to be $\frac{4.5+4.5+0+...+9+4.5+9}{45} =$ $(4.5 \times 9 + 9 \times 4)/45 = (40.5 + 36)/45 = 1.7$, and it tallies with the population average, thereby implying that this estimate is also unbiased. The variance of this estimate is given by $V_{II} = \frac{20.25 \times 9 + 81 \times 4}{45} - 1.7^2 = 11.25 - 2.89 = 8.36$ so that the standard error of the estimate is given by 2.8914.

Upon comparing the two estimates in terms of their respective sampling variances or, equivalently, in terms of the standard errors, we find that the standard error of the first estimate (based on Data Type 1/2) is much smaller than that of the second (based on Data Type 3). Therefore, the first estimate is relatively more precise than the second. This result is possibly expected since the former uses more information on the network than the latter. This result may be noted that the sampling procedure, data acquisition, and proposed estimate together constitute what is known as a sampling strategy. Therefore, we may refer to the above as Strategy I and Strategy II, respectively.

7.3.4 Inference Formulae for Data Type 3 Using Sample Size n

Our discussion on Strategy II will remain incomplete unless we explain the data analysis technique for a general sample size n. The generalization of the estimator $t_{II}(i, j)$ is given below.

Procedure   II (General Sample   Size). Upon selection of the units $i, j, k, \ldots \ldots$ of size n by the *srswor* procedure from the population of N units, we propose the estimator

$$t_{II}(i, j, k, \ldots) = [(N-1)/n(n-1)] \left[\sum_{i \neq j} a_{ij} \right], \qquad (7.13)$$

based on the available Data Type 3.

The derivation of this result rests on a general theory for unbiased estimation based on data drawn according to any method of sampling and then on an application of the HTE. Then we specialize to simple random sampling and derive the above result. We refer to Frank (1978) for technical details.

It turns out that the above estimator is unbiased for the population average out-degree. Computation of its variance and the variance estimate from the sample data (of Type 3) is a routine task for a survey statistician. (We refer to Frank [1977a, 1977b, 1978] for necessary technical details. One can follow the general and specific results presented in these articles. We, however, follow a different computational approach here, based on the same theory.) For general readers, these derivations may seem quite difficult, and it is recommended that they may skip the details altogether and follow the numerical computations given in the subsequent subsections. However, for the sake of completeness, we indicate the computational formulae below. We also show the computation of the estimate for the data set of 30 sample HHs from the village Kabilpur (1970). Note that the estimator above can be expressed as

$$t_{II}(i, j, k, ...) = [(N-1)/n(n-1)] \sum_i d_i^c, \tag{7.14}$$

where d^c refers to the "curtailed" d value based on Data Type 3. In other words, the estimate is the sample average out-degree, "inflated" by the factor $(N-1)/(n-1)$. These curtailed d values are already shown in the list of 30 sample HHs along with the d values. Computations now yield the estimate as $(238/30.29)(32) = 8.7540$.

Expression for the variance and its estimator is as follows.

We use the notation

$$b_{(i,j)} = b_{(j,i)} = a_{ij} + a_{ji} \tag{7.15}$$

for all pairs of units in the population (and also in a random sample).

Note that the population average out-degree can be expressed as

$$\bar{D} = \left[\sum_{i<j} \sum b_{(i,j)} \right] /N, \tag{7.16}$$

and furthermore, its estimate is given by

$$\hat{\bar{D}} = (N-1) \left[\sum_{i<j;s(n)} \sum b_{(i,j)} \right] /n(n-1), \tag{7.17}$$

which coincides with t_{II} given above. The variance of the estimate is, by definition, given by

$$V(t_{II}) = E[t_{II}^2] - E^2[t_{II}]. \tag{7.18}$$

To find an unbiased estimate of this variance of t_{II} based on random sample data, one way is to find an unbiased estimate of the square of $\bar{D}$, say $\hat{\bar{D}}^2$. Then an unbiased estimate of the above variance is given by

$$t_{II}^2 - \hat{\bar{D}}^2. \tag{7.19}$$

Next note that $(\bar{D}^2)$ can be expressed as

$$(1/N^2)[T_1 + T_2 + T_3], \tag{7.20}$$

where

$$T_1 = \left[\sum_{i<j} \sum b_{(i,j)}^2 \right]; \tag{7.21}$$

$$T_2 = \left[\sum \sum_{i<j<k} \sum (b_{(i,j)}b_{(i,k)} + b_{(i,j)}b_{(j,k)} + b_{(i,k)}b_{(j,k)}) \right]; \tag{7.22}$$

$$T_3 = \left[\sum \sum \sum_{i<j<k<t} \sum (b_{(i,j)}b_{(k,t)} + b_{(i,k)}b_{(j,t)} + b_{(i,t)}b_{(j,k)}) \right]. \tag{7.23}$$

It follows that an unbiased estimate of $(1/N^2)[T_1 + T_2 + T_3]$ in (7.24) is given by

$$(1/N^2)[\hat{T}_1(s(n)) + \hat{T}_2(s(n)) + \hat{T}_3(s(n))], \tag{7.24}$$

where

$$\hat{T}_1(s(n)) = \left[\sum_{i<j\epsilon s(n)} \sum b_{(i,j)}^2 \right] N^{(2)}/n^{(2)}; \tag{7.25}$$

$$\hat{T}_2(s(n)) = \left[\sum \sum_{i<j<k\epsilon s(n)} \sum (b_{(i,j)}b_{(i,k)} + b_{(i,j)}b_{(j,k)} + b_{(i,k)}b_{(j,k)}) \right]$$
$$N^{(3)}/n^{(3)}; \tag{7.26}$$

$$\hat{T}_3(s) = \left[\sum \sum \sum_{i<j<k<t\epsilon s(n)} \sum (b_{(i,j)}b_{(k,t)} + b_{(i,k)}b_{(j,t)} + b_{(i,t)}b_{(j,k)}) \right]$$
$$N^{(4)}/n^{(4)}. \tag{7.27}$$

In the above, $N^{(2)} = N(N-1)$, $n^{(2)} = n(n-1)$, and so on for other higher powers.

7.3.5 Illustrative Example of Kabilpur Village: 1971–1972

We now turn our attention to the sample network for Kabilpur village based on *srswor* sample of 30 selected HHs, as already indicated and displayed before, and carry out data analysis, restricting to Data Type 3. We propose providing an estimate of the population average out-degree along with its estimated standard error.

The sampled HHs and also their out-degree sets are already displayed above in (7.9). There we have also indicated in bold the nature of Data Type 3. We reproduce them below, indicating the sample tie-based small networks thus formed:

$$F_1 = [38, 42, 69];\ F_2 = [174, 183, 187, 194];\ F_3 = [64, 122];$$
$$F_4 = [199, 203, 215];\ F_5 = [206, 232, 235].\qquad (7.28)$$

Here, F stands for figures. It helps to understand the arguments and the computations once the figures are drawn by freehand. In each of the above, there are only two-way ties between any two HHs involved. There are no one-way ties formed of the sampled HHs. This facilitates our computation of $b_{(i,j)}$ values—namely, 0 and 2. We only list the $b_{(i,j)}$s, assuming the value 2.

$$b_{(38,42)} = b_{(38,69)} = b_{(42,69)} = 2;$$
$$b_{(174,183)} = b_{(174,187)} = b_{(174,194)} = b_{(183,187)} = b_{(183,194)} = b_{(187,194)} = 2;$$
$$b_{(64,122)} = 2;\ b_{(199,203)} = b_{(199,215)} = b_{(203,215)} = 2;$$
$$b_{(206,232)} = b_{(206,235)} = b_{(232,235)} = 2.\qquad (7.29)$$

Computations yield

$$\left[\sum \sum_{i<j\epsilon s(n)} b_{(i,j)}\right] = 3 \times 2[from\ F1] + 6 \times 2[from\ F2]$$
$$+ 1 \times 2[from\ F3] + 3 \times 2[from\ F4] + 3 \times 2[from\ F5] = 32.\quad (7.30)$$

Therefore, an estimate of the population average out-degree is computed as

$$\hat{D} = (N-1)\left[\sum \sum_{i<j;s(n)} b_{(i,j)}\right]/n(n-1) = (238)(32)/(30)(29) = 8.7540.$$
$$(7.31)$$

Next,

$$\hat{T}_1 = [N^{(2)}/n^{(2)}][3 \times 4[from\ F_1] + 6 \times 4[from\ F_2] + 1 \times 4[from\ F_3]$$
$$+ 3 \times 4[from\ F_4] + 3 \times 4[from\ F_5]]$$
$$= (239)(238)(64)/(30)(29) = 4184.4230;\qquad (7.32)$$

$$\hat{T}_2 \;=\; [N^{(3)}/n^{(3)}][3 \times 4[from\ F_1] + 4 \times 3 \times 4[from\ F_2]$$
$$+3 \times 4[from\ F_4] + 3 \times 4[from\ F_5]] = (239)(238)(237)(84)/$$
$$(30)(29)(28) = 46486.3241; \tag{7.33}$$

$$\hat{T}_3 \;=\; [N^{(4)}/n^{(4)}][(3 \times 6 \times 4[from\ F_1, F_2]) + (3 \times 1 \times 4[from\ F_1, F_3])$$
$$+(3 \times 3 \times 4[from\ F_1, F_4]) + (3 \times 3 \times 4[from\ F_1, F_5])$$
$$+(1 \times 3 \times 4[from\ F_2]) \tag{7.34}$$
$$+(6 \times 1 \times 4[from\ F_2, F_3]) + (6 \times 3 \times 4[from\ F_2, F_4])$$
$$+(6 \times 3 \times 4[from\ F_2, F_4])$$
$$+(1 \times 3 \times 4[from\ F_3, F_4]) + (1 \times 3 \times 4[from\ F_3, F_5])$$
$$+(3 \times 3 \times 4[from\ F_4, F_5])]$$
$$=\; (239)(238)(237)(236)(396)/(30)(29)(28)(27)$$
$$=\; 1915531.7057. \tag{7.35}$$

Hence,

$$\hat{D}^2 = (8.7540 + 46486.3241 + 1915531.7057)/(239)^2 = 34.3486. \tag{7.36}$$

Thus, finally, estimated variance is computed as

$$t_{II}^2 - \hat{D}^2 = (8.7540)^2 - 34.3486 = 42.2839. \tag{7.37}$$

Therefore, estimated standard error is given by $\sqrt{42.2839} = 6.5026$.

Next we compute 95% confidence limits to the population average out-degree based on the sample average, and this is given by ± 2 times the estimated standard error. This yields the interval [0, 21.7592]. Once again, we find that the population average out-degree lies in this interval.

7.3.6 Illustrative Example of Kabilpur Village: 1997–1998

We also present results of sampling of HHs from the same village of Kabilpur with reference to the period 1997–1998. During 1997–1998, there were $N = 432$ HHs, and we consider approximately the proportional sample size of $n = 55$ HHs. The sampled units and also data derived from them on all three types discussed earlier are shown below.

[24; −; 0; 0]; [27; −; 0; 0]; [37; −; 0; 0] [41; 87, 211; 2; 0];

　[55; 265; **265**; 1; 1];

　[58; 9; 1; 0]; [66; 213; 1; 0]; [71; 176; 1; 0];

　[75; −; 0, 0]; [76; −; 0; 0];

[84; 235, 265; **265**; 2; 1]; [91; −; 0; 0]; [93; 88, 189; 2; 0];

　[96; 277; 1; 0];

[107; 159, 185, 207; 3; 0]; [113; −; 0; 0]; [126; 164, 224; 2; 0];

　[133; 265; **265**; 1; 1];

[134; 232; 1; 0]; [148; 149, 177; 2; 0]; [160; 101, 116,

　209, 283, 324; 5; 0];

[170; 173, 181, 198, 261; 4; 0]; [179; 178, 180, 199, 283; 4; 0];

　[203; −; 0; 0];

[206; 178, 179; **179**; 2; 1]; [208; 249; 1; 0]; [221; 230; 1; 0];

　[226; 224, 242; **242**; 2; 1];

[242; 224, 244; 2; 0]; [252; 253; 1; 0]; [258; 256, 260; 2; 0];

　[265; 87, 199, 256, 417; 4; 0];

[275; 208, 232, 276; **208**; 3; 1]; [279; 181, 199, 269; 3; 0];

　[282; 210; 1; 0];

[294; 216; 1; 0]; [295; 270; 1; 0]; [309; 331; 1; 0]; [315; 270; 1; 0];

　[320; 199; 1; 0];

[330; 283; 1; 0]; [335; 170; **170**; 1; 1]; [341; 213; 1; 0]; [343; 181; 1; 0];

[344; 210; 1; 0]; [359; 285, 311, 313; 3; 0]; [365; 192, 298; 2; 0];

　[368; 249, 313; 2; 0];

[376; 167, 375, 378; 3; 0]; [390; 279, 388; **279**; 2; 1]; [391; 255; 1; 0];

　[399; 371; 1; 0];

[403; 265; **265**; 1; 1]; [423; 265; **265**; 1; 1]; [425; 191, 404; 2; 0].　(7.38)

It turns out that the population average out-degree is given by 1.7. In the random sample displayed above, the sample out-degrees are found to be 0(8); 1(25); 2(13); 3(5); 4(3); 5(1). The quantities in parentheses are the frequencies of the numbers shown. The sample total of d values is equal to $\sum d_i = 83$, and sum of squares of the sample d values is equal to $\sum d_i^2 = 195$. Also, the "curtailed" d values (denoted by d_i^c) are given by $0(45); 1(10)$ with a total of 10.

Estimates for the population average out-degree computed from Data Types 1/2 and 3 are respectively given by

$$\bar{d} = \sum d_i/n = 83/55 = 1.5091$$

and

$$(N - 1)\sum d_i^c/n(n - 1) = (431)(10)/(55)(54) = 1.4518. \qquad (7.39)$$

For Data Type 1/2, we now compute the value of the estimated standard error of the estimate. For this, we first compute sample variance of the d values as $[\sum d_i^2 - n\bar{d}^2]/(n - 1) = [195 - (83)^2/55]/54 = 1.2916.$

Therefore, the estimated standard error of the sample average is given by
estimated $SD \times \sqrt{[(1 - f)/n]} =$ sample $sd \times \sqrt{[(1 - f)/n]}$

$$= \sqrt{1.2916}\sqrt{[1 - (55)/(432)]/55} = 1.1365 \times 0.1260 = 0.1432. \qquad (7.40)$$

This gives rise to the 95% confidence limits to the population average out-degree as $1.5091 + / - 2 \times 0.1432 = [1.2251, 1.7931]$, which is seen to include the true population average value, which is 1.7.

We leave the computation of the estimated standard error for the estimate based on Data Type 3 to the interested reader(s).

7.4 ESTIMATION OF AVERAGE RECIPROCITY

We now turn to the problem of unbiased estimation of the measure of reciprocity given by average reciprocity $\bar{R}$ defined in earlier chapters. For completeness, we reproduce the definition below.

We refer to the adjacency matrix $\mathbf{A} = ((a_{ij}))$, where $a_{ij} = 1$ whenever there is a tie originating at i and ending at j. Likewise, $a_{ji} = 1$ whenever there is a tie originating at j and terminating at i. Reciprocity between the pair of units i and j takes place whenever $a_{ij} = a_{ji} = 1$ (i.e., whenever the units are involved in a reciprocal relation). We may denote the "reciprocity" score for a pair of units i and j as $r_{(i,j)} = a_{ij}a_{ji}$ so that $r_{(i,j)} = 1$ whenever the units are involved in a reciprocal relation. Otherwise, $r_{(i,j)} = 0$. Therefore, average reciprocity in a population network, denoted in the above by $\bar{R}$, is the average of r scores over all such $N(N-1)/2$ pairs of units in the population of N units, that is, $\bar{R} = \sum\sum_{i<j} 2r_{(i,j)}/N(N-1)$.

We now embark upon the problem of unbiased estimation of this population parameter $\bar{R}$ based on a sample network of size n.

First we will discuss the case of $n = 2$ in detail. Then we will move on to the general case.

We have a population network with N units, and we propose to unbiasedly estimate the average reciprocity $\bar{R}$ from a sample of size 2. Naturally, the *srswor* procedure of drawing 2 units, such as i and j, coupled with $r_{(i,j)}$ serves as a strategy to start with. Since there are $N(N-1)/2$ pairs of units in the population and we are adopting random sampling, the pair (i, j) is selected with probability $2/N(N-1)$. Therefore, the average of such sample estimators will be given by $\sum\sum_{i<j} 2r_{(i,j)}/N(N-1)$, which identifies itself with $\bar{R}$.

Conceptualizing a generalization of this result for a general sample size n under the *srswor* procedure is a fairly routine task. First, we draw a sample of n units by the *srswor* procedure. For every pair of units in the sample, say i and j, we compute the sample reciprocity score $r_{(i,j)}$. Then we average over all such pairs. In other words, we propose an estimate of population $\bar{R}$ by its sample analog $\bar{r}$ based on the average of r scores of $n(n-1)/2$ pairs of units in the sample. It follows that the estimate $\bar{r}$ is unbiased. Its variance computation is a routine but nontrivial exercise. Furthermore, deriving an expression for an estimate (based on sample reciprocity scores) of the variance of the estimator so derived is also a highly nontrivial exercise. We omit the derivations altogether and simply state the results. (We again refer to Frank [1977a, 1977b, 1978] for the basic theoretical derivations. Of course, as mentioned earlier, we proceed in an alternative way.)

Below $T(R)$ denotes the total reciprocity score in the population as a whole (i.e., $T(R) = \sum\sum_{i<j} r_{(i,j)}$) so that $\bar{R} = 2T(R)/N(N-1)$. Moreover, while providing sample-based estimators, we use the notation s for the selected sample. Thus, for example, while $i < j$ refers to all pairs of population units, $i < j \in s$ refers to all pairs of units in the selected sample.

$$(1)\, T(R) = \sum\sum_{i<j} r_{(i,j)};$$

$$(2)\, \hat{T}(R) = N(N-1)\left[\sum\sum_{i<j \,\in\, s} r_{(i,j)}\right]/n(n-1);$$

$$(3)\, T^2(R) = \left[\sum_{i<j} \sum r_{(i,j)}^2 + 2 \sum \sum \sum_{i<j<k} (r_{(i,j)}r_{(i,k)} + r_{(i,j)}r_{(j,k)} \right.$$

$$+ r_{(i,k)}r_{(j,k)})$$

$$\left. + 2 \sum \sum \sum \sum_{i<j<k<t} (r_{(i,j)}r_{(k,t)} + r_{(i,k)}r_{(j,t)} + r_{(i,t)}r_{(j,k)}) \right]$$

$$= [T_1 + T_2 + T_3];$$

$$(4)\, \hat{T}_1 = N(N-1)T_1(s)/n(n-1);$$

$$\hat{T}_2 = N(N-1)(N-2)T_2(s)/n(n-1)(n-2);$$

$$\hat{T}_3 = N(N-1)(N-2)(N-3)T_3(s)/n(n-1)(n-2)(n-3);$$

$$T_1(\sigma) = \sum \sum_{i<j \,\epsilon\, s} r_{(i,j)}^2;$$

$$T_2(s) = 2 \sum \sum \sum_{i<j<k \,\epsilon\, s} [r_{(i,j)}r_{(i,k)} + r_{(i,j)}r_{(j,k)} + r_{(i,k)}r_{(j,k)}];$$

$$T_3(s) = 2 \sum \sum \sum \sum_{i<j<k<t \,\epsilon\, s} [r_{(i,j)}r_{(k,t)} + r_{(i,k)}r_{(j,t)} + r_{(i,t)}r_{(j,k)}]$$

$$(5)\, V(\hat{T}(R)) = E[(\hat{T}(R))^2)] - T^2(R)$$

$$(6)\, \hat{V}(\hat{T}(R)) = [(\hat{T}(R))]^2 - (\hat{T}^2(R)) =$$

Square of (2) – Expression from (3) and (4)

$$(7)\, \bar{R} = 2T(R)/N(N-1) = 2 \sum_{i<j} \sum r_{(i,j)}/N(N-1);$$

$$(8)\, \hat{\bar{R}} = \bar{r} = 2 \sum \sum_{i<j \,\epsilon\, s} r_{(i,j)}/n(n-1);$$

$$(9)\, V(\hat{\bar{R}}) = 4V(\hat{T}(R))/N^2(N-1)^2;$$

$$(10)\, \hat{V}(\hat{\bar{R}}) = 4\hat{V}(\hat{T}(R))/N^2(N-1)^2. \qquad (7.41)$$

We will now demonstrate the computations using the example of the Kabilpur (1971–1972) network for a population of $N = 239$ HHs and a sample of $n = 30$ HHs. The sample units along with the information on Data Types 1/2 and 3 all have been displayed before. We need to ascertain values of $r_{(i,j)}$ for the sample HHs. Note that for examining reciprocity, only Data Type 3 is relevant. Here are the results, essentially along the same lines as those for ascertaining the out-degrees.

$$r_{(38,42)} = r_{(38,69)} = r_{(42,69)} = 1; r_{(64,122)} = 1;$$

$$r_{(174,183)} = r_{(174,187)} = r_{(174,194)} = r_{(183,187)} = r_{(183,194)}$$

$$= r_{(187,194)} = 1;$$

$$r_{(199,203)} = r_{(199,215)} = r_{(203,215)} = 1;$$

$$r_{(206,232)} = r_{(206,235)} = r_{(232,235)} = 1. \tag{7.42}$$

The rest of the $r_{(i,j)}$s are all 0.

Therefore, an estimate of the population average reciprocity $[\bar{R}]$, as given by the sample average reciprocity, is computed as

$$\bar{r} = 2 \sum \sum_{i<j;s} r_{(i,j)}/n(n-1) \text{ turns out to be } (2 \times 16)/(30 \times 29) = 0.0368.$$

$$\tag{7.43}$$

Furthermore, an estimate of total reciprocity $T(R)$ is given by the formula in (7.2), and it is computed as $239 \times 238 \times 0.0368 = 2093$, when approximated to a whole number.

For the computation of confidence limits to the population average reciprocity or the population total reciprocity, we follow the computational formulae given above. Note that $r^2_{(i,j)} = r_{(i,j)}$ since $r_{(i,j)}$ is equal to either 0 or 1. We also reproduce here the sample reciprocity-based networks already discussed and displayed before. Here, again, it helps to sketch the small reciprocity-based networks to follow the computations illustrated below.

$$F_1 = [38, 42, 69]; \quad F_2 = [174, 183, 187, 194]; \quad F_3 = [64, 122];$$

$$F_4 = [199, 203, 215]; \quad F_5 = [206, 232, 235]. \tag{7.44}$$

We now proceed toward computation of estimated variance using (4).

$$T_1(s) = \sum \sum_{i<j \in s} r^2_{(i,j)} = \sum \sum_{i<j \in s} r_{(i,j)}$$

$$= 3[from\ F_1] + 6[from\ F_2] + 1[from\ F_3]$$

$$+ 3[from\ F_4] + 3[from\ F_5] = 16;$$

$$T_2(s) = 2 \sum \sum \sum_{i<j<k \in s} (r_{(i,j)}r_{(i,k)} + r_{(i,j)}r_{(j,k)} + r_{(i,k)}r_{(j,k)})$$

$$
\begin{aligned}
&= \quad 2(3[from\ F_1] + 4 \times 3[from\ F_2] \\
&\quad\ \ +3[from\ F_4] + 3[from\ F_5]) = 42
\end{aligned}
$$

$$
\begin{aligned}
T_3(s) &= 2\sum\sum\sum_{i<j<k<t\ \epsilon\ s} \sum \left(r_{(i,j)}r_{(k,t)} + r_{(i,k)}r_{(j,t)} + r_{(i,t)}r_{(j,k)}\right) \\
&= 2(3 \times 4[F_1, F_2] + 3 \times 1[F_1, F_3] + 3 \times 3[F_1, F_4] \\
&\quad\ \ +3 \times 3[F_1, F_5] \\
&\quad\ \ +3[F_2] + 6 \times 1[F_2, F_3] + 6 \times 3[F_2, F_4] + 6 \times 3[F_2, F_4] \\
&\quad\ \ +1 \times 3[F_3, F_4] + 1 \times 3[F_3, F_5] + 3 \times 3[F_4, F_5]) = 198. \quad (7.45)
\end{aligned}
$$

Therefore,

$$
\begin{aligned}
\hat{T}_1 &= (239)(238)(16)/(30)(29); \\
\hat{T}_2 &= (239)(238)(237)(42)/(30)(29)(28); \\
\hat{T}_3 &= (239)(238)(237)(236)(198)/(30)(29)(28)(27). \quad (7.46)
\end{aligned}
$$

Hence,

$$
\hat{T}^2(R) = \hat{T}_1 + \hat{T}_2 + \hat{T}_3. \quad (7.47)
$$

From this, we compute

$$
\hat{\bar{R}}^2 = 4\hat{T}^2(R)/N^2(N-1)^2 = 0.00121408. \quad (7.48)
$$

Furthermore,

$$
\hat{\bar{R}}^2 = 0.00135277. \quad (7.49)
$$

Hence, finally,

$$
\begin{aligned}
\text{Estimated variance} &= 0.00135277 - 0.00121408 \\
&= 0.00013869. \quad (7.50)
\end{aligned}
$$

Thus, estimated standard error = 0.0118.

It turns out that 95% confidence limits to the population average reciprocity are given by sample average reciprocity ± 2 times the estimated standard error. This results in [0.0132, 0.0604]. The population average reciprocity value (i.e., 0.0136) lies in the above interval.

Remark 4. It follows from Table 1.7 in Chapter 1 that there are only 46 reciprocal pairs of HHs in the population of Kabilpur (1997–1998). Accordingly, the population average reciprocity is given by $2 \times 46/(432)(431) = 0.000494$. Therefore, reciprocity is a "rare" event for the Kabilpur 1998 population of HHs. This suggests that one may hardly expect any reciprocal pair of HHs among the selected 55 HHs. That is indeed the case with the sample data exhibited before. Therefore, one may have to take recourse to what is known as "inverse sampling" in the traditional sampling literature. The idea is to continue sampling of the HHs one by one and at random and, with each "new" HH thus selected, check the presence of reciprocal pairs involving the new unit and continue sampling until a "preassigned" number of reciprocal pairs are encountered (or exceeded) in the sample HHs. We will not discuss this methodology here. Also, there are other forms of sampling strategies, involving sequential drawing of the units and related inferential procedures. We refer to Goswami, Sengupta, and Sinha (1990) for an account of available results. Sinha (1997) deals with applications of the symmetrization principle in case the units are drawn in an ordered fashion and the estimators are also order based to start with. This principle provides symmetrized estimators with reduced sampling fluctuations and therefore serves as a better alternative to "ordered" estimators. A discussion of these techniques is beyond the scope of this text.

Frank (1977a, 1977b, 1978) and Thompson (2006), among many others, have studied the problem of sampling from graphs in a systematic manner. The unified theory of sampling and the celebrated HTE provide the basic frameworks to undertake this kind of study. Suitably modified for addressing the question of dyad-based responses, the results are fairly straightforward to a survey theorist, although necessarily complicated. In the above, we have adopted the approach suggested in the literature, although the computations are a bit different. Other improved sampling strategies (e.g., see Goswami et al., 1990; Sinha, 1997) use advanced techniques such as sequential search, order-based estimators, and the symmetrization principle.

This fascinating topic of sampling from graphs (of which networks involving HHs is a particular exemplary case) still holds rich rewards for those who are willing to undertake a serious study of the underlying sampling strategies for drawing inference on many meaningful network-based parameters. We have discussed only two specific features—namely, average out-degree and average reciprocity—and those too are based on relatively simple sampling strategies.

REFERENCES

Cochran, W. G. (1977). *Sampling techniques*. New York: John Wiley.

Frank, O. (1977a). Estimation of graph totals. *Scandinavian Journal of Statistics, 4,* 81–89.

Frank, O. (1977b). Survey sampling in graphs. *Journal of Statistical Planning and Inference, 1,* 235–264.

Frank, O. (1978). Sampling and estimation in large social networks. *Social Networks, 1,* 91–101.

Goswami, A., Sengupta, S., & Sinha, B. K. (1990). Optimal strategies in sampling from a social network. *Sequential Analysis, 9,* 1–18.

Hedayat, A. S., & Sinha, B. K. (1991). *Design and inference in finite population sampling*. New York: John Wiley.

Sinha, B. K. (1997). Some inference aspects of a social network. *Applied Statistical Science, II,* 77–86.

Thompson, S. K. (2006). Targeted random walk designs. *Survey Methodology, 32,* 11–24.

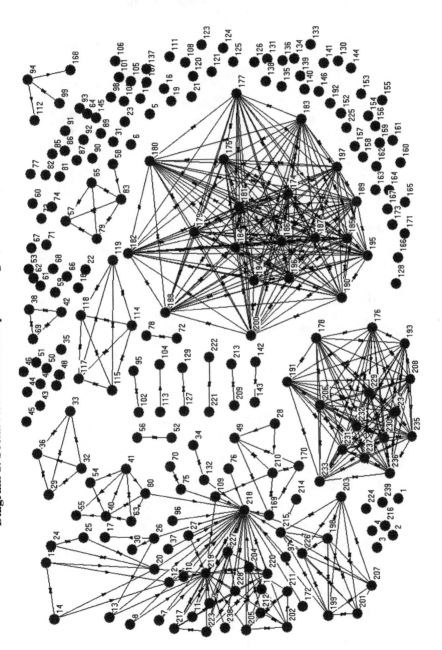

Diagram 1: Social Network of Kabilpur Village (1971–1972)

Diagram 2: Social Network of the Sadgopes of Kabilpur Village (1997–1998)

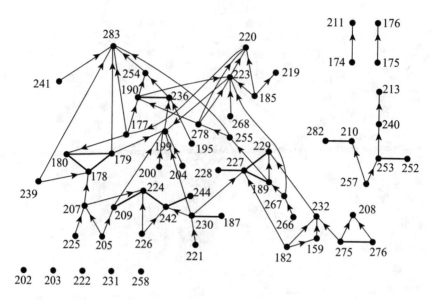

Diagram 3: Social Network of the Bagdis of Kabilpur Village (1971–1972)

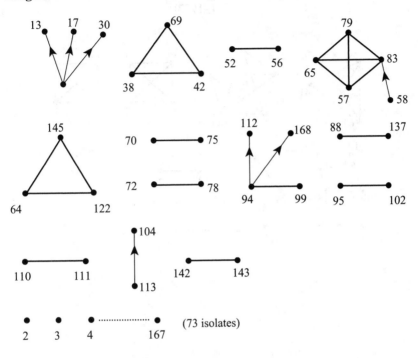

**Diagram 4: Social Network of the Santals of Kabilpur Village
(1971–1972)**

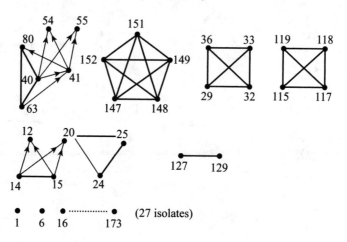

Diagram 5: Within Bagdi Network in Kabilpur, 1998

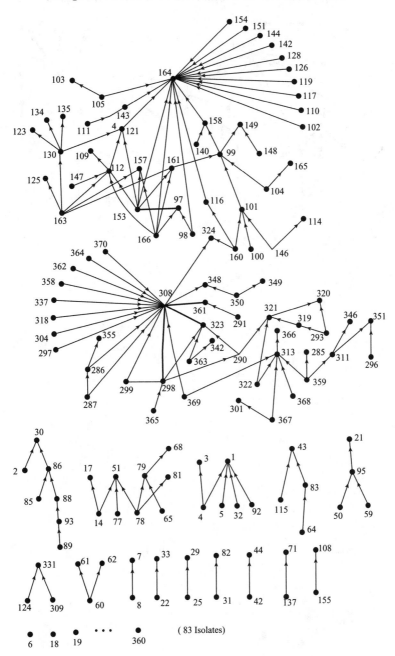

(83 Isolates)

Diagram 6: Within Santhal Network in Kabilpur, 1998

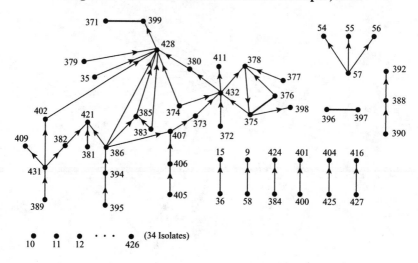

Diagram 7: Social Network of Baghra Village (2002)

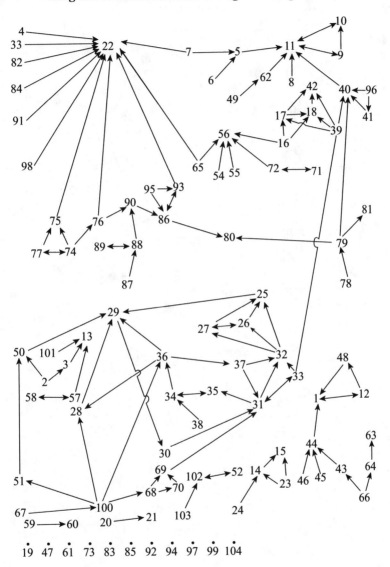

Diagram 8: Social Network of the Muslim Community of Baghra Village (2001–2002)

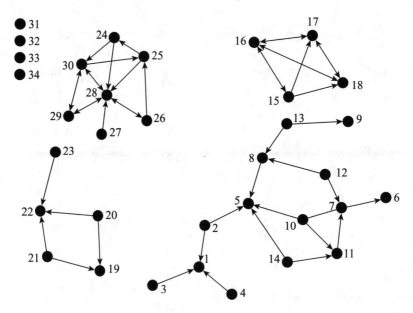

Diagram 9: Social Network of the Muslim Community of Harsingraidih Village (2001–2002)

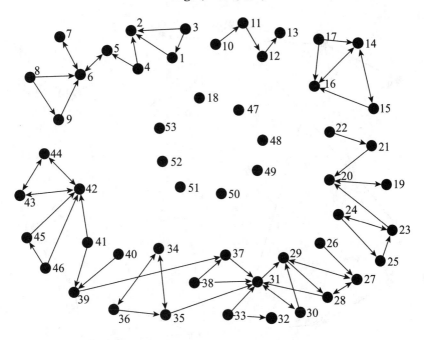

Diagram 10: Social Network of the Muslim Community of Chitmadih Village (2001–2002)

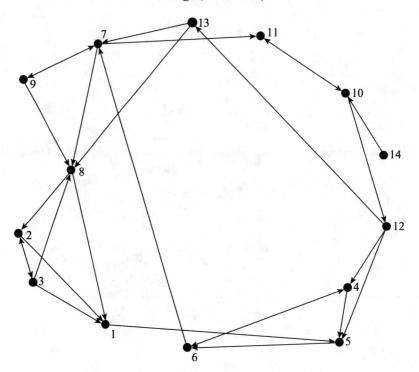

Diagram 11: Social Network of the Muslim Community of Mahacho Village (2001–2002)

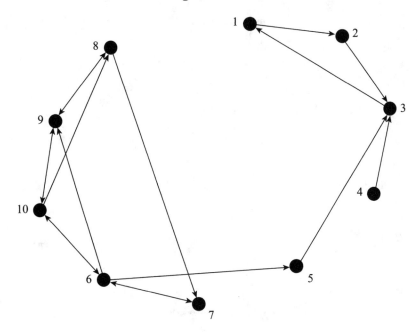

Diagram 12: Social Network of the Muslim Community of Maladanga Village (2001–2002)

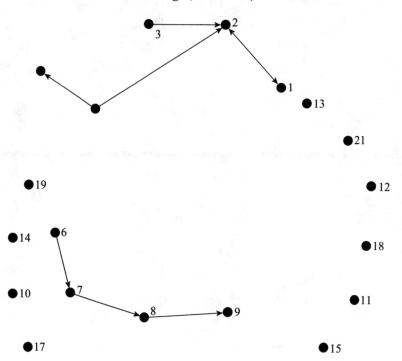

Diagram 13: Social Network of the Muslim Community of Raspur Village (2001–2002)

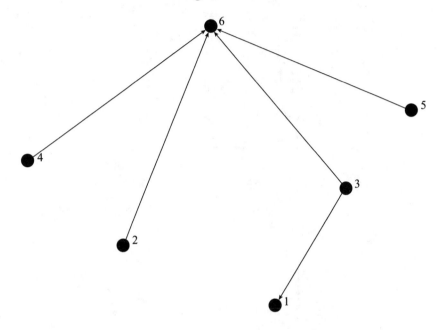

**Diagram 14: Social Network of the Santals of Baidyanathpur Village
(1971–1972)**

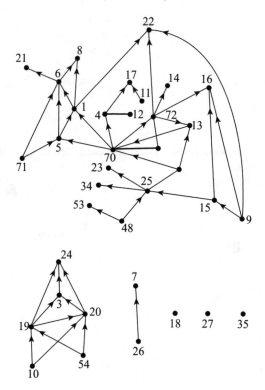

Diagram 15: Social Network of the Santals of Baidyanathpur Village (1997–1998)

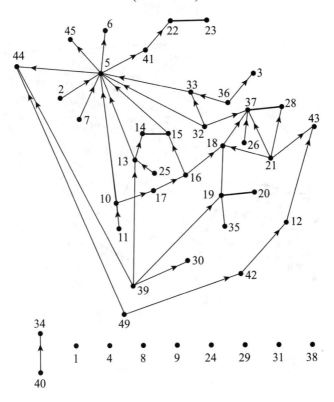

Diagram 16: Social Network of the Rajputs of Baidyanathpur Village (1971–1972)

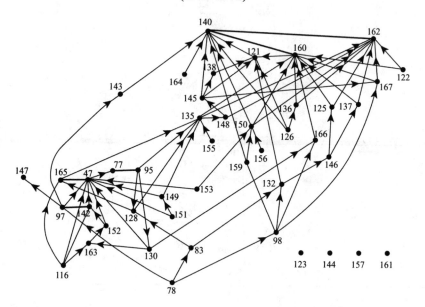

Diagram 17: Social Network of the Rajputs of Baidyanathpur Village (1997–1998)

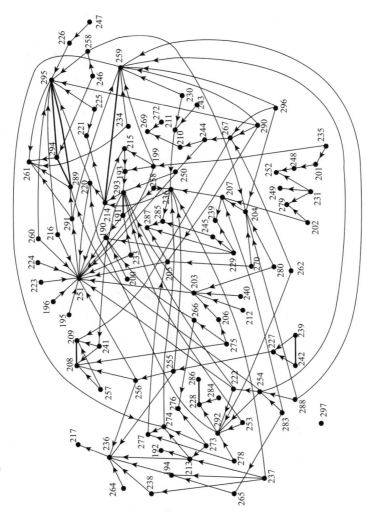

Diagram 18: Notional Diagram for D^2 Based on Three Attributes

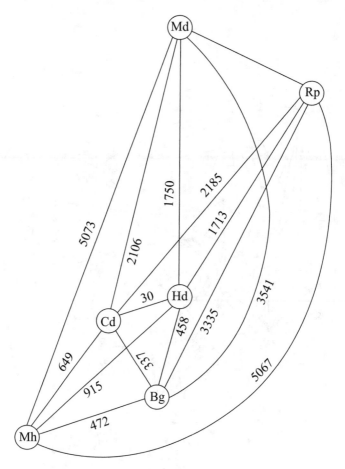

Diagram 19: Notional Diagram for D^2 Based on Five Attributes

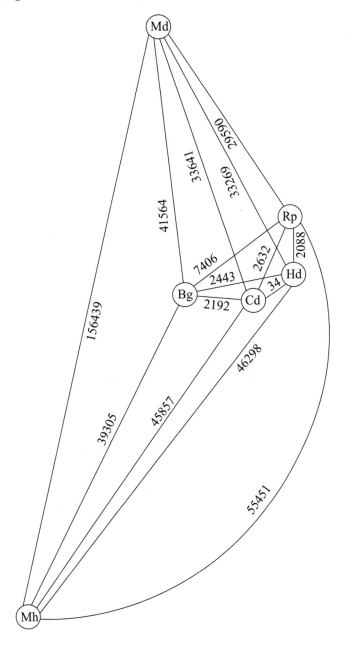

AUTHOR INDEX

SUBJECT INDEX

———•••———